HOW TO REACH AND TEACH
ADD/ADHD
CHILDREN

PRACTICAL TECHNIQUES, STRATEGIES, AND INTERVENTIONS FOR HELPING CHILDREN WITH ATTENTION PROBLEMS AND HYPERACTIVITY

SANDRA F. RIEF

**THE CENTER FOR APPLIED
RESEARCH IN EDUCATION**
West Nyack, New York 10995

Library of Congress Cataloging-in-Publication Data

Rief, Sandra F.
    How to reach & teach ADD/ADHD children : practical techniques, strategies,
and interventions for helping children with attention problems and
hyperactivity / Sandra F. Rief.
       p.   cm.
    Includes bibliographical references.
    ISBN 0-87628-413-6
    1. Attention-deficit-disordered children—Education—United States—
Handbooks, manuals, etc.   2. Hyperactive children—Education—United
States—Handbooks, manuals, etc.   3. Classroom management—United
States—Handbooks, manuals, etc.   I. Title.   II. Title: How to reach and
teach ADD/ADHD Children.
    LC4713.4.R54   1993   92-42851
    371.93—dc20   CIP

Printed in the United States of America

10 9

ISBN 0-87628-413-6

+---+

ATTENTION: CORPORATIONS AND SCHOOLS

The Center for Applied Research in Education books are available at quantity
discounts with bulk purchase for educational, business, or sales promotional use.
For information, please write to: Prentice Hall Career & Personal Development
Special Sales, 240 Frisch Court, Paramus, New Jersey 07652. Please supply: title
of book, ISBN number, quantity, how the book will be used, date needed.

+---+

**THE CENTER FOR APPLIED RESEARCH
IN EDUCATION**
West Nyack, NY 10994
A Simon & Schuster Company

On the World Wide Web at http://www.phdirect.com

Prentice-Hall International (UK) Limited, *London*
Prentice-Hall of Australia Pty. Limited, *Sydney*
Prentice-Hall Canada Inc., *Toronto*
Prentice-Hall Hispanoamericana, S.A., *Mexico*
Prentice-Hall of India Private Limited, *New Delhi*
Prentice-Hall of Japan, Inc., *Tokyo*
Simon & Schuster Asia Pte. Ltd., *Singapore*
Editora Prentice-Hall do Brasil, Ltda., *Rio de Janeiro*

Dedication

This book is dedicated to the memory of my beloved son, Benjamin, and to all of the children who face obstacles in their young lives each day with loving, trusting hearts, determination, and extraordinary courage.

About the Author

Sandra F. Rief received her B.A. and M.A. degrees from the University of Illinois in elementary and special education. She has specialized in teaching children with learning disabilities as well as attentional and behavioral problems for nineteen years. For the past twelve years she has been working as a resource specialist in the San Diego, California, schools.

As a mentor teacher, Sandra became actively involved in the Project for Attention Related Disorders (PARD). She wrote a manual for her school district on effective strategies for teaching children with attentional and learning difficulties and has presented numerous workshops, inservices, and conferences addressing this topic. Sandra is also the author of *Systematic Phonics*, published by EBSCO Curriculum Materials in 1986.

About This Book

Attention deficit/hyperactivity disorder is not something that we can "cure." A child with ADD/ADHD, like one with learning disabilities, does not "outgrow" it, though their difficulties and behaviors are manifested differently as the child matures. We, the significant adults in their lives, play a *major role* in how well these children achieve, succeed, and feel about themselves. We are the ones who can help these children best manage their lives, cope with frustrations, and compensate for weaknesses. We are also the ones who can help them see their strengths—often their giftedness—and value their uniqueness.

There are many children with ADD/ADHD who have grown up to be very successful adults. They have drawn upon their strengths, creativity, and "survival skills" to their advantage. On the other hand, there are many who have not fared well. There is a high correlation between ADHD and failure in society. A significant percentage of individuals who drop out of school, are unable to keep a job, fail in their interpersonal relationships, pack our prison system, and even commit suicide were children who had this disorder without the benefit of identification, intervention, and treatment. Many adolescents and adults with ADD/ADHD have painful memories of their childhood, particularly of their experiences and frustrations in school. Many experienced years of failure and serious depression.

The best help we can give our children is early identification and aggressive intervention at a young age to prevent the cycle of failure, frustration, and plummeting self-esteem. It is our responsibility in the schools to pull together as a team, doing everything we can to meet these children's needs effectively. This includes providing each child with the environment, skills, tools, and confidence to learn and feel good about himself/herself. We need to be patient, positive, and understanding—and try to see past the behaviors to the whole child—as we provide support and remove the obstacles in their paths.

This book is meant to serve as a comprehensive guide for school personnel trying to make a positive difference in the lives of these children. Regular and special education teachers, counselors, school nurses, administrators, psychologists, and parents will be provided with information, techniques, and strategies that will help students with ADD/ADHD succeed. Although the book is designed and written to address the specific needs of students with ADD/ADHD, the suggested strategies are appropriate and recommended for all students who appear to have attention problems, learning disabilities, or are underachieving for any number of reasons. Be aware that many gifted, intelligent children fall within this category.

For easy use, this resource is organized into thirty sections that provide you with comprehensive, practical guidance on such topics as:

✱ Preventing behavioral problems in the classroom through effective management techniques

✱ How to focus and maintain students' attention

✱ How to teach students organization and study skills

✱ Detailed, multisensory strategies for teaching academic skills—reading, writing, and math

✱ Learning styles: elements and interventions

✱ Cooperative learning techniques

✱ Questions and answers regarding medication and its management with a school nurse

✱ Techniques for relaxation and visualization, including the use of music for calming and facilitating smooth transitions

✱ Challenges and specific interventions for kindergarten and middle school and junior high school students

✱ How to help a student obtain a proper evaluation, assistance, and intervention through a team approach

✱ Protocol and steps for referring students, and documenting and communicating effectively with parents, physicians, and agencies

✱ How administrators can help teachers and students to succeed

I urge all readers to read Section 19, A Parent's Story, the poignant account by the mother of *three* children diagnosed with ADD/ADHD. One of the rewards I have gained in writing this book comes from the wonderful opportunity I had to interview teenagers and adults from across the country who have grown up with ADD/ADHD. Excerpts of these interviews are included throughout this book. By openly sharing their experiences and insights, the parent's story and the personal interviews reveal an important message about *what makes a difference* and the power we have as teachers.

Sandra F. Rief

Acknowledgments

Mrs. Linda Haughey and the Haughey family, for courageously sharing their personal, powerful story in Section 19

Decker Forrest, the illustrator of this book, and my incredibly talented former student (currently in eighth grade)

Those wonderful individuals (Joe, Spencer, Steve, Susan, Mike, Bruce, Amy, Joseph, John, Brita, Malinda, Bob, and Brad) who have grown up with attention and/or learning difficulties, and whose enlightening insights are shared throughout the book

Sandra Wright, M.S.N., school nurse and number one child advocate, for being my role model and friend, and for sharing her vast knowledge in Section 20

Susie Horn, Coordinator of Project for Attention Related Disorders (PARD), San Diego City Schools, for her support, assistance, and guidance as well as her contribution to Section 29

Dr. Jill Reilly, developer and coordinator of Mentor Program in Dakota County, Minnesota, for her contribution to Section 29

Bertha Young, music specialist in the San Diego City Schools, for her contribution to Section 17

The sixteen kindergarten teachers from San Diego County who allowed me to interview them, "pick their brains," and share their expertise for Section 21

The many teachers throughout San Diego County, especially of Benchley-Weinberger Elementary, who have inspired me through their techniques, ideas, and strategies

Matt, Shawna, David, Robert, and Ariel, my "models" for the photos in Section 15

"Turning Point" Program facilitators (San Diego City Schools) for motivating, spreading the message, and building the skills of so many teachers

All of my students—past, present, and future— who teach, inspire, and challenge me

Susan Kolwicz, my editor at Prentice Hall, Simon & Schuster, for her assistance and advice, and for making it such a pleasure to write this book

Last, but not least, my precious husband, parents and three children—Gil, Jackie, and Ariel—for their love, patience and encouragement

Contents

1

What Is ADD/ADHD?

*T*hroughout this book the terms ADD and ADHD are used interchangeably. ADD stands for Attention Deficit Disorder. At this time the most widely used term is ADHD, which means Attention Deficit Hyperactivity Disorder. A child with ADD often *is not* hyperactive. These children are generally not disruptive in the classroom and their behaviors are not necessarily annoying or noticeable to the teacher. However, ADD can be very problematic to the child, causing him or her to significantly underachieve in the classroom and experience low self-esteem.

Behavioral Characteristics of Attention Deficit Disorder Without Hyperactivity (ADD)

* Easily distracted by extraneous stimuli

* Difficulty listening and following directions

* Difficulty focusing and sustaining attention

* Difficulty concentrating and attending to task

* Inconsistent performance in school work—one day the student may be able to do the task, the next day cannot; the student is "consistently inconsistent."

* Tunes out—may appear "spacey"

* Disorganized—loses/can't find belongings (papers, pencils, books); desks and rooms may be a total disaster area

* Poor study skills

* Difficulty working independently

The term ADHD is the current descriptive diagnostic term in the revised third edition of the *American Psychiatric Association's Diagnostic and Statistical Manual* (1987). It is the label used to describe the student who may have many of the above-mentioned characteristics in addition to many associated with a hyperactivity component.

Behavioral Characteristics of Attention Deficit Disorder With Hyperactivity (ADHD):

✳ High activity level

— Appears to be in constant motion

— Often fidgets with hands or feet, squirms, falls from chair

— Finds nearby objects to play with/put in mouth

— Roams around classroom—great difficulty remaining in seat

✳ Impulsivity and lack of self-control

— Blurts out verbally, often inappropriately

— Can't wait for his/her turn

— Often interrupts or intrudes on others

— Often talks excessively

— Gets in trouble because he/she can't "stop and think" before acting (responds first/thinks later)

— Often engages in physically dangerous activities without considering the consequences (for example: jumping from heights, riding bike into street without looking); hence, a high frequency of injuries

✳ Difficulty with transitions/changing activities

✳ Aggressive behavior, easily overstimulated

✳ Socially immature

✳ Low self-esteem and high frustration

Note: Not all symptoms apply to each child, and symptoms will vary in degree. Each child is unique and displays a different combination of behaviors, strengths, weaknesses, interests, talents, and skills.

It is important to recognize that any one of these behaviors is normal in childhood to a certain degree at various developmental stages. For example, it is normal for a young child to have difficulty waiting for his/her turn, to have a short attention span, and to be unable to sit for very long. However, when a child exhibits a *significantly high number of these behaviors when they are developmentally inappropriate (compared to other children their age)*, it is problematic. These children will need assistance and intervention.

What Is the Frequency of ADD/ADHD?

The estimated incidence of ADHD varies widely, depending on the studies you read and the tools used. It is estimated by experts that 3 percent to 10 percent of school-age children are affected. The estimated figures most frequently cited in the literature are 3 percent to 5 percent. However, this is very likely an underestimation due to the fact that many ADD girls often go undiagnosed. ADHD is far more common in boys than girls. Hyperactivity affects at least 2 million children in the United States alone. Girls more commonly have ADD without hyperactivity.

What Are the Possible Causes of ADD/ADHD?

The causes of ADHD are not known at this time. The scientific and medical communities are gaining more and more knowledge about how the brain works and what affects attention and learning. As with many disorders, it is not always possible to identify a cause. At this time, ADD/ADHD is usually attributed to heredity or other biological factors.

When parents have a child who has problems of any kind—medical, physical, psychological, or social—they feel guilty typically and blame themselves. Many parents believe that they did something that may have caused their child to have problems. This feeling of guilt and blame should be dispelled. If a child has ADD/ADHD, it is no one's fault.

The following are possible causes of ADD/ADHD:

* Genetic causes: We do know that ADHD tends to run in families. A child with ADD will frequently have a parent, sibling, grandparent, or other family member who had similar school histories and behaviors during their childhood.

* Biological/physiological causes: Many doctors describe ADHD as neuro-logical inefficiency in the area of the brain which controls impulses and aids in screening sensory input and focusing attention. They say there may be an imbalance or lack of the chemical dopamine which transmits neurosensory messages. The explanation is that apparently when we concentrate, our brain releases extra neurotransmitters, which enable us to focus on one thing and block out competing stimuli. People with ADD seem to have a shortage of these neurotransmitters.

* Complications or trauma in pregnancy or birth

* Lead poisoning

* Diet: ADHD symptoms linked to diet and food allergies continue to remain controversial in the medical community. Current research has not given much support to a dietary connection. However, there are many strong proponents of this theory. Future research will perhaps shed more light on this topic.

* Prenatal alcohol and drug exposure: We are all aware of the impact of the high number of drug-exposed infants who are now of school age. These children have often sustained neurological damage and exhibit many ADHD behaviors. Currently the statistics in the state where I teach are very alarming. Over one in every ten babies born in California today are exposed to drugs in the womb. Scientific research has not yet proven a causal relationship between prenatal drug exposure and ADD. However, drug-exposed children clinically exhibit many neurological deficits and behaviors that we see in ADD children.

Critical Factors in Working With ADD/ADHD Children

*T*here are many critical factors to consider when working with ADD/ADHD students. I have attempted to provide a list that is as useful and complete as possible—one that I hope will make a difference in the way students learn and teachers teach.

1. **Teacher flexibility, commitment, and willingness** to work with the student on a personal level. This means putting forth the time, energy, and extra effort required to really listen to students, be supportive, and make changes and accommodations as needed.

2. **Training and knowledge about ADD/ADHD.** It is essential that teachers are aware that this problem is physiological and biological in nature. These children are not "out to get us" deliberately. Their behaviors aren't calculated to make us crazy. This awareness helps us maintain our patience, sense of humor, and ability to deal with annoying behaviors in a positive way. Every school site (elementary and secondary) should have inservicing to educate staff about ADD/ADHD, the effects of the disorder on the child's learning and school functioning, and appropriate intervention strategies.

3. **Close communication between home and school.** It is very important to increase the number of your contacts and establish a good working relationship with this population of parents. If you are to have any success with ADD/ADHD students, you *need* the support, cooperation, and open line of communication with their parents. (See Section 18.)

4. **Providing clarity and structure for the students.** This guide emphasizes the need for structure. Students with attentional problems need a

5

structured classroom. A structured classroom need not be a traditional, no-nonsense, rigid classroom with few auditory or visual stimuli. The most creative, inviting, colorful, active, and stimulating classroom can still be structured.

Students with ADD/ADHD need to have structure provided for them through clear communication, expectations, rules, consequences, and follow-up. They need to have academic tasks structured by breaking assignments into manageable increments with teacher modeling and guided instruction, clear directions, standards, and feedback. These students require assistance in structuring their materials, workspace, group dynamics, handling choices, and transitional times. Their day needs to be structured by alternating active and quiet periods. No matter what your teaching style or the physical environment of your classroom, you can provide structure for student success.

5. **Creative, engaging, and interactive teaching strategies** that keep the students involved and interacting with their peers are critical! All students need and deserve an enriched, motivational curriculum that employs a variety of approaches. If you haven't had training in multisensory teaching strategies, cooperative learning, reciprocal teaching, learning styles, or the theory of multiple intelligences, you need to update your teaching skills and knowledge for today's classroom. These are good topics for staff development days.

6. **Teamwork** on behalf of the ADD/ADHD student. Many teachers find team-teaching extremely helpful. Being able to "switch" or "share" students for part of the school day often reduces behavioral problems and preserves the teacher's sanity. It also provides for a different perspective on each child.

Teachers cannot be expected to manage and educate these very challenging students without assistance. A proper diagnosis is needed. With many ADD/ADHD students, medical treatment is critical to the child's ability to function in school. Management of the social/behavioral problems these children often exhibit requires help from counseling (in school and often privately). In-school counseling centers can assist in many ways, such as: behavior modification (charts, contracts), time-out/time-away, conflict resolution, training in social skills, relaxation techniques, controlling anger, and cooling down. You need cooperation and partnership with parents and support and assistance from administration. You are all part of the same team!

Elicit the assistance and expertise of your site resources. Refer the child to your site consultation team or student study team. Members of the team will probably observe the student in your classroom or other school settings. They can be of great support by attending meetings with you and parents to share concerns, provide information, and brainstorm "creative" solutions. Many outside referrals for medical/clinical evaluations are initiated at the school site. Your communication with the team is very important.

You can facilitate matters before coming to your team by:

— **Saving work samples** (Any papers or work that reflects the child's strengths and weaknesses) Collect a variety of written samples.

— **Documenting specific behaviors you see** (e.g., falling out of chair, writing only one sentence in 20 minutes of independent work, blurting out inappropriately in class) It is important that teachers document their observations and concerns about these students. This documentation is crucial for many children to get the help they need. Teachers are in a position to facilitate the necessary medical/clinical evaluation and intervention that may be needed for student success.

NOTE: Many times parents don't recognize that their child is experiencing the problems that we are seeing in school. Children with ADD/ADHD present their pattern of behavior year after year. It often takes parents a few years of hearing similar comments from different teachers to become convinced that they should pursue some sort of treatment for their child.

There is another reason for teacher documentation to be placed in the student's records. Physicians will often see the child during a brief office visit, not notice anything significant, and conclude that the student doesn't have a problem. Often the implication is that the problem is with the teacher/school. When the school records show a history of inattention, distractibility, impulsivity, hyperactivity, a physician would be more prone to take the school/parent concerns seriously. The physician/clinician needs to determine that the child's problems are pervasive (visible in a number of settings over a period of time). Good documentation (observations and anecdotal records) help supply the necessary evidence.

— **Communicating with parents.** It is important to share positive observations about their child along with concerns. Be careful how you communicate and voice concerns. Never tell parents, "I'm sure your child has ADD." Communicate your concerns by sharing specific, objective observations. "Becky is very distractible in my class. I have noticed that she . . ." Tell parents the strategies you are using to deal with the problems in the classroom. Then tell parents that you are involving your site team for assistance, and let the school nurse or counselor make recommendations for outside evaluations if deemed necessary. (See Section 27.)

7. **Administrative support.** It is critical that administrators be aware of the characteristics and strategies for effectively managing ADHD students so they can support the teacher in dealing with disruptive children. Some of these students are extremely difficult to maintain in the classroom and require highly creative intervention. You will certainly need administrative support (e.g., having a student removed from class when behaviors interfere with ability to teach or other students' ability to learn). Some intervention for highly disruptive children include: time-outs, suspensions, half-days, cross-age tutors rotating into the classroom to keep the child on-task, and having parents spend the day in class with the student and meeting with the consultation team.

It is important to distribute these students and avoid placing a large group of ADD/ADHD students in the same classroom. Loading one classroom with a high number of ADHD students would burn out the best of teachers and push them to seek another profession. However, it is rare to find a classroom without at least a few ADD/ADHD students (as well as students with learning disabilities).

One of the keys to success is home-school communication and cooperation. When parents are difficult to reach and won't come to school, follow through with home-school contracts, monitor their child's homework, and so on; administrative assistance is also very much needed. (See Section 24.)

8. **Respecting student privacy and confidentiality.** It is important that a student's individual grades, test results, special modifications of assignments or requirements, as well as medication issues are not made common knowledge.

9. **Modifying assignments, cutting the written workload!** What takes an average child 20 minutes to do, often takes this student hours to accomplish (particularly written assignments). There is no need to do every worksheet, math problem, or definition. Be open to making excep-

tions. Allow student to do a more reasonable amount (e.g., every other problem, half a page). Accept alternative methods of sharing their knowledge such as allowing a student to answer questions orally or to dictate answers to a parent, and so on.

Ease up on handwriting requirements and demands for these students. Be sensitive to the extreme physical effort it takes these children to put down in writing what appears simple to you. Typing/word processing skills are to be encouraged.

10. **Limit the amount of homework.** If the parent complains that an inordinate amount of time is spent on homework, be flexible and cut it down to a manageable amount. Typically, in the homes of ADHD children, homework time is a nightmare. Many teachers send home any incomplete classwork. Keep in mind that if the student was unable to complete the work during an entire school day, it is unlikely that he/she will be able to complete it that evening. You will need to prioritize and modify.

11. **Providing more time on assessments.** These students (often very intelligent children) frequently know the information, but can't get it down, particularly on tests. Be flexible in permitting students with these needs to have extra time to take tests, and/or allow them to be assessed verbally.

12. **Teacher sensitivity about embarrassing or humiliating students in front of peers.** Self-esteem is fragile; students with ADD/ADHD typically perceive themselves as failures. Avoid ridicule. Preservation of self-esteem is the primary factor in truly helping these children succeed in life.

13. **Assistance with organization.** Students with ADD/ADHD have major problems with organization and study skills. They need help and additional intervention to make sure assignments are recorded correctly, their work space and materials are organized, notebooks and desks are cleared of unnecessary collections of junk from time to time, and specific study skill strategies are used. (See Section 8.)

14. **Environmental modifications.** Classroom environment is a very important factor in how students function. Due to a variety of learning styles, there should be environmental options given to students that consider where and how they work. Where the student sits can make a significant difference. Lighting, furniture, seating arrangements, ventilation, visual displays, color, areas for relaxation, and provisions for blocking out distractions during seatwork should be carefully considered. Organize the classroom with the awareness that most ADD/ADHD students need to be able to make eye contact with you, have you close by to step forward and cue, be seated near well-focused students, and be given a lot of space. There are many environmental factors that can be regulated and modified to improve ADD/ADHD students' classroom functioning considerably. (See Section 15.)

15. **Value students' differences and help bring out their strengths.** Provide many opportunities for children to demonstrate to their peers what they do well. Recognize the diversity of learning styles and individual approaches in your classroom.

16. **Belief in the student—not giving up when plans A, B, and C don't work.** There are always plans D, E, F,... Success will require going back to the drawing board frequently. These children are worth the extra time and effort.

AN INTERVIEW WITH JOE
(41 years old, California)

"Watch Joseph. He's one of the most intelligent children I've ever seen." This was the comment made to Joe's parents when he and his siblings were tested at a young age by their neighbor, a professor of psychology in New York—Joe, who never received higher than a *D* from sixth grade through high school. Joe, who was constantly ridiculed by his teachers and was "a big disappointment to his parents."

Joe was "left back" in seventh grade while living in Connecticut. He remembers the trauma of all his friends moving on to another school when he repeated seventh. Joe flunked algebra four times. He graduated from high school "dead last" in his class. "After a while I had defaulted into a discipline problem. You gravitate towards those students who have absolutely no respect for the system. Otherwise, you have to agree that the only other thing that could be wrong is YOU."

Junior College was an uphill battle all over again. He saw his classmates "cruise through all their subjects" to get their degree. "The only difference between them and me was that I never knew what to do with numbers. Reading is extremely difficult for me. I have to do it very slowly and put everything into my own translator to assimilate the material and have it make sense." Joe's adult life was "a patchwork of jobs." Up until a few years ago, the average time he stayed with a job was one year. "There were so many days I was beaten to a pulp, and completely down and out until I was thirty years old. I knew there was something wrong with me, but no one knew what it was."

One significant change came in his adult life when a friend took him 'under his wing' and mentored him for three years in his business. Now I have "a good job as a technician in a good company. But it never lets up, I can't get a reprieve. In the real world of high tech, it requires constant training and schooling." Joe was identified as an adult as having learning disabilities and attention deficit disorder.

What would you like to do?

"I'd like to finish school and go to grad school. I've only started. I'll never give up."

What would have made a difference for you growing up?

"No one saw or was interested in my strengths. The spoken word came easily to me, the written word was very difficult. I was able at a young age to take an engine apart and put it back together. I have an excellent understanding of mechanical things. I was always musically talented . . . and I know everything there is to know about reptiles and amphibians.

"If one person would have interceded on my behalf. If one person would have said, 'This is not a stupid person we're dealing with . . . There's something more involved here that we need to get to the bottom of.' The weight of the world would have been lifted from my shoulders."

A List of Don'ts

A teacher says and does hundreds of things during the course of the school day. Every word, gesture, and action affect the students he/she works with. The following list of don'ts was carefully prepared for all professionals to consider when working with these special children.

1. DON'T assume the student is lazy in the classroom. A student with attention deficit disorder or a learning disability is typically not lazy. There are other reasons for their nonperformance in the classroom.

2. DON'T be fooled by inconsistency or assume the student is deliberately not performing because you have observed that at times he/she is able to do that kind of task/assignment. Students with attention deficit disorder have inconsistency as a hallmark characteristic of their disorder. Sometimes they can do the work, sometimes they cannot.

3. DON'T give up on any student. These challenging students often try the patience and could discourage any teacher. These children need your persistence and belief in their ability to succeed no matter how difficult and frustrating it is.

4. DON'T give up on behavior modification techniques. Students with ADHD often do not respond well to behavior modification and positive reinforcements for a long period of time. You will need to revamp, revise, and modify your behavior management system frequently. It is still worth the effort!

5. DON'T forget to involve your support staff. Bring students to consultation team/student study team for assistance. Your team should support you in making observations, helping with behavioral management and classroom strategies, attending meetings with parents, providing information,

and making necessary referrals. Networking with the other professionals at your site eases the load.

6. DON'T neglect to involve parents. Invite parents to visit the school, observe their child in the classroom, and meet with you to plan strategies for working together on behalf of their child. Be sensitive to parents' frustrations and fears. It is very painful and stressful for them to have a child with special problems and needs. Let them know that your primary concern is helping their child to succeed and feel good about himself/herself.

7. DON'T surround yourself with negative peers who are critical of students, aren't open or receptive to new techniques and strategies, or are not updating their skills.

8. DON'T listen to previous teachers who only want to pass on the negative traits and characteristics of their students to you. Assume the best of the child. Allow each student to start the year with a fresh, clean slate.

9. DON'T forget the quiet student in the background who can easily go through the year unnoticed and anonymous.

10. DON'T be afraid to modify, make exceptions, and alter assignments for students as needed. Your goal is the student's success and building/maintaining self-esteem. That requires flexibility and special arrangements with certain students. It is okay and fair to make exceptions for individual students with special needs.

AN INTERVIEW WITH SPENCER'S MOTHER (Colorado)

What are some of the comments you remember from Spencer's teachers that were hurtful?

"One teacher told me, 'If he gets enough *F*'s, he'll learn how to do what is expected of him in fifth grade,' referring to his homework. Another teacher said, 'He slipped a few times and has shown us how bright he is. He's just playing games with us.'"

Tell me about his best teacher

"Spencer's third grade teacher was wonderful. She read to the class with the lights off . . . made sure there wasn't a lot of clutter on the chalkboard or his desk. She seated him to reduce distractions . . . right up front near her. She spoke softly to him and every criticism was coupled with something positive."

A Comprehensive Treatment Program for ADD/ADHD

*O*nce a child is identified and diagnosed with ADHD there are many ways to help the child and the family. The most effective approach is a multifaceted treatment approach which may include:

* Behavior modification and management at home and school

* Counseling. Family counseling is recommended because with an ADHD child in the house, the whole family is affected.

* Individual counseling to learn coping techniques, problem-solving strategies, and how to deal with stress and self-esteem

* Cognitive therapy to give the child the skills to regulate his/her own behavior as well as "stop-and-think" techniques.

* Social skills training (sometimes available in school counseling groups)

* Numerous school interventions (environmental, instructional, behavioral)

* Providing for physical outlet (e.g., swimming, martial arts, gymnastics, running—particularly non-competitive sports)

* Medical intervention (drug therapy)

* Parent education to help parents learn as much as they can about ADHD so they can help their child and be an effective advocate. Parent support groups are excellent sources of training, assistance, and networking. Most communities also have parenting classes and workshops dealing with a variety of helpful management strategies.

When pursuing any treatment, it is a good idea to ask the school nurse and other parents of ADHD children (perhaps through an ADD support group) for references. Seek out doctors and therapists who are knowledgeable and experienced specifically with treating children with ADHD. Medical treatment is often extremely helpful and can make a major difference in treating children with ADHD. However, it is never to be used without the employment of behavioral, environmental and other interventions at home and school.

Physical activity is also very important. Activities such as martial arts (particularly aikido) are recommended because they increase the child's ability to focus and concentrate.

If a child displays the symptoms of possible ADD/ADHD, school interventions should be implemented regardless of whether the child has been diagnosed with ADHD. School personnel may encourage the parents to pursue the evaluation for the purpose of determining how to best help and meet the needs of their child.

AN INTERVIEW WITH JOE
(15 years old, Minnesota)

Joe was diagnosed at a young age with learning disabilities and ADHD.

Tell me about your favorite teacher in elementary school.

"My second grade teacher was my favorite. When I was held back a grade, she always checked on me and asked how I was doing. I still go back and visit her."

I understand you have seen many different doctors over the years. How do you feel about that?

"Yeah. I saw all kinds of doctors including different psychologists and psychiatrists. I took those psychological tests so many times, but the doctors didn't really talk to me. I went to two doctors at the same time, one who took care of my medication, and one because of my psychological problem. I didn't like him. He talked down to me, and I didn't like that."

How did you get along with other kids?

"I'm really good with adults. It's kids that are kind of tough for me. I took offense at what they said. I tried to ignore it, but it took a while. I realize that those kids I had trouble with were just jerks. I'm getting much better now. I've learned that it doesn't happen overnight. It takes a while—everything takes time."

What do you want teachers to be aware of?

"Teachers should be as respectful of kids as kids are to be respectful of them. Class should not be stressful, but relaxed. Teachers shouldn't ever make fun of students. I like active things like research, projects, and reports (especially oral reports)."

What do you want to tell parents?

"Parents need to be aware that kids have a tough time, too, and don't need problems at home. Parents may have a hard time at the office. Well, we have a hard time, too. My dad (a lawyer) does every day what he learned to do and likes to do. In school we're learning new things and we have to do what we've never done before, and reach our teacher's expectations. It's tough. Parents have to be aware and know what their kid is doing in school . . . be involved and make teachers tell you more."

Preventing Behavioral Problems in the Classroom Through Management Techniques

*T*he most critical factors for preventing behavioral problems, particularly for students with special needs (e.g., ADD/ADHD, learning disabilities), include:

*   Clarity of expectations

*   Teaching what is acceptable/unacceptable in your classroom

*   Structure and routine

*   Predictability, consistency

*   Much practice, modeling, and review of behavioral expectations and rules

*   Clear, fair consequences

*   Follow-through

*   Teacher understanding, flexibility, patience

*   Heading off problems with preventive tactics

*   Teacher assistance on a personal level

These children are in particular need of a classroom that is structured, not chaotic. They need to feel secure within the parameters of their classroom, knowing precisely what is expected of them academically and behaviorally.

Teach Your Rules

✳ Make rules few, clear, and comprehensive. Many teachers have students discuss, decide on, and write the classroom rules to give more ownership in class.

Example A:

1. Come prepared to work.

2. Follow directions and stay on task.

3. Keep hands, feet, and objects to yourselves.

4. Be kind and courteous to others.

Example B:

1. Follow directions.

2. Pay attention.

3. Work silently during quiet time.

4. Do your best work.

✳ Explain the rationale for your rules. Any time spent on teaching your rules and modeling all behavioral expectations is time well spent.

✳ Post rules (written or pictorial) in at least one visible spot. Teach with examples. Role-play rules in action. This is appropriate at all grade levels. Review and practice frequently throughout the school year.

✳ With every behavioral expectation you communicate: (1) explain, (2) write it down, (3) demonstrate it in action, and (4) let students practice. Example: Practice 12-inch voices. "What does it sound like? Is this a 12-inch voice?"

✳ Communicate rules and expectations to parents in writing.

Positive Reinforcement

There is no substitute for positive reinforcement in the classroom. It is the best behavioral management strategy and the one that builds self-esteem and respect. Catch students doing what you want them to do. Recognize and praise specific instances. Examples:

"I like the way Cathy remembers to raise her hand and waits to be called on. Thank you, Cathy."

"Adam, I appreciate how quietly you lined up."

"Joey, you did such a good job paying attention and staying with the group."

"It makes me so happy when we are all settled down, and ready to listen."

Some Examples of Positive Reinforcement in the Classroom:

* Legitimate praise and acknowledgment are the best reinforcers.

* Reward students with privileges (e.g., classroom jobs and responsibilities).

* It's generally a good idea not to use the "big guns" (major incentives and rewards) unless they are needed in the classroom. Start with easy, small rewards and incentives.

* Many students are motivated to work for tangible rewards (stickers, prizes, food).

* Other suggested reinforcers include:
    — Choosing a game to play with a friend
    — Earning "free time"
    — Earning breakfast or lunch with the teacher
    — Reading or looking at special interest magazines
    — Using the computer alone or with a friend
    — Listening to music with tape recorder and earphones
    — Working with clay, special pens/paper, whiteboards
    — Leading a game, perhaps as captain of team
    — Removing lowest test grade
    — Skipping an assignment of student's choice
    — Bringing to class/demonstrating something of the student's choice
    — Reducing detention time
    — Chewing gum privileges at specified times

Classroom Incentives

Classroom incentives are great motivators. Here are two that work particularly well for many teachers:

* Students earn tickets or play money to be used towards a weekly, bi-weekly, or monthly auction or raffle. Students can use their accumulated tickets/money to buy assorted toys, items, or privileges from their teacher.

* Marbles or chips are placed in a jar by the teacher when students are caught doing something well or behaving appropriately. When the jar is filled, the class earns a special party (e.g., popcorn, pizza, ice cream), activity, or field trip of some kind.

Assertive Discipline

Have clear consequences for following and not following the rules. Use warnings with incremental consequences when students do not follow the rules. Give positive attention when students are behaving appropriately. Various classroom management systems include the following:

Color-Coded Cards

This is a graphic system for monitoring behavior which is used in many classrooms. There are many variations of this system. It usually involves a pocket chart with an individual envelope or compartment for each student (identified by name or number). All students start the day with one color (e.g., pink card) in their envelope. When there is an infraction of the rules—after a warning—the color is changed (e.g., to yellow) resulting in a consequence such as five minutes of time-out. With the next infraction, the card is changed to the next color (e.g., blue) resulting in stronger consequence. After another infraction, the red card appears, resulting in a more severe consequence.

With this system students start each day with a clean slate. For greatest effectiveness, allow your class to devise the consequences associated with each change of color. Teachers who do not want to post the cards for everyone to see may choose to pass out a pink card at the beginning of each day. As a student's color needs to be changed, the teacher may go to the student's desk and change the card with the student quietly and privately.

Some teachers use a variation of this system. They link each of their classroom rules to a certain color. When a student breaks a specific rule, the teacher places a color card corresponding to the rule broken into the child's pocket. In this way, students are clearly aware of what it is that they did inappropriately. The progressive consequences follow the change of card.

Numbered Cards

Some teachers have students with behavioral monitoring needs go home each day with a number card.

> 5 — Very well behaved. Great day!
>
> 4 — Good day.
>
> 3 — So-so day.
>
> 2 — We had some trouble today
>
> 1 — We had a very difficult day.

Home/School Communication

Many teachers send home some type of notification to parents as to how their child behaved that day or week. Often teachers using the colored card system send home the final color card at the end of the day with each student (or only with those students in need of close home/school monitoring).

Many teachers send home some type of form or slip indicating how well the student behaved during the week. These notices are usually sent home every Friday or on Mondays for the previous week. It is the student's responsibility to return the forms to school with their parent's signature. (See Section 18 on Communication with Parents and Mutual Support.)

Response Costs

Some teachers use a system of payment/fines (response cost) with students. Example: Using plastic colored links (found in catalogs selling math materials), the teacher awards monetary value to the four colors of the links: yellow=penny, red=nickel, green=dime, blue=quarter. The teacher "pays" students for good behavior: (a) the whole class earns points and the teacher awards all students a certain value for their links; (b) individually, for on-task behavior; (c) groups, for cooperative work assignments/projects. The possibilities are limitless. Students are "fined" for offenses such as: no homework, getting out of seat, and off-task behavior. Every week or every other week students get to "buy" small treats or privileges with their money (value of links).

How to Avoid Behavioral Problems

Behavioral problems often occur when the students are undirected. Planning well and beginning instruction promptly are generally good deterrents to behavior problems.

Try to greet students at the door as they arrive in class. Offer directions as needed before they enter the room. A smile and "hello" is a nice way to start the day. Handing the students a brief assignment to work on as they enter the room is also a deterrent to behavioral problems.

The same applies for claiming students after recess, lunch, gym, art, or music. Be there on time. These transitional times are frequently the worst times for ADHD students.

Time Outs and Time Aways

Time outs or time aways for ADHD students are necessary in most cases. These children often can't handle all of the stimulation in a classroom and become worked up and sometimes out of control. Time away from the group is often needed to calm them down and help them regain self-control.

Use time outs and time aways as needed:

* In the classroom, away from distractions.

* Buddy or partner up with another teacher (preferably cross-grade) for time outs. Student is brought to the receiving classroom with an independent assignment to work on for a specified amount of time. This is usually a very effective system.

* In the counseling center.

Here are some tips for time outs and time aways:

* Try directing the student to time out calmly and positively. Example: "Michael, I would like for you to sit with your hands and feet to yourself. If you can't handle that, go back to the table. You can join us when you are ready to sit without touching others."

✳ Some teachers use a "think-about-it" chair for a specified amount of time, for example, 3 to 5 minutes to think about their inappropriate behavior.

✳ Other teachers have students sit away from the class until they feel ready to join the class again. A typical rule of thumb is one minute of time out per year of age. So, a six-year-old may have about six minutes time out or away from the group

✳ As a next step, other teachers send the student to sit outside the room. When the student feels that he/she can behave properly, he/she comes voluntarily inside the door, and waits there quietly until the teacher acknowledges him/her. The teacher might say something like: "I am glad you're ready to follow our rules. Please join us."

✳ If the student continues to be disruptive, the next step is often to be sent to the counseling center or another classroom for time away, and then the office.

✳ Teachers with access to telephones have good results since they can call home or the parent's work place together with the student.

Note: Primary teachers should read Section 21, What About Kindergarten? This section contains many behavior management suggestions successful with young students.

Caution: Teachers need to be careful not to overuse time outs and to be sure that the child is aware of the behavior that caused him/her to receive the time out.

Behavioral Contracts

Write a contract specifying what behavior is expected and what the reinforcement will be when the behavior/task is completed. Behavior modification methods are often effective with students and should always be tried. Be aware that effectiveness for ADHD students may be short-lived and your rewards/systems will need to be revamped frequently. Don't be discouraged. Give it a try. Involve your school counselor for assistance. Of course, you will need parental involvement and support. (See samples at end of this section.)

Proximity Control

Stay close to students with attentional or behavioral problems. Circulate in the classroom. A hand on the shoulder or a direct look with quiet reminder is effective.

Students with ADD/ADHD should be seated close to teachers and next to or between well-focused students. Avoid seating them along the periphery. Often second row is better than first row for teacher-pupil eye contact. Avoid seating near learning centers, the door, windows, or other disractors. (See Section 7 and Section 15.)

The Personal Connection

Take students aside to talk about their behavior. Talk calmly and matter of factly. Give warnings and explain what the consequences of their breaking rules will be. Then, follow through.

Talk it out. When there is a problem, talk to the student about it in private conference. Try (a) passive listening—hear the student out without interrupting; (b) acknowledgment responses—give verbal and/or nonverbal feedback that the student has been heard by you; (c) active listening—respond, ask reflective questions, such as "Come sit with me . . . Maybe we can find a solution." "I'm not sure I understand what you mean. Can you tell me more?"

Try to state the problem in terms of the specific behavior and avoid messages to the student that he/she is "bad." Restate the guidelines, limits, and consequences in a quiet, calm manner.

Parent contacts are crucial. Elicit parental support through conferences, phone calls, and regular, frequent reporting of behavior and work completion. Remember: With all parental contacts communicate that you care about the student. Always include positives and recognition of what student is doing right along with your concerns.

Appropriate Behavior Modeling

Use cross-age tutors or peers to model specific types of behavior that the student is having difficulty with.

Take photos of students engaged in positive behaviors (which can be photographed during role play) and display them in the classroom. Rather than hanging them in the room, you may show them when needed to remind about your expectations. It is very effective to have a photo of the student seated properly and appearing to be on-task. Tape the photo directly to the student's desk. Cue the child by walking over and pointing to the picture—encouraging him/her to look like the photo.

Preventive Cueing

Preventive cueing is a technique for stopping disruptive behavior before it begins and for avoiding confrontation or embarrassment of the student in front of peers. The teacher arranges privately with the student a predetermined hand signal or word signal to cue the student to calm down, pay attention, stop talking out, stop rocking in chair. These are all quiet reminders.

Examples of cueing:

* Use traffic light or stop sign signal to indicate slow down/stop behavior.

* Go over to the student, look directly into his/her eyes and tap your chin a few times to indicate that you want him/her to focus on you.

* Use the two-thumbs up sign indicating that the student can get up and move to another part of the room or outside the door. (See Section 7—Attention . . . Getting It . . . Focusing It . . . Keeping It.)

* Students to whom you have taught relaxation strategies (see Section 17) can be cued with a word or two to start using the specific strategies to relax and regain control.

How effectively they will be able to use the strategy will depend on how much they practice and internalize the technique. For example, I have taught some students to visualize a color that is calming and peaceful to them. The students are taught to "breathe in" that specific color and to send it throughout their bodies to relax and feel peaceful and in control. When one of those students begins to "lose it" in class, the goal is for me to be able to walk over to that student and try cueing him/her to apply the strategy. With a word or a few quiet words and cues (e.g., "Breathe, . . . send the turquoise through your body," the student may be able to calm himself/herself and regain control.

✳ Student "help" signs or colored cards can be given to students to place or prop up on their desks. Examples:

— I'm working. (green card)

— I'm finished. (blue card)

— I need help. (red card)

✳ Send student short, handwritten notes. "Please remember to _____."

✳ Use reminder cards on desks of students (written directions or picture clues).

Try to keep in mind that these children are not "out to get you," and annoying, disruptive behaviors are often not intentional or even in the child's awareness. Help by doing the following:

✳ Avoid criticism and "don't" statements. Teach and explain what behaviors you do want to see. Make your expectations clear.

✳ Show respect for the student and, whenever possible, keep your sense of humor!

What Should I Do About . . . ?

1. The child who is totally out of control—yelling, swearing, hiding under desk:

First, have the child removed from your classroom immediately. Some schools have a crisis team to deal with such problems. When a child is totally out of control, the office is immediately alerted and someone from the team (e.g., principal, VP, counselor) comes to the classroom to deal with the child while the teacher takes the rest of the class out of the room. For extreme cases you need administrative support and immediate involvement from your site consultation team to meet with parents, plan strategies, and give you support and assistance.

2. The child who can't stay seated and who is constantly falling out of the chair:

In private time with student, explain your concern and expectation that he/she remain seated. Ask student why he/she can't stay seated. Sometimes the size of the chair is inappropriate and not comfortable. Sometimes seat cushions help. Other times allowing the student to straddle the back of the chair is helpful.

Most of these children generally have a physiological need for mobility. Make sure your instruction allows for active involvement and some movement. Work out a system with the student that gives him/her more opportunity to get up when needed and to move around. Some students need the structure of masking tape boundaries on the floor indicating the space they are allowed.

Try a contract for "sitting in chair" with positive reinforcement. Start with a baseline of time they may be able to stay seated and work to build up that amount of time. Try a private cue with the student.

A logical consequence for a student who cannot sit in a chair without causing a disturbance is to temporarily lose the privilege to sit. Have the student remain standing for a specified amount of time. Seat work might have to be done standing or kneeling. Some children cannot physically remain seated for any length of time. You will have to be tolerant and willing to ignore some of this behavior, allowing some children to stand up by their seats as needed.

3. The impulsive child who blurts out in class all the time:

Try a contract and positive reinforcement for raising a hand. A token system may be effective for reminding a student who does not have the inner controls to stop himself/herself. Begin the day by giving the student a certain amount of chips/tokens in a little cup. Whenever he/she blurts out inappropriately in class, remove a chip from the cup with a quiet reminder or signal to raise a hand. Don't acknowledge this student's answer or response during blurt-outs. Ignore what he/she said. When all chips are gone, the negative consequence follows (time out, loss of privilege, and so on). If chips remain at the end of the day (or specified amount of time), positive reinforcement follows.

This child needs proximity control with teacher reminders that are physical (gentle touch) and auditory (e.g., whispering to student or talking in a soft voice): "Robert, you need to raise your hand." Then call on someone else.

4. The child who is constantly angry or upset about something:

Find time to talk with and listen to the student. Refer to the counselor for assistance. Acknowledge the child's feelings and offer acceptable, more appropriate responses or alternatives.

* Provide for a release of physical tension—running track, writing about anger in a journal or on paper.

* Teach relaxation strategies. (See Section 16.)

* Teach the student to become aware of his/her internal feelings when he/she is becoming upset and to practice techniques such as: deep breathing, giving self reminders ("chill out," count backwards from 25 before doing or saying anything).

* ADD/ADHD students often have peer problems due to generally weak social skills. Incorporate social skill training/awareness whenever you can, especially in cooperative learning groups.

* Try a contract with positive reinforcement. Obvious negative consequences will occur if the student breaks rules out of anger.

5. The child who is always irritating peers:
Often this child is unaware of how annoying he/she is to others and it is best to bring it to the child's attention at a time when he/she would not be humiliated in front of peers. Talk about how it makes others feel and how it would make them feel if their 'space was invaded.' Take a good look at environmental alternatives. Give this student space—leg room, extra tabletop space, extra seating space. Reward the student (praise) when he/she is facing forward and seated properly. Make a big deal out of how great it is to see the child seated appropriately.

AN INTERVIEW WITH STEVE
(16 years old, California)

Steve has learning disabilities and ADHD

What is your advice to teachers?

"Don't embarrass kids in front of the whole class. If you need to talk to them about something they did, the teachers should tell them in private. Otherwise, you just end up hating the teacher and then you're not going to listen to what they say. . . . When somebody is frustrated, give them a couple of minutes to cool down before they get in trouble."

Sample Contracts

	Monday	Tuesday	Wednesday	Thursday	Friday

✳ Choose one, two, or three behaviors (together with the student) to monitor daily or two times a day. The above example is designed to monitor two times a day (before lunch/after lunch).

✳ Student brings you the card for your initials, stars, or whatever symbol you choose if student earns.

✳ Reinforce according to contract agreement.

Examples of possible behaviors to choose from:

1. I pay attention.

2. I control my temper.

3. I listen to my teacher.

4. I keep my hands and feet to myself.

5. I raise my hand before talking.

6. I do my best work.

7. I sit appropriately in my chair.

8. I speak politely to others.

Contract Examples to Use with Monitoring Card

Example A

If I earn _____ stars on my chart by Wednesday afternoon, I will earn

_____ .

Signature _____

Date _____

Example B

If I earn _____ stars on my chart by Friday, I will earn _____

_____ .

Signature _____

Date _____

Example C

Every time I earn _____ stars, I will earn _____

_____ .

Signature _____

Date _____

Date _____

Next time we will be better at

_____
(behavior)

Signed   _____   _____

              _____   _____

Date _____

We will

_____
(behavior)

Signed   _____   _____

              _____   _____

section

6

Preventing Problems During Transitions and Noninstructional Time

*T*ransitions and noninstructional time are typically the most disastrous times of the day for ADD/ADHD students. The time between activities and periods takes 15 percent of the school day in an average classroom. Hyperactive children have major problems during recess, riding the bus, waiting in the lunch line, on the way to the bathroom, and so on.

What Are Some Ways to Help?

1. Avoid catching the student off guard. Prepare him/her for any change in routine (e.g., assemblies, guest speakers, field trips, substitute teachers).

2. Talk about what will take place and teach the necessary behaviors. Role play is helpful, especially for young students, in preparing for upcoming changes.

3. Use signals (e.g., flashing the lights, ringing a bell, playing music) to indicate that an activity is coming to an end and the children need to finish whatever they are doing. Five-minute warnings are often used. Kindergarten teachers are masters of these techniques. Such signals are helpful at all grade levels.

4. Build in stretch breaks and brief exercise between activities, particularly ones that require a lot of sitting or intense work.

5. Use relaxation and imagery activities and exercises for calming after recess, lunch, and P.E. (See Section 16 relaxation strategies.)

6. Help physically guide students through transitions. Some children may need you, an aide, or another student to give extra help, stay close, and model appropriate behavior during transitions.

7. Reward smooth transitions. Some teachers use individual points or table points to reward students or table clusters of students who are ready for the next activity.

8. Some teachers use whole class incentives for transitions. One technique is to place a circle on the chalkboard. Prior to making the transition (e.g., cleaning up after an art activity and settling down before the next activity), the teacher signals the students, tells them he/she will count to a certain number, and then proceeds to count. If everyone in the class manages to be ready with the cleanup by the time the teacher finishes counting, the teacher places a checkmark in the circle. If the whole class is not ready, the teacher says, "Oh, well, maybe next time." If the class earns a specified number of checks in the circle by the end of the week, there is a class reward.

9. For the behavioral problems that take place during out-of-classroom activities, you need to plan site strategies above and beyond what may be spelled out in your site discipline plan. Brainstorm strategies with your colleagues, including the administration and consultation team.

10. There may need to be more structuring of recess activities. ADHD students often have difficulty waiting turns and entering games. They may do better with hula hoops, jump ropes, relay races, and Simon Says activities. Cross-age student helpers may assist with some great activities at your site.

11. Clue in aides and other staff members who are working with these students and have difficulties with them out of the classroom. They may benefit greatly from some awareness training about these children's behavior and special needs. Include them when possible in staff development about ADD/ADHD or learning disabilities. Make sure the classroom teacher is aware of out-of-classroom behavioral problems so that he/she can alert parents.

12. Prepare for independent seat work time:
    — Make sure activities/assignments are clearly explained.
    — Write down what students should be doing during that time.
    — For certain students clarify and structure even further.

Examples to Consider:

✴ Write a list of what to do. Have student cross out each task when completed.

✴ Use a timer to complete a reasonable amount of work. Reward for completion/on-task behavior.

✱ If assignment is difficult or lengthy, shorten or modify as needed. Don't give independent work that is very difficult.

✱ Assign the student a buddy or use cooperative learning groups to clarify questions as needed. When teacher is with another group, avoid interruptions by telling class that they must ask a classmate or their group first. Only if no one in the group can answer the question may the teacher be asked.

✱ Provide study carrels and quiet areas for students who tend to be distracted during seat work time.

✱ Some students need complete quiet and may benefit from earphones or ear plugs to block out noise.

✱ Make sure necessary supplies are available so students can work during independent time without excuses. Remember to have extra (but less desirable) materials available for unprepared students.

Attention: Getting It, Focusing It, Keeping It

*B*eing able to catch and hold our students' interest and attention is not always an easy task. Keeping an ADD/ADHD student focused and on-task is a monumental challenge to teachers, and one that requires experimenting with a variety of approaches.

Ways to Get Students' Attention

1. Signal your students by any number of techniques—turning off the lights, flashing the lights, ringing a bell, raising your hand which signals the children to raise their hands and close their mouths until everyone is silent, playing a bar of music on the piano or guitar, and so on.

2. Vary tone of voice: loud, soft, whispering. Try making a loud command: "Listen! Ready! Freeze!" followed by a few seconds of silence before proceeding in a normal voice to give directions.

3. Eye contact. Student should be facing you when you are speaking, especially while instructions are being given. Teachers who have students seated with desks in clusters need to work out and structure with those students who face away from them, how to turn their chairs and bodies around to face the teacher when signaled to do so.

4. Model excitement and enthusiasm about the upcoming lesson.

5. Ask the class an interesting, speculative question to generate discussion and interest in the upcoming lesson.

6. Try "silliness" and theatrics at times. Sometimes props such as a crazy hat or music are helpful in getting your students' attention.

7. Mystery. Bring in an object relevant to the upcoming lesson in a box, bag, pillowcase. This is a wonderful way to generate predictions and can lead to excellent discussions or writing activities.

8. Other "into" strategies prior to reading (See Language Arts, Section 10). Bring in past experiences of students through discussion, poems, visuals, and so on prior to reading the story/chapter.

9. Make sure it is quiet before proceeding with instruction.

How to Focus Students' Attention

1. Employ multisensory strategies when directions are given and a lesson is presented. (See Section 9.)

2. Use visuals. Write key words or pictures on the board or overhead projector while presenting.

3. Use color. Use colored chalk to highlight on the chalkboard, and colored pens on the overhead. Write key words, phrases, steps to computation problems, tricky letters in spelling words, and so on in a different color.

4. Frame the visual material you want students to be focused on with your hands or with a colored box around it.

5. Point to written material you want students to focus on with your finger, a dowel, a stick/pointer.

   Note: Overhead projectors are the best tools for focusing students' attention in the classroom. The teacher is able to write down information in color without having to turn his/her back on the students, thus improving classroom management and reducing behavioral problems. On the overhead, teachers can model easily, frame important information, and students love to be called up to write on the transparency.

   Transparencies of material can be made in advance, saving the teacher time. The transparency can be partially covered up, blocking out any distracting visual stimuli. The room can be darkened, and the light on the screen holds students' attention. I urge teachers who do not have access to an overhead projector to try any available means to get one.

6. Use a flashlight. Turn off the lights and get students to focus by illuminating objects or individuals with a flashlight.

7. Incorporate demonstrations and hands-on presentations into your teaching whenever possible.

8. Explain purpose and relevance whenever possible to hook students in to your lesson.

9. Maintain your visibility.

10. Project your voice and make sure you can be heard clearly by all students. Be aware of competing sounds in your room environment such as heaters and air conditioners.

Tips for Helping Distractible Students

1. Seat students up close near the teacher.

2. Make direct eye contact with this student.

3. Clear hands and desk of distractions.

4. Make sure child is seated among attentive, well-focused students.

5. Use physical contact (e.g., hand on shoulder or back).

6. Positive reinforcement and behavior modification techniques/incentives can be employed (e.g., table points for being attentive and on-task, individual charts, contracts and cards for teacher to give points, stickers, initials, and so on).

7. Praise the student when focused: "I like the way Adrian is sitting up and looking at the board."

8. Use private signals and cues that have been arranged with this student to help focus attention. Examples: When teacher points to his/her eyes, it means "look." Pointing to the teacher's ear means "listen." When the teacher points to and taps his/her chin it means "watch my face and pay attention."

Maintaining Attention and Keeping Students' Involvement

1. Keep the lesson clear.

2. Present at a snappy, brisk pace.

3. Reduce lag time by being prepared.

4. Use pictures, diagrams, gestures, manipulatives, and high-interest material.

5. Structure the lesson so that it can be done in pairs or small groups for maximum student involvement and attention. Cooperative Learning is the ideal strategy and structure for keeping students engaged and participating. It is a critical teaching skill to learn for today's classrooms! (See Section 14.)

6. Use higher-level questioning techniques. Ask questions that are open-ended, require reasoning and stimulate critical thinking and discussion.

7. Have students write down brief notes during instruction.

8. Use cloze techniques. Provide a study sheet or study guide with key words omitted. Have students fill in the missing words during instruction. Using a teacher-provided study sheet, have students HIGHLIGHT in color the key points.

Example of cloze method: "This chapter provides suggestions on how to get students' _____ and keep them _____ _____."

9. Call on students with equity. Many teachers inadvertently ignore certain students in the classroom. Teachers are generally unaware that they overlook students seated in certain parts of the room, or that they may call on males more frequently than females. Some teachers tend to call on those students who typically can 'feed back' the information that the teacher is looking for. Other teachers will deliberately call on students who they think are not prepared or will not know the answer. Statistics in gender/ethnic expectations and student achievement (GESA) prove this to be overwhelmingly so. (See Bibliography and Recommended Reading section for reference by Dolores A. Grayson and Mary D. Martin, *GESA*.)

   Students are very astute and quickly learn their teachers' habits and system and their chances of being called on to contribute in class. Students who perceive that they will be required to contribute and speak in front of their peers will remain more attentive. GESA training suggests strategies to ensure that students are called on with greater equity. Teachers may want to try some of the following:

   — Use a deck of cards with each student's name on it. Pick from the deck randomly to call on students, replacing the card back in the deck each time.

   — Write the students' names on popsicle sticks and pull them at random to call on students.

   — Videotape yourself or tape record yourself on occasion to check your own tendencies and observe who you respond to the most. This awareness helps us make a conscious effort to respond to students we may have been ignoring in the past. ***Note:*** I noticed that I look toward the left side of the room and respond to those children more frequently than students on the right. I also tend to give more attention to those students who are disruptive than to the quieter students. With this awareness, I am trying to change.

   — Have students keep a tally card on their desk. Tell them that you are trying to make sure you are being fair in who you call on in class. Ask them to put a tally mark on the card each time that you call on them in class. This can be done for a day, or over a period of a few days or a week. The results can be very revealing to the teacher, and kids are generally happy to cooperate. Students also view random methods as being fair.

10. Allow at least 5 seconds of wait time. Many students need more time to process the question, gather their thoughts, and be able to express them. Try rephrasing, ask probing questions, and wait longer for a response. Tell students who cannot answer the question that you will come back to them later—then do it.

11. Make special arrangements. Be sensitive to students who are often viewed by peers as poor students who never know the answer. Be open to making a special arrangement in private with a student to help bolster their self-esteem. You may try telling the student to go ahead and raise his/her hand with a fist closed, and you will not call on him/her at that time. When the student raises an open hand, you will make every effort to call on the student at that time.

I have heard from my colleagues that this technique is very effective in changing peer perception of individuals who seldom raise their hand. Other classmates are not aware of the fist or open hand and only notice that the student appears to know the answer and wishes to contribute in class.

12. Have students actively participate in the lesson to keep them involved and focused. Try the following techniques:

— Brainstorm. Have students generate ideas related to the topic orally. Teacher writes down all ideas/contributions on the chalkboard, butcher paper, or overhead transparency.

— "Turn to your partner (or person across from you, behind you) and discuss for a few minutes." or "Write down with your partner all the things you can think of that _____ ."

— Quickwrites. Give students a brief amount of time to write in a response to your question or prompt. They then have to read what they wrote to a partner, group, or the whole class.

Methods for Unison Response

Rather than calling on individual students (which gives the distractible student the opportunity to "zone out"), try other methods for checking for understanding:

1. Use individual whiteboards or chalkboards. Each student can keep one at their desk or the teacher can pass them out as needed. When the teacher asks the class a question or has them do a math problem, the students write on their boards, and at the teacher's signal, hold them up under their chins for the teacher to see.

Note: Many teachers who use individual chalkboards have students bring an old sock or baby bootie to class to store their piece of chalk and use as an eraser.

2. Direct instruction methods. Hold your hand out with a straight arm while asking your students a question. Make sure they are instructed to watch you carefully. After giving some "think time," drop your arm—preferably with a snap of your fingers or other auditory signal. At this prompt, students all call out the answer in unison.

3. Point/tap method. Point to the left of a word (e.g., from a list of words written on the chalkboard or overhead projector). Tell students that whenever you are pointing to a word, they need to be trying to read the word silently. Tell them that when you tap the word with your pointer or chalk, they are to say the word out loud. Give some think time and then cue: "What word?" Then tap. At that signal, all students respond in unison. This direct instruction technique is very effective for keeping all students' attention when reading lists or charts.

4. Yes/no whole class responses. These can be done in a variety of ways. It is recommended that hand signals or held-up cards should be done in such a way that there is communication only between the teacher and the individual students. Teach students to hold up fingers, cards, and so on under the chin, close to the body, facing forward. This way the rest of the class can't easily look around and check your answer. Examples may include:

— Thumbs up (yes), thumbs down (no)
— Green card (yes), red card (no)
— Open hand (yes), closed hand (no)
— Happy face card (yes), sad face card (no)

5. Operation sign cards (for word problems). Students hold up the sign of the operation that is needed to solve the problem.

6. Number fans. These are excellent for whole group responses to math problems or other questioning. They can be used for responding to questions such as: (1) I strongly agree; (2) I kind of agree; (3) I disagree.

Number fans can be made by writing numerals on cardboard tag cards, hole punch one end and attach with a brad. Students hold up their answer to math problems or math facts.

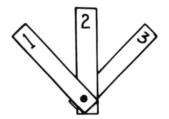

Keeping Students On-Task During Seat Work

1. Check for clarity. Make sure directions were clear and understood before sending students back to their seats to work independently.

2. Give a manageable amount of work that student is capable of doing independently.

3. Give other 'failproof' work that student can do in the meantime if he/she is stumped on an assignment and needs to wait for teacher attention or assistance.

4. Scan classroom frequently. All students need positive reinforcement. Give positive comments frequently, praising students you observe to be on-task. This serves as a reminder to students who tend to have difficulty.

5. Consider using a timer for some students who work well with a "beat the clock" system for work completion.

6. Use contracts, charts, and behavior modification systems for on-task behavior.

7. Use response costs and natural consequences for off-task behavior. Student might "owe you time" at the end of the day, before school, or for part of recess time. If they are on a point system, they may be fined points if a reasonable amount of work isn't accomplished.

8. Make use of study carrels or quiet office areas for seat work.

9. Study buddies or partners may be assigned for any clarification purposes during seat work, especially when the teacher is instructing another group of students while part of the class is doing seat work.

10. Signals to the teacher/aide for "I need help!" Some teachers use a sign or a colored signal that students may place on their desk that alerts any adult scanning the room that he/she needs assistance.

AN INTERVIEW WITH BOB
(49 years old)

Bob grew up in New England. He has a Master of Science degree, is retired from the Navy, and is currently a business consultant and government contractor.

Tell me how your attentional problems affected you in school.

"Reading was my biggest frustration. I would avoid it at all costs. I loved picture books and resources like *National Geographic*, but read the captions only. That was the extent of my attention span. I couldn't concentrate on a page five minutes. I often didn't test well. I had trouble paying attention to the test and would get frustrated. Sometimes I would just draw little designs all over the test."

Tell me about your coping skills.

"I always had the ability to take a very small piece of information (hard data), look at it, touch it, hear it, and then turn around and draw you a picture of the finished product. One experience I remember was in sixth grade when we had to do oral reports in front of the class. Earlier in the year I had no problems because we could make or draw something, then just get up and talk about what we made. This time the teacher required a written report to get up and share. I never did it because it was very difficult for me to concentrate and focus long enough to get it down in writing. I remember that I memorized all of the data and information and presented the report orally from memory. My teacher was furious. She tore me up one side and down the other."

What memories do you have of secondary school?

"Teachers branded me as a nonachiever. I vividly remember my history teacher in my senior year of high school. In my family there was no question that I would be going to college. Everyone in my family was a college graduate. This teacher did everything in her power to prove that I was not 'college material.' She would exclude me from class and had me sitting in a back room drawing maps for her instead of letting me participate in class. People say that with time you forget those kinds of experiences, but you don't. I still can feel the anger and animosity towards that teacher."

What advice can you give teachers? What would have made a difference?

"I guess I would tell teachers that there are a thousand roads to roam. Not everyone is going to choose the same path. Everybody has different ways of assimilating data—different filters, different life experiences that affect how they look at things and process information. To be fair, teachers need to first evaluate if some other method of learning is available to help one child or another to do what they have to do. Some might be adept at reading. Others are like me: If you touch it and feel it, you own it. For me to do my best, put me in a group with three or four people (of whatever aptitude). I get the most from a group structure where there is a lot of verbal interchange."

8

How to Teach Students Organization and Study Skills

Students with ADD/ADHD have major problems with organizational and study skills. This is, in fact, one of the key characteristics of the disorder. These students need direct assistance, structuring, and training in how to:

* Organize their material

* Organize their work place

* Record their assignments

* Make lists

* Prioritize activities

* Plan for short-term assignments

* Break down long-term assignments

* Know standards of acceptable work

* Read and use a calendar

* Read a clock and follow a schedule

* Know what to take home and leave home

* Know what to take home and return

* Know when and where to turn in assignments

* Know what to do specifically during seat work

* Know what to do when seat work is completed

* Know what materials are needed and expected

Critical Skills to Teach ADD/ADHD Students

There is an outstanding program that is being used in many school districts that trains students in the above skills as well as in several learning strategies such as active reading, taking notes, mapping written material, proofreading, studying for tests, and using reference books. The program, *Skills for School Success*, by Dr. Anita Archer and Mary Gleason, Curriculum Associates, Inc. (see bibliography and recommended resources) is very effective and successful in teaching students these important lifetime skills. Many schools are using *Skills for School Success* as a school-wide program, so students have the training and consistency across grade levels and the opportunity to truly internalize the organizational and study skills taught.

A major component of the *Skills for School Success* program is the consistent use of a standard three-ring notebook with subject dividers and side pockets (for take-home/leave home and take-home/return papers). Students are also given a plastic pouch for supplies and a monthly calendar for recording all assignments.

Students need to be taught how to use a monthly calendar and record assignments on their due date. As Dr. Archer points out, the "due date" is not, as many students believe, the day you are supposed to "do" the assignment. Parents need to expect notebooks home *daily* and check the assignment calendar and side pockets with the student. Dr. Archer recommends having a laminated card stating "no homework tonight" which is given to students to place in the side pocket of their notebooks when indeed there is no specific homework assignment that evening.

Methods for Recording Homework Assignments and Organizing Work Area and Materials

ADD/ADHD students often have trouble recording homework assignments in any format (on a monthly calendar or daily/weekly homework sheet). Try the following to assure that assignments are being recorded accurately:

1. Assign a peer study buddy. This student will assist in making sure all assignments are recorded on the assignment sheet or calendar. Usually study buddies are seated at the same table or next to each other.

2. Make sure all assignments are written on the board, not just given orally.

3. At the time you give assignments for each subject, have students open to their assignment calendars and record along with you at that time. If you have an overhead projector, it is ideal to make a transparency of the assignment calendar and lead students through the recording of their assignments.

4. Students who have particular trouble with these skills may do better with a daily action list. After recording assignments on the calendar (including tests, book reports, and any projects due), help students with writing a

things-to-do list. Daily things-to-do lists where students cross off items as they are completed are very effective.

5. Leave a couple of minutes at the end of the school day to review all homework, have a quick check to make sure necessary books and supplies are going home, and so on.

6. Communicate with parents when there is a problem with homework. Make sure they know your system and what you are doing to provide extra help. Parents need to do their part to help with homework, organization, and study skills.

7. Teach your expectations for materials that you expect in class at all times (e.g., sharpened pencils with erasers, notebook paper). When students come to class unprepared, give them inferior, less desirable materials as substitutes (e.g., backside of ditto paper; old, chewed-up pencils). This will show that you are serious about your expectations. Don't reinforce poor study skills and irresponsibility by allowing them to borrow desirable materials from you or their neighbors, particularly on a regular basis.

8. Have schedules and unscheduled notebook checks/desk checks, and reward students for good organization (e.g., special certificates, "no homework tonight" passes, special privileges).

9. Collect homework! Either have a specific place for turning assignments in each day or go student-to-student and collect it directly.

10. Provide for clean-out times for students to sort and clean out their desks and notebooks. Students with problems in organization need an adult to help them sort and dump ("recycle") unnecessary papers periodically. Use an aide, volunteer, or very organized student buddy for this purpose.

11. Make sure homework is review work or practice work, not new information that the student has to figure out on his/her own with a parent.

12. If student/parent reports that he/she is spending hours each night on homework, modify that work, cut the workload!

How to Help Students With Written Work Organization

1. Teach consistent standards of work (e.g., on notebook paper, write on every other line, include a heading with name, date, subject, and page number). *Skills for School Success* is excellent for teaching students these standards and the importance of neat, quality work.

2. Teach student to space properly and avoid crowding by placing his/her index finger between each word to avoid crowding.

3. Lightly draw in left and right margins on paper for students and teach them not to cross the boundary lines.

4. Many students try writing without anchoring their paper on the desk. Often they write while propping up their heads with their other arm. Teach/require that one arm or hand should anchor the paper. If it's a real problem, try adhesive to keep paper down on desk.

5. ADD/ADHD students make numerous careless errors and frequently need to make erasures—resulting in torn, messy papers. I recommend that they use heavier, thicker paper that doesn't rip so easily. It is also easier and kinder to accept neat cross-outs (one line through word) with caret (^) and correction above the line. Even if you don't allow this for the rest of your class, it is very helpful for students who struggle with written output.

6. Teach proportion of letters for younger students by referring to the top line as the "head line," middle line as the "belt line," and the bottom line as the "foot line."

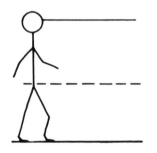

Remind students about the relative size of their letters: "Remember, the humps on the letter *m* come up to the belt line and not higher."

7. Math problems are often hard to organize on paper. Require students to leave lots of space between problems and to number and circle the number of each problem. It is often helpful to have students use graph paper for math problems or to use notebook paper written on sideways (with lines going down the page, rather than across the page). Any pre-lined paper that helps students keep their columns aligned properly is helpful.

How to Avoid Visual Clutter

Students with ADD/ADHD and/or students with visual processing problems have trouble focusing when there is visual clutter distracting them.

Help these children focus by trying the following:

1. Provide handouts and tests that are dark copies, double- or triple-spaced and easy to read (not too cluttered).

2. Try to erase unnecessary writing on the chalkboard. Use color whenever possible to catch attention. White boards are preferable to chalkboards (because of lack of dust and ability to use different colors).

3. Avoid clutter on desks. Help students keep as little as possible on their desk tops.

4. Color-coded file folders for student's use are helpful.

5. Placing colored sticker (dot) on outside cover of texts often helps student locate books more quickly. (For example, blue dot = Writer's Corner, green dot = Reader's Corner.)

6. Make sure student has adequate storage space and as few materials to worry about as possible.

7. Require students to carry a backpack or bookbag.

8. If younger students don't use a notebook, you may want to use a large, laminated envelope with students' names printed on it for the take-home system.

9. You may want to try an organizational system in your room with tubs or trays labeled "To be checked," "Corrected work to return," "Needs help." Students know precisely where to turn in work to be checked by the teacher. Teacher assistants, aides, and parent volunteers can come into your room, pull assignments from the "Needs help" tray and assist individual students.

10. Divide all long-term, major projects into smaller segments. Give time frames and sequence for each segment. Teach your specific expectations for each part and communicate clearly the date each part is to be done. Make sure you collect and give feedback on each segment. Remember that ADD/ADHD students have particular difficulty on such projects. Tap their interests, give extra assistance and communicate with parents so they can help.

Time Management/Organization Techniques

1. Help with individual time management and organization by taping a cardboard clock face to their desks with the hands on the time that individual students need to leave the room for various pull-out services. Write the time in words and numbers as an extra reminder for student.

2. Help students make schedules. Tape them to desk.

3. Some students could be helped with time management by using a 10-minute or 15-minute timer. If you don't find this system too annoying or distracting, allow an ADD/ADHD student to set the timer for individual seat work. If the assignment is completed with accuracy within that time frame, the teacher or aide reinforces according to a contract.

Helping Students Organize Their Ideas

Specific strategies for cognitive organization such as pre-writing, story mapping, learning how to read and determine the "meat of the text," knowing how to organize steps for solving math problems, and other skills will be discussed in the academic strategy sections. These are all difficult skills for a number of children, particularly students with learning disabilities and attention deficit disorder. Teachers need to break down these skills and be able to teach them to their students.

Parental Involvement

Parents need to share the responsibility of teaching organizational and study skills to their children. Teachers need to work with parents to provide assistance for their children at home. Parents need to:

* provide a quiet work place at home, away from the TV;

* have appropriate materials, supplies, and lighting for homework;

* provide a place and system for checking their assignment calendar or homework sheet with the child (as well as checking for notices, permission slips, and other school communication);

* assist with prioritizing activities and things to do in the evening;

* enforce as consistent a routine as possible (e.g., homework, dinner time, bedtime);

* make sure books, notebooks, etc., are in the child's backpack for the next day;

* help write lists, schedules, reminder notes for their children; and

* reward good organizational skills at home.

Parents need to call the teacher for clarification if their child comes home with minimal homework on a regular basis or claims that he/she has no homework or finished it in class. This is often not the case. It could be the child's lack of awareness, perception, or wishful thinking that he/she is caught up with homework. Parents should also communicate with the teacher when the student is overloaded with homework. In either case, home/school communication and flexibility are required.

Obviously there are many chaotic homes where assistance in these skills will not be provided. As teachers, we need to do everything we can to supply the structure and model these skills for our students.

More information about *Skills for School Success* is available through Curriculum Associates, Inc., 5 Esquire Road, North Billerica, Massachusetts 01862-2589, 1-800-255-0248.

AN INTERVIEW WITH JOHN
(23 years old, a senior at a university in Colorado)

John was diagnosed as having ADHD as an adult.

Tell me what you remember as being difficult for you in elementary school.

"From first grade I felt that I was one of the 'dumb kids.' Teachers always said that I had the ability but just didn't apply myself. I remember in sixth grade that for a school project I worked very hard and built a solar house all on my own. I didn't have any help from my parents. I knew what I wanted to do, but I didn't have the tools to get it all together. I got a poor grade on the project because it didn't look like I spent much time on it. My teacher said 'You could have done better than that!'

"In elementary school, storytelling time was difficult for me. I fell asleep. My teacher would ask all the time, 'John, do you feel all right?' because I couldn't listen to her stories. She didn't understand . . . I had to sleep to stay quiet.

"In one of my grades one of the kids in the 'top' group did a project on optical illusions. I remember thinking how her project didn't look like much . . . I know I could have done a better job. But because I was in the lower group, I never had a chance to do all the special projects."

What do you wish could have happened when you were younger?

"If I could go back now, I would like to relearn how to learn. If there were only teachers who really cared and tried to find out what my problem was. For a long time I could hardly read a story. I had to keep rereading it because I was 'off somewhere else,' and not paying attention to what I was reading. I would read a sentence over and over again, and read it out loud, and still not have any idea what I read."

What about junior high?

"Most of the problems I had in school were disciplinary, especially in junior high. I started ditching class because algebra was so difficult for me."

What is your advice to teachers?

"The most important thing is to be there for the kids. Those kids that have problems early and are identified are the ones who can be helped!"

section

9

Multisensory Instruction

A good part of this book deals with the need to teach through multisensory techniques in order to reach all of the students in a classroom. Learning style statistics show that the majority of the students learn best through visual and tactile/kinesthetic input. Only 15 percent tend to be stronger auditory learners. This is particularly important for secondary teachers to be aware of. If your teaching style emphasizes lecturing, with you doing all of the talking, there is a high percentage of students you're not reaching. According to statistics, students retain:

* 10 percent of what they read;

* 26 percent of what they hear;

* 30 percent of what they see;

* 50 percent of what they see and hear;

* 70 percent of what they say; and

* 90 percent of what they say and do.

The obvious implications of the above are that we need to present lessons with a combination of methods. Students need hands-on experience. They also need the opportunity to verbalize their understanding frequently during the school day. Cooperative learning situations (with partners, triads, or groups of four) are very effective for getting students to verbalize and share in the classroom.

Students who have the opportunity to work together and discuss with peers and who are actively, physically involved and participating in the lesson will have the most success.

The following is an example of how to teach multiplication facts and multiples of a number (in this example, 4) using a multisensory approach.

Auditory

Teach the sequence of skip counting by fours through use of rhythm, melody, song, or rap. There are tapes and records on the market that teach multiplication tables. Musically inclined students can be given the assignment of writing their own 'rap' or melody and teaching it to the class.

Visual and Tactile

1. Practice the multiples of four on the computer. There are a number of computer programs that have fun drill and practice games.

2. Practice multiples of four on a calculator. Have students punch in the fact, then write down the answer.

3. "Donut Math"—Make a paper circle with the center cut out. On the circle, write the numerals 0 through 9 in random order. Attach the "donut" to a piece of string or yarn and hang it on a hook over the chalkboard. Write "× 4" in the center of the circle on the chalkboard. Give students practice coming to the board and writing the products along the outside of the circle. This same "donut" can be used for practicing any other math fact by simply writing in a different number or operation in the center of the circle. With a few donuts on the board, competitive students can have multiplication races.

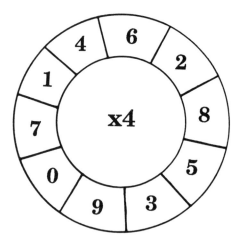

4. Play games with rolling a die and multiplying it by four. Since students can only practice up to 4 x 6 with the use of one die, the same technique can be used by spinning a spinner that has numerals that go higher. An alternative is to have students first roll two dice together and add the numbers (e.g., 6 + 3 = 9); then they roll a third die and multiply whatever

the sum was by the number they just rolled (9 x 4 = 36). Other variations work just as well.

5. Use traditional flash cards that students make and color.

6. Make visual/tactile flash cards by writing the facts in glue, sprinkling with sand or salt, and shaking off the excess when dry. Students then use these flash cards by tracing the numerals with their finger while they say the fact out loud.

Spatial

1. Use designs and color for helping students visualize the pattern and sequence of multiples. The program "Touch Math" has posters and designs for each of the multiples. They use the pattern of "bowling pins" for the multiples of four.

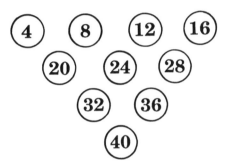

— Have students color the first two single-digit numerals (4 and 8) in yellow. The next two numerals which have a 1 in the tens place (12 and 16) are colored in orange. The second row of "pins" with numbers in the twenties (20, 24, 28) are colored red. The next row of "pins" with numbers in the thirties (32, 36) are colored purple. The numeral 40 is colored blue.

— Students make their own charts, filling in the numbers in sequence and coloring them.

— Make large, laminated, colored "pins," shuffle them, and have students lay them out on the floor in proper sequence. Then they hop on the correct circle to a prompt: "Jump to the circle that is 4 x 6." This is also a kinesthetic technique—involving body movement.

Note: Many students with learning disabilities have severe difficulties memorizing multiplication facts. The "spatial" approach seems to be the answer for some of these children. It is amazing to watch them close their eyes and picture where the number is placed spatially. You can observe them rapidly visualizing and pointing to where 4 x 8 or 4 x 3 is placed with their eyes shut, and most can tell you without looking what color that "pin" is. Yet these same children may not be able to ever skip count or memorize the sequence of fours—even with repetitive practice. Many children with learning disabilities who have significant weakness with left brain/se-quential tasks are gifted spatially.

2. Use a number chart or matrix of the numerals 0 to 99 and/or 1 to 100 and have students count by fours. Then they color or put an *X* in each box on the multiple of four in sequence. When they color in each of the boxes, students will see the pattern.

3. Have students use interlocking plastic cubes that are combined into groups of four, using a different color for each group. As they stack ten groups of four, have them count by fours. This can be done similarly with plastic links or other manipulatives.

4. The following is another design that is fun for students and helpful for visually oriented students.

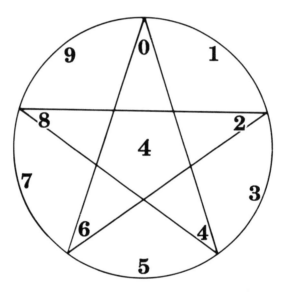

Draw a circle and space the numerals 0 through 9 along its circumference. Write a 4 in the center. Have students write out the multiples of four in sequence (4, 8, 12, 16, 20, 24, 28, 32, 32, 40). Begin by putting their pencil on the numeral 4, then have them draw the pattern by connecting the digits on the circle in order by looking at the digit in *the ones place* of each multiple. Draw a straight line from the 4 to the 8, from the 8 to the 2 (which represents 12), from the 2 to the 6 (which stands for 16), then to 0 (which represents 20), and continue the pattern. The same digits (4, 8, 2, 6, 0) will be repeated over and over as students continue the sequence (24, 28, 32, 36, 40, 44, 48, and so on). Students love to make these designs for each of the numbers.

Verbal

It is critical, of course, that students understand the concept of multiplication. They should have many opportunities to make up their own word problems to share with the class. One way to do this is to have students brainstorm as a class and generate a class chart and lists of "things that come in fours." This is an excellent activity which is very helpful for students. From the list (which might include wheels on a wagon, quarts in a gallon, legs on a horse, suits in a deck of cards), students make up problems for their classmates to solve.

Conceptual

There are hundreds of hands-on games and activities that students can and should be doing in the classroom to understand multiplication at the conceptual level. Memorizing multiplication facts and solving problems at the symbolic level does not accomplish this. Books and sourses such as *Mathematics: A Way of Thinking* and *Math Solutions* are excellent resources. See Math, Section 12.

The following sections on specific reading, writing, and math strategies will explain multisensory techniques in greater depth. It is only through a variety of approaches—and teacher recognition that students do learn differently—that all students will be given the opportunity to learn effectively.

AN INTERVIEW WITH BRITA
(37 years old, California)

Brita was diagnosed as an adult with learning disabilities and ADD.

What are your memories of elementary school?

"My family was one of avid readers. I grew up surrounded by books. I loved to be around books, but I couldn't read them. I remember how much I loved hearing my teacher read *Charlotte's Web* to the class in third grade. Hearing the stories was so powerful. My biggest frustration was not being able to get further in my reading."

Tell me how your attentional difficulties affected you in school.

"One of the pitfalls with ADD is that I would have my good days and my bad days. I never knew when the trap door would open and I'd lose my train of thought. For example, in class I would want to ask a question. I would raise my hand and repeat in my head over and over the question I wanted to ask, so I wouldn't forget. In the meantime, I would miss everything in between the waiting and getting called on. I lost a lot, and it was very frustrating. I spent hours on homework. Reading, processing and writing were very difficult for me."

What about junior high and high school?

"One of my survival skills was being 'Miss Goody Two Shoes.' I wasn't popular, but that didn't matter much to me. Friends came second to my wanting to do well. Teachers always liked me. I would always tune in to what the instructors wanted and did what I could to please them.

"I had some very good teachers. A lot of my trauma was self-inflicted. I used to have teachers so fooled. I fooled everybody, but in fooling people (i.e., hiding that I couldn't read), I thought I was cheating. In speaking with a lot of other adults who have learning disabilities, many of us felt that we were cheating by not doing what was expected of us the traditional way. We might have squeaked through the system, but we had to find our own methods. Most of us knew when we were very young that something was wrong, but we just didn't know what.

"In junior high I remember being the last to get started. I would sit down to write something, but I just couldn't get started. I would get so frustrated, and my anxiety level would go up and up, making it worse. I often felt that my body and I were separate. My body was next to me. My brain and body weren't coordinated with each other."

How did you cope with your difficulties?

"I had trouble coping. In fact, I went through periods of serious depression. I saw psychiatrists when I lived back East. No one ever figured out that I couldn't read.

"I have learned how to accommodate myself. In class I sit up front, close to the teacher, and do as much one-to-one with the teacher as possible. In college I never missed a single class. I am a very disorganized person, but I have an office that I am responsible for organizing. I can do this successfully by setting up visual cues for myself. I set things up in neat little boxes and color code them all. I use tools to help me compensate, like my Franklin Language Master, and I take advantage of Recordings for the Blind which will record books and texts on tape for individuals with learning disabilities. If I can't reach the top shelf, I can with a ladder—so what if you need aids to compensate! I can do a lot of things that others can't do. I'm very creative. I'm learning to pat myself on the back now, so I don't go back into that black hole I was in for thirty years."

section

10

Language Arts Strategies

Children with ADD/ADHD and other students who are at risk for failure in the classroom are among the students who will benefit the most from current teaching strategies that are taught and recommended throughout the country. These include whole language strategies, the writing process, reciprocal teaching, and other higher-level questioning and critical thinking strategies.

There are numerous strategies that teachers can use to best teach an integrated language arts curriculum. The following pages summarize many strategies one can use in teaching literature and writing.

Ideas come from a wide range of sources. I would like to credit and thank some of the following teachers and sources whose ideas I am sharing: Arlene White-Gruber, Darlene Rios-Smith, Wendy Wright, Sumi Holzman, Carol Fisher, Valerie Kear, Meijean Chan, Ethel Daniels, Ann Sturm, C.L.P., Yellow Pages: California Literature Project, Dominguez Hills Teacher Leaders (summer, 1989), Chancer/Asher (1990).

These strategies are excellent for students who have difficulty focusing and maintaining attention because:

* they are high-interest, relevant, and motivating;

* they are multisensory in nature;

* they involve active participation;

* they involve interaction with peers, resulting in greater acceptance, social skill development, and improved self-esteem; and

* they allow for choices, tapping students' learning styles and strengths.

As we experiment with introducing some of the following activities and strategies in our classrooms, all of our students will benefit, particularly those with special needs.

With an integrated language arts approach, it is difficult to focus separately on reading and writing strategies. However, I will be discussing writing problems in more detail in the following chapter.

Pre-Reading Strategies

Relate stories to prior experience or knowledge by:

* Class discussions

* Brainstorming/charting prior knowledge

* Using visuals/audiovisuals relating to topic of literature (e.g., maps, music, filmstrips)

* Story predictions, charting, graphing predictions

* Setting a purpose

* Previewing the visuals in the text

Graphic Organizers and Other Meaning-Making Strategies

Graphic Organizers

Graphic organizers are visual depictions of a concept and allow the student to organize visually what they have read. Good readers visualize and form an image while they read; poor readers do not.

1. **Storyboards**. Divide sections on a board or piece of paper and have students draw or write story events in sequence in each box/section.

2. **Story charts/maps**. Identify characters, setting problem, sequence of events, resolution of conflict.

3. **Plot profiles**. After reading a book, choose a number of events and produce a class graph of which events students found to be the most exciting. Plot on a large graph the majority opinion of the class (by show of hands or applause) how exciting each event was.

4. **Favorite part graph** (similar to above). Class identifies a number of scenes or parts of the book which are plotted on a graph. Everyone records their favorite part on the bar graph.

5. **Circle stories** (For stories that are cyclical, e.g., *If You Give a Mouse a Cookie, The Ox-Cart Man*). Write on the chalkboard all the main events. Whole class decides where they fit on the circle. Then on individual paper

plates divided into sections, students reproduce the story in sequence (pictures/words) and retell it.

6. **Wanted posters**. Students create posters listing identifying characteristics of a character in the book.

7. **Venn diagrams**. Use diagrams to compare and contrast two similar pieces of literature, compare a book with its movie version, or to compare characters within a book. Example:

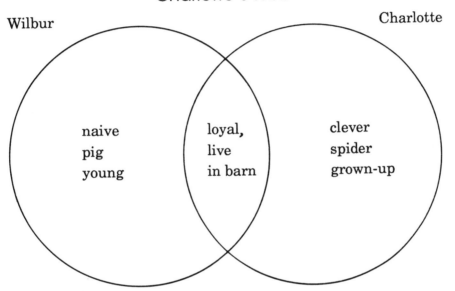

Charlotte's Web

8. **Character web**. Put the character's name in center of the web with traits and descriptions stemming from the center.

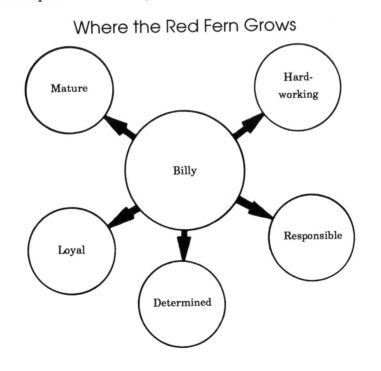

Where the Red Fern Grows

9. **Plot charts.** Make a chart for stories such as *Sleeping Beauty* and *The True Story of the Three Little Pigs*. Use the following format:

| Somebody | Wanted | But | And so . . . |

10. **Prediction charts.** Create charts that are modified as story is being read. Based on the title and illustrations, students make initial predictions. As they read, stop and predict what will happen next. Continue questioning, predicting, and recording. Make clear to students that predictions are best guesses based on the information we know at the time and that good readers are constantly predicting when they are reading.

Other Meaning Making Strategies

1. **Hot seat.** A student volunteers to be on "the hot seat," representing a particular character from the story. Students ask him/her questions that must be answered in the way the character would answer them.

2. **Quick-writes.** Give students two or three minutes to write anything they can think of about the topic. Students are instructed not to worry about punctuation, spelling, grammar; just write.

3. **Think-about protocol.** Pairs of students read aloud and exchange their interpretations and concerns.

4. **Directed reading/thinking activity (DRTA).** Guide students in predicting what the story will be about, reading to verify hypothesis, checking their comprehension with peers and teacher, predicting what will occur next, and starting the process over again after a certain amount of passages/pages are read.

5. **Guided imagery (visualization).** Develop meaning by creating personal pictures of the text in the mind as sensory descriptions are suggested or read by the teacher. Students close their eyes as teacher either reads aloud or tells the setting. Students are guided in creating personal mind pictures using their five senses.

6. **Teacher modeling.** The teacher models thinking aloud and summarizing.

7. **Journal entries.** Include reflective journals, metacognitive journals, and double-entry journals.

Reflective Journal

WHAT HAPPENED	HOW I FELT	WHAT I LEARNED

Metacognitive Journal

WHAT I LEARNED	HOW I CAME TO LEARN IT

Double-entry Journal

QUOTATION—PHRASE OR SENTENCE I especially like	**MY THOUGHTS** ABOUT THIS QUOTATION

8. **Literature logs/journals**. Have students record their personal reflections, summaries, and predictions.

9. **K-W-L**. Create a three-column chart as follows:
   K (What do you *know*?)
   W (*What* do you want to find out?)
   L (What did you *learn*?)

K	W	L

10. **Reciprocal teaching**. Use a questioning strategy that teaches students to focus intently on what they are reading by designing and asking questions and summarizing their understanding. Research has found that good readers spontaneously use strategies of predicting, questioning, clarifying, and summarizing. Poor readers don't self-monitor or use strategies for asking themselves questions that lead to understanding. In a reciprocal teaching format, students are asked summarizing questions such as: "What is this paragraph mostly about? What would be a good title for this passage?" Follow-up with in-depth questioning: "Who is the most important person in this paragraph? Which details support the main idea?" Clarifying questions might include: "Has anyone heard this expression before? What do you think it means?"

11. **Reader's theater**. Work on scripting a piece of literature into dialogue, then read it aloud dramatically.

12. **Retelling**. Review the literature students have read through storytelling, summarizing, time lines, quick-writes/quick-draws, tape recordings, plot charts, or any of the graphic organizers.

13. **Teach** students the following:

    — vocabulary within context

    — point of view

    — writing style, author's use of language (including figures of speech)

14. **Reading aloud**. Read to the class at all grade levels, modeling fluency, expression, and metacognition.

15. **Additional tips**:

    — When using "Big Books," point to the print with a dowel or pointer. Frame key words and phrases with your hands.

    — Use pocket charts and colored sentence strips to retell the story and discuss vocabulary.

    — On wall charts, use "stick-em" papers to cover key words and have students supply the missing words.

"Beyond" Activities and Book Projects

Draw:

    — A scene from a book

    — A map or diagram of the setting of the story

    — A poster advertising the book

    — A bookmark with pictures or symbols on one side, and a list of important events or summary on the other

    — A comic strip page that highlights important action

Design:

— A picture postcard of the setting. On the back, write to a friend as if you were the main character in the book and describe the setting and events happening there.

— A T-shirt for your main character that represents attributes of the character's personality

— A T-shirt with symbols representing events in the book

Make:

— A diorama of the setting

— A literary scrapbook about a character in the book with postcards, pictures, award certificates, report cards, etc.

— A cube on which you draw the key events of the story

— A word and picture collage of the main events

— A board game based upon the book

— A mobile of the plot

— A roll-movie of the book

— A pop-up book, mini-book, accordion book, or big book

— A flannel board story

— A memory basket with items representing events or themes in the story

— Foods mentioned in the book

Pretend:

— You are a TV interviewer. Audio- or videotape an interview with a character in the book.

— You are a prosecuting attorney. Put one of the characters in the book on trial for a crime. Prepare your case, giving all your arguments and support them with facts.

— You are a movie director. Cast your book with movie stars. Explain why you selected a particular actor for a role from the book.

— You are a news reporter on a particular scene ("You Are There" program).

Write:

— A letter to a friend telling her/him about the most exciting parts of the book

— A letter to the main character suggesting what might have happened if he/she acted in another way

— A soap opera using the characters from the book

— A "Dear Abby" letter from the point of view of one of the characters in the story, and a solution letter

— A new ending or sequel

— Poems about your character/story

— A TV commercial advertising your book

— A diary entry by the main character describing a major event in the story

— Some riddles about the story

— A scene from the story in a different time, past or future

— A moral for the story and relate it to your own life

— A short report on a topic related to the story

— A travel diary describing the places you have traveled in the story

— A promotion campaign for a movie about the book

— A letter to the author

— An event in the story from a different point of view

Find:

— Figures of speech (metaphor, simile, personification, etc.) in the book

Create:

— A book jacket

— A crossword puzzle using words and characters from the story

— A dice game that follows development of the plot or events

— An animation of a scene on adding-machine tape

Perform:

— An original song related to the story

— Pantomime scenes from the story

— A phone conversation between two or more characters

— A reader's theater scripted from the book

Storytelling

Storytelling is very powerful in the classroom—both for the teacher telling stories to students and for teaching students the technique. Storytelling promotes good attention and invites active involvement. It encourages visualization and the active use of imagination. It develops children's sense of story and listening skills. Storytelling brings literature to children in a particularly satisfying way.

Teach students to take a short story, read it four or five times, "block the story" by diagramming, making a story map, drawing key pictures, or writing down key scenes. Then teach students to watch in their mind's eye each scene like a silent movie, observing every sensory detail. Then practice retelling. (See Catherine Farrell, *Word Weaving: A Guide to Storytelling*. San Francisco: Word Weaving, Inc., 1987).

Storytelling teaches inner concentration. It is an excellent vehicle for motivating and helping students, particularly distractible, harder-to-reach students.

Oral Reading Strategies

Oral reading in the classroom is necessary, but can be problematic. To discuss a story or text, it is naturally important that all students have read the material. However, "round robin" reading with the students taking individual turns reading aloud to the class is often not the most effective or productive, especially in a large classroom.

Students who have reading difficulty have a hard time following along and paying attention. These students lose the continuity, flow, and, consequently, the meaning of the passage. They may become so fearful of being embarrassed by their poor skills in oral reading that they spend the whole period in panic, trying to predict what will be their portion to read and practicing ahead. Therefore, they are not listening or following along.

Try the following:

1. Teacher orally reads and models for fluency, expression, and interest; students follow along in the text. Perhaps have students orally reread certain passages at teacher prompts. Have students locate information in the passages at teacher prompts and questioning, and orally reread those passages containing the information.

2. Have students first read silently before the class or group reads orally. Students (particularly older ones) who are uncomfortable reading orally should never be forced to read out loud to the class. They should be able to volunteer when they wish to read in front of the class. Buddy reading or reading in small groups is a much "safer," preferable way for students to practice their oral reading.

3. Buddy or partner reading: Assign (or let students pick) a reading buddy. After the pairs of children have read their stories silently, explain that the partners will take turns reading orally and listening. Indicate how many lines the children should read before letting their buddies have a turn. Often only one book is used by each pair during this activity, but for distractible children it may be better for each to have a copy of the book.

   Sometimes buddy reading is conducted with students sitting in pairs back to back, taking turns or reading in unison. Teachers can assign questions that each pair of students will need to be able to answer. It is important that students be given a lot of space to spread out away from other pairs of students, so they won't be distracted by all the voices reading at different paces.

Problems ADD/ADHD Students May Have With Reading

1. **Silent reading**. They often need to subvocalize or read quietly to themselves so they can hear their voice, maintain attention, and get meaning. If students do this, then permit them to do so. Many students need the auditory input and can't get meaning by reading silently.

2. **Maintaining attention during whole class instruction**. If possible, seat ADD students among well-focused students during this part of instruction. These children benefit the most from the opportunity to hear the selection on tape, and then reread with partners and small groups after the initial reading.

3. **Losing their train of thought** and not being able to concentrate on what they are reading. A large percentage of individuals with ADD report this difficulty. They may have excellent decoding skills and fluency. However, due to their distractibility, they struggle tremendously with focusing on what they are reading, particularly if they find it dry, uninteresting, or difficult material. They report having to read and reread numerous times. Techniques such as reciprocal teaching, note taking, self-monitoring, and questioning are helpful strategies to teach your students.

4. **Difficulty with the language/vocabulary** of books being read. This is naturally one of the disadvantages of having everyone read from the same book. Some students will find the story or book far too difficult for independent reading and decoding. They will, however, benefit from listening to the teacher read, rereading the story or hearing it reread. They will definitely gain tremendously from all of the creative, motivational whole language techniques and activities related to the literature.

   However, these children very likely need more *word attack/phonics* training than they may be receiving in their reading programs. They need to develop strategies for independently decoding new, unfamiliar words. Not all students can be taught independent reading skills with whole word/sight techniques. There are many children who still need to be taught specific strategies for sounding out unfamiliar words. They need to see and recognize common visual patterns in words, for example:

   consonant—vowel—consonant (<u>hat</u>)

   consonant—vowel—consonant—final e (<u>hate</u>)

   Elementary (particularly primary grade) teachers need to work at their sites by grade level to brainstorm ways to provide this extra assistance to any students in need of more intensive decoding skill instruction. Not all students have this need, but many do. There are many good supplementary programs for providing extra training in phonics. See Bibliography and Recommended Resources.

5. **Difficulty visually focusing on the print,** losing their place (tracking): Encourage students to use strips of cardboard for markers or to use their finger to track, if needed. Some students may benefit from using a "window box." A sample pattern follows. Any number of variations may work. On

the sample window box, the notches along the sides of the card are different sizes to accommodate different sized print in the book. Students select an appropriate notch and place it at the beginning of each line (sliding it down the left side of the page). Other children may need to place the window box over the page, blocking out the print except for the words that are exposed in the window. They slide the card across the page to reveal a few words at a time. The window can be cut as large as desired.

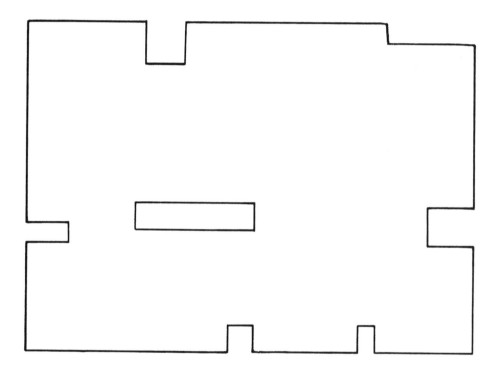

6. **Needing more one-to-one assistance, small group skill work:** Once again, each site needs to use all of its resources to provide additional assistance to students who need more help (reading specialists, basic skills teachers, aides, parent volunteers, cross-age tutors, peer-tutors, teacher-directed skill groups, tutoring before or after school, computer-lab assistance, tape-recording selections for students to listen to and follow along with).

AN INTERVIEW WITH MALINDA
(14 years old, California)

Which of your classes did you like the most during elementary school?

"I don't remember too much about a lot of my classes. I liked the teachers who made what we were studying a reality. For example, if we were studying something in history, they would explain and discuss what was currently in the news and tie it in to what was happening in the world now."

What is your advice to teachers?

"Teachers need to give students more time to try to understand. You need to explain carefully, see if there are any questions, and take more time to teach it before you move on."

Written Language Strategies

Of all the academic skills, it is writing that students with ADD/ADHD tend to struggle with the most. These students are poor spellers and typically have poor handwriting, difficulty organizing their thoughts in written expression, weakness in mechanics and written organization (e.g., spacing on the page), and tremendous difficulty with speed of written output. There are often numerous erasures and illegibility of product. These children experience enormous frustration trying to keep up with the pace of teacher expectations and the rate of peers when it comes to writing.

Teaching Spelling

Many students with learning disabilities and/or attentional deficits are poor spellers for a number of reasons. Children with attentional difficulties are often inattentive to visual detail, and don't notice and recall the letters and sequence of words. They aren't visually aware of patterns in words and are careless in their writing and spelling.

Children with learning disabilities often have auditory sequential memory deficits, causing them great difficulty with learning letter/sound association and hearing and remembering the sounds in the correct order. For example, they may spell the word *trust* as *turts*, *blast* as *bats*.

Other children have deficits in visual-sequential memory, causing them difficulty recalling the way a word looks and getting it down in the correct order/sequence. These students will incorrectly spell many of the common little words that they have seen and used thousands of times. For example, they may spell *said* as *sed*, *from* as *form*, *when* as *wen*, *they* as *thay*, and so on. (See Section 28 for an explanation of learning disabilities.)

How Can We Help?

Teach high frequency words as a top priority in your spelling instruction. Just one thousand words account for nearly 90% of the words adults find necessary for their everyday writing. Many of the one hundred most frequently used words (listed below) account for a significant number of spelling errors made.

the	or	out	its
of	by	them	who
and	one	then	now
a	had	she	people
to	not	many	my
in	but	some	made
is	with	so	over
you	all	these	did
that	were	would	down
it	when	other	only
he	we	into	way
for	there	has	find
was	can	more	use
on	an	her	may
are	your	two	water
as	which	like	long
with	their	him	little
his	said	see	very
they	if	time	after
at	do	could	words
be	will	no	called
this	each	make	just
from	about	than	where
I	how	first	most
have	up	been	know

There are a number of books containing lists of high frequency words, for example, Rebecca Sitton's *Instant Spelling Words for Writing*, Curriculum Associates, (800) 225-0248.

What About Phonics?

The move away from phonics instruction is cause for concern, because the students' ability to learn the letter/sound association necessary for decoding unknown words and encoding (spelling) words will decrease even further. Phonics is a system for reducing larger words to a workable number of component parts. Approximately four-fifths of all words can be decoded with phonics.

Include phonetically regular words in your spelling instruction. When pulling words for weekly spelling tests, it is a waste of time to select many low-frequency, irregular words from the literature or content areas that students may never need to use in their writing. Choose, instead, words that will teach students the pattern and regularity of most English words (including prefixes and suffixes). Examples: *hop / hope, hid / hide, quit / quite, star / stare, pond / pound, fond / found, plan / plain, clam / claim, nation / vacation / imagination, native / active / relative,* and so on.

You should also select words from the literature or content area that are phonetically irregular but useful in their everyday writing, for example, *country, science, Wednesday, laughter, character.*

Multisensory Teaching Techniques for Helping Students with Spelling Difficulty

* Write the word in the air while sounding it out.

* Write words in glue or starch on a piece of cardboard. Then sprinkle sand or any powdery material to create a textured, 3-D spelling word for tracing.

* Prepare a tray of sand or salt and have students write words with their finger while spelling out loud.

* Fingerpaint spelling words using shaving cream squirted on the desk top or spread a small amount of pudding or frosting on a paper plate, and have students write words with their finger.

* Pair students and have them write the spelling words on each other's backs with their finger.

* Use individual chalkboards with colored chalk or whiteboards with colored pens for high motivation in practicing spelling words.

* Practice typing words on a typewriter or computer. There are numerous software programs for reinforcing practice of word lists in motivational games, or just practice typing on a regular word-processing program.

* Write words in large letters on a large piece of newsprint and have students trace the word several times with different colored markers or crayons.

* Dip a clean paintbrush in water and practice writing words on the chalkboard or desk top.

* Have oral drills (spelling bees).

* Pair a movement with learning spelling words (e.g., clap each letter, jump rope while spelling the word, bounce a ball while spelling each word).

* Sing spelling words to common tunes/melodies.

* Use manipulative letters (magnetic letters, alphabet cookies, sponge letters, etc.) for practicing words.

* Use configuration clues. Print a word and then outline its shape in a different color.

```
┌─────────────────┐
│ f i g u r e │
└─┐         ┌─────┘
  └─────────┘
```

* Search for memory clues (mnemonics) within the word to help students memorize and recall the spelling. Examples:

  friend — I am a friEND to the END.

  what — It has the word *hat* in it.

  church — You are (U / R) in church.

* Create a sentence from the words that will help students to recall irregular words. Example: "The *naughty daughter* was *taught* a lesson when she got *caught*."

Testing for Spelling

* Enunciate each word slowly, exaggerating or stretching out the sounds when dictating. This helps students hear the sequence of the sounds as they spell.

* Test slowly. Give these students the time they need to get the word down carefully before going on to the next word. You could also give additional time after the test to go over and redo words they couldn't get down on paper fast enough.

* For students with significant difficulty in this skill, shorten the list of required words. You could give extra credit for additional words above the shortened list that students may study for and be tested on.

* Allow students to take spelling tests orally for credit. Have them also take the written test, but use the grade of the oral test if it is higher than the written test score. Quite a few of these students could get *A*'s on spelling tests if tested orally, though they fail on the written test.

Handwriting and Penmanship

A frequent characteristic of ADD/ADHD students is poor handwriting. They often have trouble writing neatly on and within the given lines and form letters awkwardly. Their written work is messy and immature looking. They often have trouble copying from the board or book onto paper. They tend not to anchor their paper on the desk when writing and write extremely slowly when they are trying to do their best work. Others write so rapidly that the product is totally illegible. Many of these students were not attentive in the grades where proper letter formation strokes were taught. They learned their own creative, sometimes bizarre way of forming letters.

One amazing effect of medication (particularly ritalin) in some children is a dramatic improvement in handwriting and speed of written output. I have seen many students whose coloring, drawing, penmanship, and general neatness of written products improved so greatly that it was almost unbelievable that it was produced by the same child.

Strategies for Teaching Students Who Struggle With Handwriting

✱ Carefully teach and model on an overhead projector if possible. Show the strokes as you talk through the steps of forming the letters.

✱ Do the same talking through while demonstrating with large, exaggerated movements/strokes in the air.

✱ Have students stand up (maybe one side of the room at a time) and write the letters in the air with large motions as you observe.

✱ While students practice on paper or individual chalkboards, walk around the room and try to identify which students are in need of one-to-one, small group assistance or immediate reteaching.

Note: Once letters are learned incorrectly, it is almost impossible to break children of poor habits. They find their own way of writing that becomes permanent, such as making strokes from bottom up and making circles clockwise instead of counterclockwise.

✱ When teaching the correct relative size of letters and their formation, it is helpful to introduce the graphic of a person with the head reaching the top line (head line), the trousers' belt at the middle line (belt line), and the feet on the bottom line (foot line). Then, when instructing how to form each letter, refer to those lines by name.

Example: "To make the letter *h*, start at the head line and go straight down to the foot line. Trace back up to the belt line and make a hump that goes back down to the foot line."

* Have students use pencil grips, thick pencils, and lined paper as needed.

* Practice handwriting using a variety of writing implements (e.g., crayons, felt-tip pens, paintbrushes).

Necessary Compensation for Students Who Struggle

There are a number of upper grade students who find cursive writing so tedious and awkward, they prefer to print in class. Allow them to do so, while trying to provide the reteaching of cursive skills. Many teachers in the upper and secondary grades accept print in lieu of cursive writing as long as it's readable.

For children who struggle with speed and neatness of writing, the best service you can provide is to teach them proper keyboarding. These children should have the opportunity to develop this skill at a young age, because they will need to compensate for their difficulty in speed, neatness, and production. Allow students to turn in typewritten assignments, and encourage them to use the word processor/typewriter, particularly in the upper grades.

Organization on Paper

* Teach students your standards of how a proper, acceptable paper should look. Include heading (name, date, subject, page number), margins (left and right), blank lines (at top, bottom, between numbers, etc.), neat erasures or cross-outs, and words legible and numbers on/within the lines.

  To further help you teach students the proper organization of a paper, I recommend *Skills for School Success,* by Anita Archer and Mary Gleason, published by Curriculum Associates. (See Bibliography and Recommended Resources.)

* It is helpful when schools have consistent standards so that each year students are expected to use the same format.

* Teach students to space between words by placing an index-finger space between the words.

* Some students need larger-spaced, larger-lined paper. Have some available in the room for them.

* It is helpful for some younger students who confuse directionality to place a green dot on the left side of the paper indicating where to begin. A red dot indicates where to stop. (Green dot the ones/units column on math papers for the same reason with these students.)

* See Section 12 on Math Strategies for recommendations on paper organization of math problems, which is typically problematic for these students.

* Keep good models and samples of written work visible for reference.

✱ Encourage students to proof their own written work for your require-ments:

— "Did you remember your heading?"

— "Did you remember to skip a line (or two) between each vocabulary word?"

— "Did you check for finger spacing between words?"

✱ An alternative is to have students pair up to proofread each other's work before handing it in.

✱ The "writing process" does not require that all written work be edited for correct spelling, mechanics, and organization. Certainly work should not be graded down for mechanical and spelling errors unless specified in advance. However, it is a good idea to remind students in their daily work to check over their work before handing it in. "Check that you have capital letters at the beginning of your sentences." "Did you remember punctua-tion at the end of your sentences?"

The Writing Process

Students need to be given numerous opportunities to write for a purpose using the stages of this process.

1. **Prewriting.** This stage is frequently overlooked, but is most important. It involves oral or written experiences to stimulate writing. Examples: brainstorming, clustering, semantic mapping, diagramming, listening to a song or poem, partner talk.

2. **Writing.** Ideas from prewriting are developed at this stage. Students must know a specific purpose for writing and who their audience is.

3. **Responding.** This stage is a quick first reaction to the writing. Students share with their peers and get feedback that should be positive and constructive. You may require the class to respond to individual writing that is shared by students by stating something they liked—a particular descriptive word or phrase, vocabulary word or expression or a feeling or emotion described. Example: "I like the way Michael used the word *inquired* rather than *asked*."

4. **Revising.** Rearranging, expanding, substituting, deleting.

5. **Editing.** Cleaning up and correcting a piece of writing. Not all writing assignments need to reach this stage. Many teachers will have students select one piece of work from their weekly writing that will be edited carefully for form, syntax, mechanics, and spelling and be recopied.

6. **Developing skills.** The writing becomes the basis to determine which skills need to be learned by students. Teachers teach skills as needed.

7. **Evaluation.** All skills do not need to be assessed in every piece of writing. Overemphasis on this part of the process should be avoided.

8. **Postwriting.** Sharing, publishing, displaying, and reading of written products.

Written Expression

Many students have difficulty knowing what to write about, sharing their ideas on paper, and using interesting descriptive vocabulary. The following are a variety of strategies to assist students in these skills.

✳ **Cluster and brainstorm topics of interest** (e.g., sports, favorite places to visit, scary things, weird things, and so on). This class list can serve as a stimulus or prompt for writing in journals or other writing activities.

✳ **Semantic mapping** (recommended in prewriting stage). This strategy helps organize thoughts. Make categories around a central topic and generate details pertaining to those categories. See the example on page 79:

✳ **Give alternatives to over-used words**. Generate a class word list or word bank of over-used, dull words (1-cent words) that can be substituted for more interesting words (10-cent words, 25-cent words, 1-dollar words). Use a thesaurus to have students find "more valuable" words. Examples:

1 cent	10 cents	25 cents
run	race	sprint
	dash	scramble
	speed	hasten
fast	hasty	swift
		speedy

✳ **Teach descriptive language**. Keep class and individual lists of metaphors, similes, personification, and other figures of speech found in the literature. Point out examples of the above found in books read together in class as well as independently by students. This makes a great bulletin board—find examples and illustrate.

— *Metaphors* are figures of speech that compare two things, but do not use the words *like* and *as*. Examples:

The road was a snake coiling around the mountain.
The theater was a refrigerator.

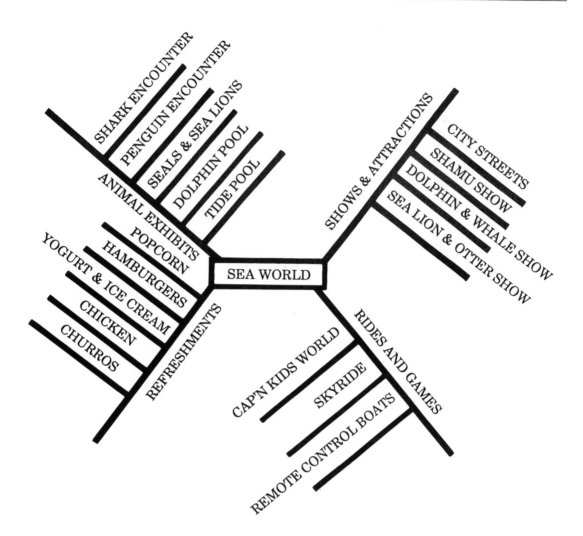

The blasting music was a hammer pounding on my head.
— *Similes* are comparisons that use *like* or *as*. Examples:

Angry as a wounded bear
As white as milk
As hard as flint
As skinny as a beanpole
Sparkled like diamonds

* Encourage students to find and bring into class good examples of sensory description (how something sounds, looks, smells, tastes, feels).

* **Show—not tell**. Teach students to create a scene with descriptive language. This can be done with a number of activities such as the following:

— Have students close their eyes and ask them to visualize a scene (e.g., a boy fishing in a stream with his grandfather, a thunderstorm, winning a raffle). Then brainstorm as a class what is in their mind's eye, what the scene sounds like, feels like, tastes like, looks like. Then students write a paragraph about it.

— Provide magazine pictures (e.g., *National Geographic*) or picture postcards of various scenes to students. Have them each select one picture and describe it in detail using colorful vocabulary. Then randomly pass out students' written descriptions and ask students to try to find the picture that was described in the paper they read.

✳ Encourage students to write about themselves: "It Happened to Me . . ."

✳ **Maintain a writing folder**. Students should keep a folder where they can jot down thoughts, feelings, topics, ideas for future writing.

✳ Encourage students to write about field trips or special assemblies.

✳ Have students write about what they learned in a science lesson, math lesson, or any other lesson.

✳ **Correspondence**. Provide opportunities for note or letter writing between two classrooms. This can be done with a special delivery system between the classes or a note box for the teacher.

✳ **Student writing journals**. Students should have daily opportunities to write and express themselves, not for evaluation purposes, but for confidence and fluency. Journal writing is highly recommended during a specific period of time on a regular basis (e.g., after lunch or homeroom). The teacher should model journal writing, quick-writes, and other sustained writing during the same time that students are required to do the activity. It helps students to see that teachers get stuck just as students do and can't always make the words flow easily.

The following are some possible topics for journal starters if students need some direction and prompts:

— How do you feel when you have a fight with your best friend? How do you think your friend feels?

— If I could write a new law for our country, it would be . . . . This would be a good law because . . .

— I wish all animals could . . . . This would be wonderful because . . .

— What would happen if there were no more television? Why would this be good? Why would this be bad?

— If I could be changed into any animal for one week, I would like to be a . . . . Why?

— When do you feel proud of yourself?

— If I won a million dollars, I would . . .

— Have you ever played a practical joke on someone or had someone play one on you? What was it?

— If I could become invisible whenever I wanted to, I would like to . . .

— If my parents would let me have lessons, I would love to learn . . .

* **Buddy journals**. Another recommended technique for making the reading/writing connection is a journal that a pair of students keep together. In this buddy journal they write back and forth to each other, "conversing" in writing. With buddy journals students read each other's entries and respond in writing. Students love to read what other students have written, and the journals, therefore, are motivating and build self-esteem. Students may be buddies with a number of classmates throughout the year.

Teaching Mechanics

Students with ADD and/or learning disabilities are often very weak in capitalization and punctuation skills. They are inattentive to mechanical errors and have great difficulty self-correcting their written work.

* Remind students frequently to check their work for capitalization and punctuation.

* Help students to identify their errors.

* Model frequently how to edit. Show examples of sentences with mechanical errors and walk students through editing and correcting. It is helpful to show copies of student work (anonymous so as not to embarrass) and edit as a class.

* Let students work in groups of two or three to edit each other's work.

* Give students brief dictation practice. The teacher dictates one or two sentences for students to write. The teacher reminds students to check the beginning of the sentence, the end of the sentence, commas, apostrophes, and quotation marks. Then the teacher writes the sentences correctly on the overhead or chalkboard for students to check. Use this technique for nonthreatening, nongraded practice in writing and editing.

* Have students dictate a few sentences or a paragraph. Then, the teacher copies exactly what the student says on large chart paper. As the teacher records what the student dictates, he/she leaves off all punctuation and capitalization. Students are asked to identify where all capital letters and punctuation marks should be placed. Then they are inserted as appropriate with a different colored pen.

* Try using puppets to teach quotation marks and commas in conversation. Using puppets, students can carry out a dialogue or conversation. The teacher records the conversation between the characters as dictated on chart paper, omitting punctuation. Students then identify how the dialogue should be punctuated.

Other Helpful Techniques and Materials

✱ Do rough draft writing and creative writing on legal-size computer paper (with white and shaded spaces). Businesses are often willing to donate a carton of computer paper to schools for this purpose. Either use individual sheets of paper, or make little booklets (folding computer paper in half and stapling). This works perfectly if students are to write on every other line (the white spaces). When it comes to conferring with the teacher, editing and revising, the shaded lines can be used for inserting words and showing correct spelling.

✱ Word processing/keyboarding skills are among the most valuable we can teach our students. A variety of software programs is available that effectively teaches students proper keyboarding/typing/word processing.

✱ Allow and encourage the use of tools and aids that help students compensate for difficulties accessing regular reference materials such as dictionaries. For students who struggle using a conventional dictionary and can't look up the words easily because they cannot spell them, there are a number of wonderful resources available.

Word Finder is a reference book that lists words by their consonant sounds only. For example, if the student wants to know how to spell *weather*, he/she needs to sound out and look up *WTHR*. Under the entry for *DSTRKTBL*, the student will find two words to choose from, *distractible* and *destructible*. *Word Finder: The Phonic Key to the Dictionary* is available through: Pilot Light, 2708 47th Street S., Gulfport, Florida 33711.

Franklin Learning Resources has a number of electronic aids from the simple to the sophisticated that allow students to easily find correct spelling and definition, access a dictionary or thesaurus, and check vocabulary and grammar. Some of their products are: Language Master™, Spellmaster™, Speaking Dictionary™, and Wordmaster™. Their address is: Franklin Learning Resources, 122 Burrs Road, Mount Holly, New Jersey 08060, (800) 525-9673.

section

12

Math Strategies

Students with ADD and/or learning problems often have specific difficulty with math computation skills:

* computing carelessly and with inaccuracy

* misalignment of problems on paper

* difficulty organizing, and copying problems from the book or board

* inattention to processing signs

* trouble memorizing and recalling basic facts

Specific recommendations will be provided in this chapter to address interventions to improve these skills.

Of far greater concern is the weakness our students—U.S. children in general—demonstrate in their understanding of mathematical concepts and their ability to problem solve and apply their skills. "The National Assessment of Educational Progress reports that students are sorely lacking in the areas of mathematics that require higher-level cognitive skills and understanding to solve problems beyond routine, step-by-step situations."[1]

In addition, many of our students experience fear, dread, and dislike of math and suffer from low self-esteem because of failure to understand the language and concepts of mathematics. This section will focus mainly on what we need to do in the classroom to instill a love of and appreciation for mathematics and to help students see the relevance of mathematics in their lives. They must learn to solve

---

[1] Marilyn Burns, *About Teaching Mathematics* (Sausalito,CA: Math Solutions Publications, 1992), p. 3.

problems by taking risks, and using the tools of technology. Many of the techniques presented here are based on recommendations in *Mathematics: A Way of Thinking*, and *Math Their Way* (courses from the Center for Innovation in Education) and *Math Solutions I* (the course from Marilyn Burns Education Associates).

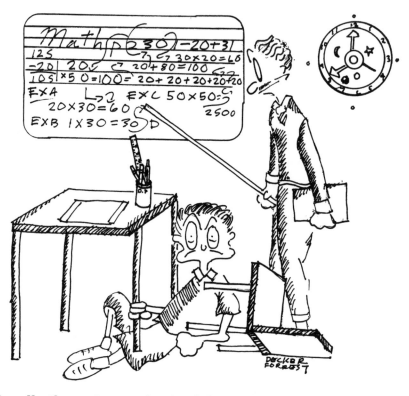

Traditionally the major emphasis of the K–8 curriculum has been on arithmetic, practice drills with paper and pencil, and copying and computing problems from textbooks. Arithmetic is only one strand of a balanced math curriculum. The mathematics framework calls for inclusion and strong emphasis, on other mathematical strands as well, including:

* geometry

* logic

* measurement

* number

* patterns and functions

* probability and statistics

Many teachers feel pressured to cover all the chapters of a textbook, and barely touch these other strands, which are generally found at the back of textbooks. In addition, many teachers are more familiar with and comfortable teaching arithmetic than they are the other strands.

Note: Students with learning disabilities and attention deficit, and other typically underachieving students, often have learning strengths (and are sometimes highly gifted) in spatial awareness, logical thinking and reasoning, and visualization. They have the ability to excel in a balanced mathematics curriculum which emphasizes patterns, geometry, measurement, probability, and logic.

These students are frequently hands-on, visual learners by nature and would benefit greatly from the use of manipulatives (pattern blocks, base-ten blocks, interlocking cubes [e.g., Unifex®] cubes, tiles, etc.), graphing activities, searching for patterns, and other nontextbook, nonworksheet strategies.

We need to question our instructional emphasis on arithmetic, particularly the practice of assigning our students problem after problem, page after page of tedious computation in isolation from problem-solving situations. The problem with this common practice is that many times students can compute pages of problems, without ever understanding the algorithms or knowing how and when to use them. Many adults report using calculators and mental math far more frequently than paper-and-pencil computation in their personal and professional lives. Our students should be trained in, exposed to, and permitted to use all tools and strategies available to solve problems.

Benefits and Importance of Teaching Through a Hands-on Cooperative, Problem-Solving Approach

Marilyn Burns states, "Instruction to children must present material in the context that gives it meaning. There is no place for emphasizing procedures without relating them to situations in which they are required. Children should expect to understand what they are asked to do and why." (*About Teaching Mathematics*, p. 159.)

Mathematics Their Way (K–2) and *Mathematics: A Way of Thinking* (3–6) are two wonderful, fun, exciting programs at the elementary level that teach mathematical concepts through a hands-on discovery approach using a variety of accessible concrete materials to teach concepts. Arithmetic/number concepts are taught, as well as graphing, patterning, sorting/classifying, probability, logical thinking, and so on. Students are guided to making their own discoveries, moving from the concrete to the symbolic level. By working together in cooperative groups, students explore, solve problems, and discover together.

Marilyn Burns' *Math Solutions I* (K–8) is another worthwhile course that presents an innovative approach to teaching mathematics. The focus is problem solving in meaningful situations. The course covers all strands of mathematics, with a host of activities to be worked on in cooperative learning groups. This program also utilizes manipulatives. Marilyn Burns stresses the need for requiring students to share the reasoning and strategies they used to solve the problems. This is done by teacher questioning: "Can you tell me what this means?" "Can you guess about how much the answer will be before doing it?" "Can you draw a picture to show what is happening in the problem?" Students are also asked to frequently *write*—put their thinking/reasoning on paper, explain and illustrate their discoveries.

With a problem-solving approach in the classroom, the emphasis is on the importance of working with persistence on solving problems, not merely getting the right answers, and not speed. The teacher structures the instruction so students are given the necessary time to "grapple with problems, search for strategies on their own and to evaluate their own results. Students describe their methods and solutions not only to the teacher, but their classmates as well. Time for discussion is needed to accomplish this, when students are encouraged to listen, question and learn from each other." (*About Teaching Mathematics*, p. 29.)

By valuing and sharing individual reasoning and problem-solving strategies, students realize that there are a number of ways that problems can be solved, not just one "right" way. Typical problem-solving strategies include:

* looking for a pattern

* constructing a table

* making an organized list

* acting it out

* drawing a picture

* using objects

* guessing and checking

* working backwards

* writing an equation

* solving a simpler (or similar) problem

* making a model

* eliminating possibilities

In *Math Solutions, Mathematics Their Way, Mathematics: A Way of Thinking* and similar approaches, the teacher's role is very different than in a typical math class. The teacher doesn't show formulas or algorithms and explain how to do the problem. The teacher, instead, models and stages the problems, leads the students to make their own discoveries, and organizes/manages the class in cooperative settings. Most important, the teacher recognizes the validity and encourages students to use a variety of approaches and methods to solve problems.

Benefits for Children With ADD/ADHD

What does this have to do with how to teach my students with attentional difficulties? Students with attentional or learning "differences" have the most to gain from the above strategies and approach to teaching mathematics. The benefits of such a program include:

* High motivation

* Students perceive the relevance and better grasp concepts

* Challenging and nonthreatening

- ✳ Interactive, cooperative group work ensures that students are participating and attention is engaged

- ✳ Promotes higher self-esteem

- ✳ Utilizes students' strengths and taps all learning styles

- ✳ Students who may not have great skill in arithmetic may very likely excel in other strands. You may be salvaging some future mathematicians, scientists, and discoverers.

Recommendations for Math Instruction

1. If you find that your math instruction relies heavily on textbooks and worksheets and that you aren't very familiar with or comfortable teaching math with other strategies and tools, consider taking advantage of the excellent training that is offered in many districts and counties across the nation. Some school districts have grants available to teachers for reimbursement on tuition or fees for courses and conferences that will improve teaching skills in math, or science, or both. Contact your district's math or science department to inquire about available courses.

2. Make a real effort to use **computer programs** for drill and practice. If your students have access to computers in the classroom or computer lab, make use of the many software programs available that make learning math skills fun for students. Computer programs are able to hold an ADD student's attention because of the rapidly changing stimuli.

3. **Math portfolios/assessment**. Have students keep a journal of their thinking, reasoning, questions, and understanding of math concepts. Encourage PYBOP: "Put your brains on paper." It is interesting to see students' understanding of a concept (through journal entries in their own words/illustrations) before and after a unit is taught.

4. **Team teach!** If you personally dislike math, or feel threatened by it . . . don't teach it (if possible). Take advantage of the many courses, workshops, and training to help you feel more comfortable and enthused about teaching mathematics. (See Section 25 on team teaching.)

5. Try **graphing** on a regular basis at all grade levels (bar graphs, picture graphs, Venn diagrams, circle graphs, line graphs). Graphing is a way to present and organize data so that relationships in the data are seen easily. In order to interpret and use graphs as a problem-solving tool, students need to make their own first.

6. Include many **estimation** activities in your curriculum.

Interventions and Strategies for Computational Problems

- ✳ Allow extra time on written math tests so students experiencing difficulty aren't rushed to make careless errors.

✳ Permit and encourage the use of calculators. Marilyn Burns calls calculators "every student's birthright."

Many students with ADD or learning disabilities have enormous difficulty copying problems from their book to paper, and lining problems up on paper so that numerals are in correct columns to compute accurately. Solutions include:

1. **Allow a choice of paper**. Keep available in class some graph paper that is already 3-hole punched. Require students to show their work and write problems neatly, either: (a) on regular paper with two or three lines of space between problems; (b) on lined notebook paper, thin lined or wide-lined held sideways (see illustration); or (c) on graph paper.

2. **Reduce the number of problems that you assign**. There is no need to assign every problem on a page to assess your students' understanding or provide practice. Allow students to do odds, evens, multiples of. Ten problems required to be written neatly, spaced well, with work shown is preferable to requiring thirty problems on a page, which will be done carelessly.

3. **Avoid anxiety of timed tests of basic facts**. There are a number of students (ADD and learning disabled) who have extreme difficulty memorizing basic facts. This is not due to laziness or lack of practice. Even if these students do basically know their facts by memory, they often choke and cannot perform on a timed test. Consider allowing some extra time for students who can't recall facts and write them down rapidly. Give credit for being able to respond orally if writing rapidly is too difficult. If some students have serious difficulty memorizing facts and rely on counting with fingers (or other manipulatives), don't penalize them.

4. **Reduce the amount of copying** required of students who struggle with written output by photocopying pages for certain students. Another possibility is to have someone else (aide, parent, volunteer, peer tutor) help the child by copying the problems onto paper for him/her.

5. **Color highlight** processing signs for students who are inattentive to change in operational signs on a page.

6. **Color dot** the ones (units) column to remind students where to begin computation.

7. **Remove individual pages** from consumable workbooks. Give students one page at a time instead of cumbersome full workbooks.

8. **Use mnemonics** (memory devices) to help with recall of steps. Examples: Steps of long division can be remembered by "dad, mother, sister, brother" or "Dear Miss Sally Brown" (for divide, multiply, subtract, bring-down).

9. **List steps** clearly.

10. **Illustrate operations** on number charts and matrices.

11. **Use overhead projectors** in daily instruction if at all possible. This is the ideal instructional tool. It is possible to buy transparent manipulatives for the overhead, including clock faces, coins/bills, pattern blocks, base-ten blocks, plastic interlocking cubes, tangrams, and calculators. All computational problems are easily modeled with colored pens on the overhead. These tools are of great assistance in helping students to visualize and grasp abstract mathematical concepts.

12. **Touch Math** is an excellent supplementary technique for helping elementary students (especially primary grades) who struggle with computation. Through the use of touchpoints strategically placed on the numerals 0 through 9, students learn to touch and count. This is a concrete, hands-on, simple method for computing rapidly and accurately without students needing to count slowly and awkwardly with their fingers, toes, or other methods. The Touch Math technique is used for addition, subtraction, multiplication, and division.

For information about *Touch Math*, call toll-free, 800-888-9191. Their catalogue is available through Innovative Learning Concepts, Inc., 6760 Corporate Drive, Colorado Springs, Colorado 80919-1999

Math Solutions courses and workshops are held in more than eighty cities across the United States. For more information, contact Marilyn Burns Education Associates, 150 Gate 5 Road, Suite 101, Sausalito, California 94965.

For more information about the courses *Math Their Way* and *Mathematics . . . A Way of Thinking*, write to: Center for Innovation in Education, 19225 Vineyard Lane, Saratoga, California 95070.

Recommended Math Resources

Baretta-Lorton, Mary. *Mathematics Their Way*. Menlo Park, CA: Addison-Wesley Publishing Company, 1976.

Baretta-Lorton, Robert. *Mathematics: A Way of Thinking*. Menlo Park, CA: Addison-Wesley Publishing Company, 1977.

Burns, Marilyn. *A Collection of Math Lessons for Grades 1–3*. Sausalito, CA: Math Solutions Publications, 1988.

Burns, Marilyn. *A Collection of Math Lessons for Grades 3–6*. Sausalito, CA: Math Solutions Publication Company, 1987. (Distributed by Cuisenaire Company of America)

Burns, Marilyn. *About Teaching Mathematics*. Sausalito, CA: Math Solutions Publications, 1992. (Distributed by Cuisenaire Company of America)

Burns, Marilyn. *Math for Smarty Pants*. Boston, MA: Little, Brown, and Company, 1982.

Burns, Marilyn. *The I Hate Mathematics Book*. Boston, MA: Little, Brown, and Company, 1975.

Cook, Marcy. *Mathematics Problems of the Day*. Palo Alto, CA: Creative Publications, Inc., 1982.

Downie, D., Slesnick, T., and Stenmark, J. *Math for Girls and Other Problem Solvers*. Berkeley, CA: Lawrence Hall of Science, University of California, 1981.

Saunders, Hal. *When Are We Ever Gonna Have to Use This?* Palo Alto, CA: Dale Seymour Publications, 1981.

Stenmark, J., Thompson, V., and Cossey, R. *Family Math*. Berkeley, CA: Lawrence Hall of Science, University of California, 1986.

There are numerous publishers that specialize in mathematical resources. A few of these publishers include:

Addison-Wesley Publishing Company
    2725 Sand Hill Road
    Menlo Park, California 94025

Creative Publications, Inc.
    P.O. Box 10328
    Palo Alto, California 94303

Cuisenaire Company of America
  12 Church Street, Box D
  New Rochelle, New York 10805

Dale Seymour Publications
  P.O. Box 10888
  Palo Alto, California 94303

Didax Educational Resources, Inc.
  One Centennial Drive
  Peabody, Massachusetts 01960

Prentice Hall
  113 Sylvan Avenue, Route 9W
  Englewood Cliffs, New Jersey 07632

Tips for Giving Directions

*I*t is worth spending extra time to make sure directions are clearly understood by all of your students. The following tips will help your students successfully follow your directions.

1. Don't give directions until the class is completely quiet.

2. Wait until you have everyone's attention. You may need to walk over and touch or physically cue certain students for their focus.

3. Explain clearly, slowly, and concisely.

4. Face students when you talk.

5. Use multisensory instructions. Provide visual and verbal instructions. For example, write on the overhead or chalkboard a few key words, phrases, page numbers, picture cues.

6. Model what to do. Show the class.

7. Don't overwhelm students with too many instructions at one time.

8. If the assignment is due the next day or later in the week, have students record it on the assignment calendar. Help walk them through the correct recording and leave the assignment written on the board or other visible place until the end of the day as a reminder.

9. Check for understanding with the whole class by asking for specifics. For example:

    Teacher: "Will we do problems 8 and 12?"
    Class: "No."
    Teacher: "Why not?"
    Class: "We are supposed to do only the odd numbers."

10. Have individual students repeat or rephrase directions to check for understanding.

11. Make sure to give complete directions, including what you expect them to do once the task is finished.

The Advantages of Cooperative Learning With ADD/ADHD Students *

N ational authorities on cooperative learning explain that all learning situations can be structured so that students either *compete* with each other ("I swim, you sink; I sink, you swim"), ignore each other and *work independently* ("We are each in this alone"), or *work cooperatively* ("We sink or swim together"). With individualization there is no correlation among goal attainments. With competition there is a negative correlation among goal attainments. Through cooperation there is a positive correlation among goal attainments. Cooperative learning is supported by a great deal of research as the most beneficial (and least used) structure in the classroom.

The Five Elements of Cooperative Learning

1. **Positive interdependence.** Establishes and includes mutual goals, joint rewards, shared materials, and assigned roles.

2. **Face-to-face interaction.** Three or four children (maximum) are grouped together, arranged "eyeball to eyeball."

3. **Individual accountability.** Structure this in the group by giving each group member an individual exam or randomly selecting one member to give an answer for the whole group.

---

*The information presented in this chapter is quoted or summarized from *Cooperation in the Classroom*, by David Johnson, Roger Johnson, and Edythe Holubec (Interaction Book Company, 1990), and is used with permission.

4. **Interpersonal and small group skills.** Students do not come to school with all the social skills they need to collaborate effectively. Teachers need to teach the appropriate skills.

5. **Group processing.** Give time and procedures to students to evaluate how well their group is functioning.

Positive interdependence and the desire to work cooperatively don't come automatically by grouping students together. They must be carefully structured by the teacher. Only then will you see students sharing answers and material, encouraging each other, putting their heads together, drilling each other, and talking about their work.

When your class has *not* been structured to foster cooperation and interdependence, you may see students leaving the group impulsively, talking about other topics, ignoring the group and doing their own work, not sharing answers or material, and not checking to see if others in their group learned the material.

How to Provide Structure and Minimize Problems in Cooperative Groups

Many students (particularly those with ADHD) do not know how to work well in a group. The following suggestions will help teachers provide the structure and minimize problems.

1. Make up groups that are heterogeneous and small in size: pairs, triads, and eventually groups of four.

2. Seat students close to fellow group members (eye to eye, knee to knee).

3. Integrate cooperative learning experiences throughout the curriculum.

4. Assign each student a role or job to do (for example, reader, recorder, checker, praiser, encourager, materials handler).

5. Make your expectations of group behavior clear: explain, model, role play, demonstrate. "I expect to see everyone staying with the group/contributing ideas."

6. Observe and question while students are working.

7. After each session have groups answer: "What did we do well in working together today? What could we do even better tomorrow?"

Structuring to Achieve Positive Interdependence

Helping students realize that they achieve their goals only if all members of the group also attain their goals can be achieved by using the following structures and techniques:

1. Require one answer from the group. Collect only one product that is signed by all (meaning that all contributed, can explain, and defend).

2. Establish a mastery level required for each member; for example, the group goal is for every member to demonstrate 80 percent mastery on a particular test. The group is rewarded with extra points if all members attain the goal. Another example: The goal of each triad (group of three) is to reach a total score of X points.

3. Randomly select a product (report, worksheet) that represents the group for evaluation (signed by each member).

4. Give bonus points or other rewards when all members in the group achieve the criteria.

5. Give a collaborative skill score added to the academic average for an overall grade.

Teaching Social Skills Through Cooperative Learning

Cooperative skills are the keystones to maintaining a stable family, a successful career, and a stable group of friends. These skills must be directly taught—especially to students with attentional and behavioral problems who are so lacking in social skill awareness and application. There is no better place or structure for teaching and practicing appropriate social skills than in the context of cooperative learning groups.

One excellent system for making students aware of how it sounds and looks to be working cooperatively is to form a T-chart like the following.

Skill: *Reaching Agreement*

LOOKS LIKE	SOUNDS LIKE
heads together	"Good idea."
looking at each other	"What do you think?"
"What about this?"	"Oh, yeah!"
smiling	"How do you feel about that?"
everyone looking at the paper	"What is your idea?"
shaking hands	"That helps!"
thumbs up	

✳ Select a skill to practice and work on.

✳ Model the skill, explain the need, demonstrate.

✳ Brainstorm with the class what it would look like and sound like.

✳ Roam around the room and record from each group things you observed or heard that looked like or sounded like the skill being practiced. Share observations at the end of the lesson.

✳ Reinforce by giving points for positive behavior observed in groups.

✳ Have visual displays of positive social skills, for example, bulletin boards and room displays.

Photographs of students engaged in appropriate behavior are powerful reinforcers of good social skills, particularly for ADD/ADHD students. Take photos of groups and individuals engaged in cooperative behavior and hang them in a prominent place.

It is also effective to take photos of groups role playing the proper social skill. Hang those photos on the board or make copies to distribute to each group as a visual reminder when they go into their cooperative learning groups.

Also, take a photo of an ADD/ADHD student sitting properly at his/her desk and "looking like a student." He/she may have to role play and pose for this picture. Tape it to the child's desk as an individual reminder.

Some Learning Outcomes Promoted by Cooperative Learning

1. Higher achievement and increased retention.

2. Greater use of higher-level reasoning strategies and increased critical reasoning competencies.

3. Greater ability to view situations from others' perspectives.

4. Higher achievement and greater intrinsic motivation.

5. More positive, accepting, and supportive relationships with peers regardless of ethnic, sex, ability, social class differences or handicapping conditions.

6. More positive attitudes toward subject areas, learning, and schools.

7. More positive attitudes toward teachers, principals, and other school personnel.

8. Higher self-esteem based on basic self-acceptance.

9. Greater social support.

10. More positive psychological adjustment and health.

11. Less disruptive and more on-task behavior.

12. Greater collaborative skills and attitudes necessary for working effectively with others.

Cooperative Skills to Teach

Forming

1. Move into groups without noise and bothering others.

2. Stay with the group.

3. Use quiet voices.

4. Encourage everyone to participate.

5. Use names, look at the speaker, no "put-downs," keep hands and feet to oneself.

Functioning

1. Direct group's work (state and restate purpose of assignment; provide time limits; offer procedures).

2. Express support and acceptance verbally and nonverbally.

3. Ask for help or clarification.

4. Offer to explain or clarify.

5. Paraphrase others' contributions.

6. Energize the group.

7. Describe feelings when appropriate.

Formulating

1. Summarize out loud as completely as possible.

2. Seek accuracy by correcting and/or adding to summaries.

3. Seek elaboration.

4. Seek clever ways of remembering ideas and facts.

5. Demand vocalization.

6. Ask other members to plan out loud how they would teach the material.

Fermenting

1. Criticize ideas, not people.

2. Differentiate when there is disagreement within the group.

3. Integrate different ideas into a single position.

4. Ask for justification on conclusions or answers.

5. Extend other members' answers.

6. Probe by asking in-depth questions.

7. Generate further answers.

8. Test reality by checking the group's work.

Cooperative Learning Forms

Social Skills Planning Unit

What are the social skills you are going to teach?

1. _____

2. _____

3. _____

4. _____

STEP 1: *How are you going to communicate the need for the social skills?*

_____ 1. Room displays, posters, bulletin board, and so forth.

_____ 2. Telling students why the skills are needed.

_____ 3. Jigsawing materials on the need for the skills.

_____ 4. Having groups work on a cooperative lesson and then asking students to brainstorm what skills are needed to help the group function effectively.

_____ 5. Giving bonus points or a separate grade for the competent use of the skills.

_____ 6. Other(s):_____

STEP 2: *How are you going to define the skill?*

1. Phrases (list 3):

_____

_____

_____

2. Behaviors (list 3):

_____

_____

_____

3. How will you explain and model each social skill?

_____ *a.* Demonstrating the skill, explaining each step of engaging in the skill, and then redemonstrating the skill.

_____ *b.* Using a videotape or film to demonstrate and explain the skill.

_____ *c.* Asking each group to plan role-play demonstrations of the skill to present to the entire class.

_____ *d.* Other(s):_____

STEP 3: *How will you ensure that students practice the skill?*

_____ 1. Assigning specific roles to group members, ensuring practice of the skills.

_____ 2. Announcing that you will observe for the skills.

_____ 3. Having specific practice sessions involving nonacademic tasks.

_____ 4. Other(s):_____

STEP 4: *How will you ensure students receive feedback and process their use of the skills?*

Teacher Monitoring

_____ 1. Structured observation with the Social Skills Observation sheet, focusing on each learning group an equal amount of time (30 minutes, 6 groups, each group is observed for 5 minutes).

_____ 2. Structured observation with the Social Skills Observation sheet, focusing only on the learning groups in which target students (emotional/behavior problem students, handicapped students, low achieving students, and so forth) are members.

_____ 3. Anecdotal observation (eavesdropping) to record the significant, specific events involving students engaging in interaction with each other.

_____ 4. Other(s):_____

Teacher Intervening

1. If the social skills are not being used in a cooperative group, I will:

_____ *a.* Ask the group what it has done so far and what it plans to try next to increase the use of the controversy skills.

_____ *b.* Other(s):_____

2. If the social skills are being used in a cooperative group, I will:

_____ *a.* Note it on the observation sheet or anecdotal record and come back to the group during the processing time, call attention to the use of the skills, and compliment the group.

_____ *b.* Interrupt the group, call attention to the use of the skills, and compliment the group.

_____ *c.* Call attention to it during the whole-class processing.

_____ *d.* Other(s):_____

Student Observing

1. Student observers will be selected by: _____

2. Student observers will be trained by: _____

3. Time for the student observers to give group members feedback will be provided by: _____

During the group processing time, students will:

_____ 1. Receive feedback from the teacher.

_____ 2. Receive feedback from the student observer.

_____ 3. Complete a skills checklist or say/write: *Things I did today that helped my group are . . .*

_____ 4. Say/write: *Things I plan to do differently next time to help my group work better are . . .*

_____ 5. Say/write: *What I learned about being a good group member is . . .*

_____ 6. Other(s): _____

STEP 5: *Ensure that students persevere in practicing the skills*

I will provide continued opportunity for students to practice and repractice the collaborative skills by:

_____ 1. Assigning the collaborative skills to group members for _____ sessions.

_____ 2. Assigning the collaborative skills to the groups as a whole with all members being responsible for their use _____ sessions.

_____ 3. Asking another teacher, an aide, or a parent volunteer to tutor and coach target students in the use of the skills.

_____ 4. Asking the groups to process how well each member is using the skill for _____ sessions.

_____ 5. Intermittently spending a class session on training students to use and reuse the skill.

_____ 6. Intermittently giving any group whose members use the skill above a certain criterion a reward of _____

STUDENT CHECKLIST: Cooperation

I contributed my ideas and information.

Always	*Sometimes*	*Never*

I asked others for their ideas and information.

Always	*Sometimes*	*Never*

I summarized all our ideas and information.

Always	*Sometimes*	*Never*

I asked for help when I needed it.

Always	*Sometimes*	*Never*

I helped other members of my group learn.

Always	*Sometimes*	*Never*

I made sure everyone in my group understood how to do
the school work we were studying.

Always	*Sometimes*	*Never*

I helped keep the group studying.

Always	*Sometimes*	*Never*

I included everyone in our work.

Always	*Sometimes*	*Never*

Best Advice

I. DECISIONS

LESSON: Start with a short lesson, something you feel comfortable with.

GROUP SIZE: Start small, a pair or a threesome. (With larger groups more skills are necessary to be successful.)

ASSIGNMENT TO GROUPS: You can randomly choose or assign students depending on the group's task.

MATERIALS: Give each student materials, or the group can have one set of papers. One group set helps create interdependence among members.

II. SET THE LESSON

WHAT IS/ARE:

Academic Task:
Clearly state what you want students to do: Make a mural, complete the worksheet, answer the questions.

Criteria for Success:
State how they will know they have been successful with the task:

90% Fantastic (A)
80% Very Good (B)

Positive Interdependence:
The groups need to know they have to be concerned with each other's learning. They sink or swim together.
—This can be done by testing each one.

Individual Accountability:
Students should know they are each responsible for knowing the work.

Expected Behaviors:
Specify how you want them to behave while they work. Name specific, observable, describable behaviors.

III. MONITORING *(Start with the teacher as the observer to model observation.)*

WILL BE DONE BY:

Teacher/Student _____   Teacher_____

FOCUS WILL BE ON:

Individual Groups _____   Whole Class _____

Individuals _____

OBSERVATION SHEET INCLUDES THE BEHAVIORS OF: Start small with just two or three behaviors. They should be positive behaviors, not negative:

ᴛᴀking turns, sharing, praising, checking (Refer to Expected Behaviors above.)

IV. PROCESSING/FEEDBACK: Take time to give feedback to your students. Refer to the behaviors you asked them to try, pointing out positive behavior you noticed.

Observation Sheet

DIRECTIONS FOR USE: (A) Put names of group members above each column. (B) Put a tally mark in the appropriate box each time a group member contributes. (C) Make notes on the back when interesting things happen that are not captured by the categories. (D) It is a good idea to collect one (or more) good things that each group member does.

	Student A	Student B	Student C	Student D	Student E	Totals
1. Contributes ideas						
2. Describes feelings						
3. Paraphrases						
4. Expresses support, acceptance, and liking						
5. Encourages others to contribute						
6. Summarizes						
7. Relieves tension by joking						
8. Gives direction to group's work						
Totals						

Trusting: 1,2; Trustworthy-Acceptance: 3,4; Trustworthy-Reciprocation: 1,2; Leadership-Task: 1,2,6,7; Leadership-Maintenance: 3,4,5,8; Communication: 1,2,3 (and, technically, all the rest); Conflict Resolution: 1,2,3.

CLASSROOM OBSERVATIONS

Teacher observed _____

My focus as an observer for this lesson is: _____

			COMMENTS
Subject Matter			
Social Skills Objective			
Positive Interdependence	Group goal	❑	
	Group grade	❑	
	Division of labor	❑	
	Materials shared	❑	
	Bonus points	❑	
	Roles assigned	❑	
	Materials jigsawed	❑	
	Other:	❑	
Group Composition	Homogeneous	❑	
	Heterogeneous	❑	
Seating Arrangement	Clear view of others	❑	
	Clear view of materials	❑	
Individual Accountability	Each student evaluated	❑	
	Students check each other	❑	
	Random student evaluated	❑	
	Other:	❑	
Observation	Teacher	❑	
	Student	❑	
	Observation form used	❑	
	Informal	❑	
Teacher Feedback: Social Skills	Class as a whole	❑	
	Group by group	❑	
	Individual	❑	
Group Processing	Observation data	❑	
	Social skills	❑	
	Academic skills	❑	
	Positive	❑	
	Goal setting	❑	
General Climate	Group products displayed	❑	
	Group progress displayed	❑	
	Aids to group work displayed	❑	

Observer _____ Date _____

section
15

Learning Styles

I have come to a frightening conclusion
that I am the decisive element in the classroom.
It's my personal approach that creates the climate.
It's my daily mood that makes the weather.

As a teacher, I possess a tremendous power
to make a child's life miserable or joyous.
I can be a tool of torture
or an instrument of inspiration.
I can humiliate or humor, hurt or heal.

In all situations, it is my response
that decides whether a crisis will be
escalated or de-escalated
and a child humanized or dehumanized.[1]

—Haim Ginott

There is a growing awareness throughout the country that we all have different learning styles that affect our way of thinking, how we behave and approach learning, and the way we process information. Through learning style training, teachers first need to go through a self-awareness process. A variety of instruments may be used to make learning style assessments. First, teachers take a close look at their own functioning as learners—their own propensities, strengths, weaknesses, and preferences, and how that is transferred into the classroom they teach.

---

[1] Haim Ginott. *Teacher and Child*. (New York: The Macmillan Co., 1972), p. 15.

It is enlightening to see the variety of styles among us, to better understand ourselves and our colleagues. This awareness and sensitivity to learning styles helps us become better equipped to *teach* all kinds of learners, especially those students who struggle academically, emotionally, and behaviorally in the classroom.

Definitions, Statistics, and Elements

There are a number of definitions of learning styles. Dr. Rita Dunn defines it as "the way in which each learner begins to concentrate on, process, and retain new and difficult information."[2]

Learning styles have also been described as how one deals with ideas and day-to-day situations, one's learning preferences and propensities, how one approaches thinking, and how one best perceives and processes information.

Statistics to Consider:

✱ One third of our students do not process auditorily.

✱ Over 60 percent of our students prefer and perform better with a tactile-kinesthetic learning activity.

✱ At least 50 percent of our students are frustrated by left-brain, sequential-type assignments and are global, holistic, and random in their organization and processing of information.[3]

According to Drs. Rita and Kenneth Dunn, authors of *Teaching Students Through Their Individual Learning Styles: A Practical Approach* (Prentice Hall, 1978), there are a number of specific elements that comprise a person's learning style, including:

✱ **Environmental elements:**

— Sound

— Light

— Temperature

— Design (formal or informal)

✱ **Sociological elements:**

— Pair-oriented

— Peer-oriented

— Team-oriented

— Self-oriented

— Authority-oriented

---

[2] Rita Dunn, "Introduction to Learning Styles and Brain Behavior: Suggestions for Practitioners." *The Association for the Advancement of International Education*, Vol. 15, No. 46, Winter (1988), p. 6.

[3] Sally Botroff-Hawes, "Understanding Learning/Teaching Styles." *Thrust*. September 1988.

✳ **Emotional elements:**

— Motivation

— Persistence

— Responsibility

— Structure

✳ **Physical elements:**

— Perceptual strengths (visual, auditory, tactile, kinesthetic)

— Time of day

— Need for intake (eating/drinking)

— Need for mobility

Teachers who offer their students a balance of instructional methods, groupings, structures, and environmental adaptations that take into account the various learning styles in their classroom, will be most effective in reaching all of their students.

Learning Style Adaptations to Meet the Needs of All Students

✳ Present all new information through multisensory instruction. Involve all of the senses, providing auditory, visual, and tactile-kinesthetic input.

✳ When you have to reteach information, try it in a variety of different ways.

✳ For **visual learners**, supply maps, graphs, pictures, and diagrams and write on overhead/board with colored markers, pens, or chalk.

✳ Point, highlight, model, and demonstrate.

✳ Teach through clustering, mind mapping, and other graphic organizers.

✳ For **global learners** who need to see the whole picture before making sense of the parts, show the end products.

✳ For **auditory learners,** read aloud, paraphrase, employ music, rhythm, melody, discussion, and tapes.

✳ It is very helpful to have material that students need to learn on tape so they can listen to it. Allow students to bring in small tape recorders to record teacher lectures (to supplement notetaking).

✳ For **tactile/kinesthetic learners,** provide lots of hands-on experience that promotes learning by doing. Use manipulatives for teaching math, role playing, dance and movement, acting-out.

✳ Use computers and games.

✳ Offer many choices (for example, book reports, science projects, oral reports).

✳ Hook the students into the instruction emotionally.

✳ Let students know why the material you are presenting is important to them.

All lessons can be structured individually, competitively, or cooperatively. There is a place for all three structures in the classroom. However, research shows that the least used but most effective structure is cooperative learning. Structure your lessons cooperatively whenever possible. Provide many opportunities for students to work with partners or in groups of three or four.

Students with attentional difficulties—indeed, most students—have a lot to gain from the cooperative learning structure because:

✳ they can receive more immediate feedback;

✳ they have a shorter wait before being able to share/respond; and

✳ a small group is the best place for learning and practicing social skills.

Even though these students may have difficulty staying on task with the group, they are typically better engaged than they would be working individually or competitively.

There are many other learning style adaptations:

✳ Alter the instructional groupings in your class (for example, by interest, skill or topic).

✳ Individualize activities and assignments (for example, provide contract packages for students to choose activities from).

✳ Offer some competitive activities (team games) in the class.

✳ Allow students to use learning aids (tape recorder, reference charts, calculators, typewriter, word processor, spell-checks).

✳ Use meaning-making strategies (metacognition, reciprocal teaching, think-alouds) in all content areas.

✳ Teach visualization strategies. Help students develop the strategy of making a detailed mental picture.

✳ Encourage students to look for and identify patterns (in math, literature, poetry, nature, music, dance).

✳ Use a "discovery" approach as often as possible in your teaching. Let the students do the experimenting and discovering on their own.

✳ Teach students to explain their reasoning and describe their thinking processes in writing. (Ask, for example, "How did you go about solving the problem?")

✳ Bring humor into your classroom.

✳ Consider student interests in planning your lessons.

* Teach your students mnemonics (memory devices or tricks to memorize things). Examples: "Every Good Boy Does Fine" for learning "line notes" on the treble staff; the state of Louisiana looks like a boot; or "Roy G. BIV" for the seven colors in the visible spectrum/rainbow (red, orange, yellow, green, blue, indigo, violet).

* Allow for physical needs. When students are physically uncomfortable (need to go to bathroom or are hungry, hot or thirsty), they will not be able to focus on instruction. Many teachers allow students to bring water bottles to class, especially on hot days. Many teachers (at the elementary level) keep some crackers or other snack foods available for hungry children.

Experimenting With Environmental Adaptations

Alter your seating arrangements. Some possibilities include:

* staggered arrangement of desks/rows

* semi-circles

* table clusters

* mix of clusters with individual desks

Teachers wishing to design their classroom for accommodating different learning styles have an infinite number of choices and possibilities. A "learning styles classroom" at the secondary level may have desks arranged in traditional rows or in semi-circles, clusters or rows split in the middle and facing each other.

The advantage at the secondary level for most students is that they are typically exposed to a large variety of teaching styles and environmental arrangements throughout the day. Even if they have some classes where the teacher's style is incompatible with their learning style, at least it isn't for the whole day. On the other hand, for many ADD/ADHD students, this need to adjust to so many different personalities and expectations can be a problem. They often do better in a core structure, staying with the same cluster of teachers.

At the elementary level, a classroom designed for a variety of learning styles may include:

* Learning centers, interest centers, and listening posts or centers. Be careful not to seat distractible students near these areas.

* Informal areas of the classroom (e.g., carpet area, beanbag chairs, couch).

* Variation in desks, seats, and tables. Allowing some students more desktop space and taller tables and chairs to accommodate longer legs and the need for more room.

One or two kidney-shaped tables are excellent in the classroom for small group work with students. Teachers are able to sit with a group of students, directly facing them, within arm reach and cueing distance.

One of the best environmental modifications for students at the elementary level with attentional problems is study carrels, office areas, or privacy boards. These block the visual distractions from at least two sides. Study carrels can be constructed from three pieces of heavy chipboard bound together, large appliance boxes, or other cartons cut to size, etc. (Stores will gladly give these to teachers.) Some teachers allow students to decorate or personalize their study carrel in some way as long as it's not a distractor. It is very helpful to have at least three or four "office areas" in the classroom for use during seat work/concentration time (particularly test-taking). By making them desirable areas and available for anyone who requests using them, you are preventing them from being viewed by the class as areas of punishment.

* Another useful provision for students with attention problems is headphones to be used during seat work or other times that require concentration (e.g., silent reading). The kind of earphones that construction workers use are the most effective for blocking out noise. However, soft-foam earplugs and other kinds of headphones are effective, too.

* Try altering the amount of light in the room. Experiment with turning off the lights at certain times of the day. Many students with ADD/ADHD report extreme sensitivity to the buzz of fluorescent lights and the intensity of some artificial lighting.

* Provide for students (particularly ADHD students) who have a physiological need for mobility. Allow exercise breaks, running the track, and doing errands for the teacher that enable them to leave the classroom (to bring something to the office, for example).

* Move students periodically in the classroom. Be responsive to student complaints about their seating and honor reasonable requests to move.

* Experiment with background music at different times to relax, motivate, and stimulate thinking. Many distractible students enjoy and benefit from having music in the classroom. Others do not, and cannot tolerate it. Make provisions for those who can and cannot.

Multiple Intelligences in the Classroom

Howard Gardner in his book, *Frames of Mind*, identifies seven distinct intelligences and styles of learning. These include:

1. **The linguistic learner** who learns best by saying, hearing, and seeing words.

2. **The logical/mathematical learner** who learns best by categorizing, classifying, and working with abstract patterns and relationships.

3. **The spatial learner** who learns best by visualizing, using his/her mind's eye, and working with colors/pictures.

Using privacy boards at outside tables

Privacy boards for in-class use during tests, or to block distractors during seatwork time. Constructed from chipboard, these are easily stored inside desks.

Office area space—These painted plywood boards block visual distractions from either side.

Learning center area for students to work at during "free time"

Room arrangement of tables facing forward. Study carrels are in the back of the classroom, which are optional areas for seatwork and test-taking times.

Informal classroom area—Students reading in beanbag chairs at library center.

Students working cooperatively on "Mini City" learning center activities

Outdoor reading group seated or lying on carpet squares

Informal classroom area in the corner of the room

Computer corner in the classroom.

Students at the overhead projector demonstrate their comprehension of the lesson presented.

Quiet corner—Students can use earphones for background music or with no music to block out auditory distractors.

4. **The musical learner** who learns best through rhythm, music, and melody.

5. **The bodily-kinesthetic learner** who learns best by touching, moving, and interacting with space.

6. **The interpersonal learner** who learns best by sharing, relating, and cooperating with others.

7. **The intrapersonal learner** who learns best by working alone, having self-paced instruction, and individualized projects.

Section 29 describes Key School, an elementary school in Indianapolis that is based on Gardner's theory of multiple intelligences. It is designed to provide a curriculum that gives equal emphasis to the seven intelligences.

Gender/Ethnic Expectations and Student Achievement

Teachers need to appreciate that our students have strengths in areas that we may not be tapping in the classroom. To build self-esteem and address the whole child, we must give students the opportunity to develop, use, and demonstrate their strengths to their peers.

There is a program in the school district where I teach called Turning Point, which is funded by a federal magnet assistance grant. Currently there are thirteen project magnet elementary schools in San Diego that have been receiving intensive training in learning/teaching styles, and teacher expectations and student equity (TESA/GEESA). Our school is one of the project schools, and we are very fortunate that all of our teachers are able to participate in the training.

It is important for teachers to evaluate their own way of teaching and relating to their individual students. TESA/GEESA training helps teachers look at how they interact with students consciously and subconsciously. Teacher expectations greatly affect student achievement. Teachers are not always aware of those expectations (along gender and ethnic lines as well as what we expect from "good students" and "weak students"). Our expectations affect many of our student-teacher interactions, including the following discussed in *Gender/Ethnic Expectations and Student Achievement*, by Dolores Grayson and Mary D. Martin:

✳ response opportunities

✳ acknowledgment and feedback

✳ organizing and grouping

✳ physical closeness to students

✳ touching

✳ reproof (giving a verbal or nonverbal indication that a student's behavior is not acceptable)

✳ asking probing questions

✽ listening

✽ asking higher-level questions

TESA/GEESA training helps teachers analyze how they interact with their students and rectify any inequities. For example, according to Grayson and Martin:

"The average time a teacher waits for a student to respond to a question is 2.6 seconds. Teachers wait an average of 5.0 seconds if a correct response is anticipated, and curtail wait time to less than 1.0 seconds if the student is expected to give an incorrect answer or to not respond at all."

Consider the implications for our students who have difficulty processing the questions and responding rapidly. It is critical that we provide all of our students with the chance to be "seen" and "heard" by their teachers and peers. Everyone's contribution needs to be valued and encouraged in the classroom.

Teachers can self-evaluate how equitably they respond to students in their classroom by:

✽ Tape-recording themselves

✽ Videotaping themselves

✽ Having another teacher or aide observe and tally the frequency of their specific interactions with children

   Examples: How many times do I call on students? How often do I acknowledge or reprove individual students?

✽ Have children keep track (on a card) the number of times they are asked to respond in class for the period or morning.

Learning style philosophy is powerful and makes quite a difference in the lives of students. We need to help teach students to understand, respect, and value differences in themselves and others. We need to help students find their strengths and nurture them. We all benefit from being exposed to a variety of strategies and seeing the diversity of how we each look at the world and solve problems. It is a wonderful discovery that there are many ways to do things, not one right way.

Students with attentional disorders are among the population of students who would benefit the most from a teacher flexible enough to try environmental modifications and learning styles techniques/strategies.

As a result of my training as a Turning Point project teacher, I developed the following learning styles interview to be used with students in grades 3 through 12. If we want to help our students know and appreciate themselves better and if we want insight into our students' thinking processes and feelings, we need to take the time to ask and listen. I have found that students are very articulate about their needs and preferences and will gladly tell you.

Learning Styles Interview

Based on Rita and Ken Dunn's Learning Styles Model Interview, designed and written by Sandra Rief, Resource Specialist.

1. Think back over the past few years of school. Whose classroom was it easiest for you to: Learn in? Feel comfortable in? Pay attention in? Tell me some of the things that you enjoyed in any of your classes. *For this question the student is asked not to tell about the teacher, but about the classroom environment and his/her feeling of success.*

2. Lighting: Do you prefer lots of light when you are studying? Low light? Do you like to sit by the window? Do you like when the lights are turned off or shades closed?

3. Temperature: Do you like it best in the classroom when the windows are open? Do you like being in air conditioning? Do you like having the heater on in the class on colder days?

4. I want you to imagine that you can set up the perfect classroom any way you want. Think about it and tell me or draw for me how you would like the class to be arranged. Would you like the tables or desks in rows? Tables in clusters? Tell me (show me) where you want the teacher to be, and where would be your choice of seating in this room.

5. How much noise do you mind in the classroom when you are trying to study/concentrate? Do you like it very quiet? Do you like it with some amount of noise? Would it make you feel good to have some music in the background or would it bother you?

6. At home, where do you usually do your homework? If you had your choice, in what place in the house would you like to do your homework/study? Pretend that your parents would build you or buy whatever you needed in your home for a good study space. What would it look like and have in it? Do you like to be alone or with someone else around you when studying/doing homework? Do you need it to be real quiet? Do you like having some music or noise when studying?

7. Do you like to do projects alone, or would you prefer to work with others?

8. If you had to study for a social studies test, would you like to study alone? With a friend? Small group? Parent or teacher helping you?

9. In your classroom, if you had a study carrel (private office area or partition) available, would you choose to do your seat work in it if some other students in your class were also using them?

10. When do you feel you are able to do your best work and concentrate best: In the morning before recess? After recess but before lunch? After lunch in the afternoon?

11. When do you concentrate best and prefer to do your homework: Soon after you get home from school? Have a break (play first) after getting home from school, but do it before dinner? Do it after dinner?

12. Do you usually get hungry and start wishing you could have a snack during the school day? Would you like it if you were allowed to eat (healthy) snacks in your classroom?

13. If your teacher assigned a big project, giving you choices of how to do it, would you prefer to:

    — make an oral presentation in front of the class?

    — tape-record something?

    — act it out/drama?

    — build something? (e.g., from clay or wood)

    — draw something?

    — write something/type it or have someone else type it?

14. Do you think you are good at building things? Taking things apart and putting them back together?

15. Do you like listening to stories? Are you good at learning words to songs?

16. Do you like to: Read? Write stories? Do math? Do science experiments? Do art projects? Sing? Dance? Use math manipulatives? Play any sports—which ones?

17. How is it easier for you to learn: When someone explains something carefully to you or when someone shows you?

18. If you have to give someone directions to somewhere or instructions for how to do something, is it easier for you to explain and tell that person or is it easier for you to draw a map or write it down for them?

19. Tell me what you think you are really good at. What do you think you are not so good at?

20. What are your favorite things to do at home? If you had the chance, what would you love to learn to do?

21. Do you ever feel you cannot concentrate in class? Have problems paying attention? What kinds of things distract you?

22. If you were promised a trip to Hawaii with your family and also $10,000 for spending money only if you got an *A* on a very difficult test (for example, a social studies test covering the last four chapters, with lots of information and stuff to memorize and learn):

    — How would you want your teacher to teach it to you? Tell me exactly what you would like your teacher to do in class so that you can learn the information.

    — How would you go about memorizing all the information you were taught?

— How would you need to study at home? What kind of help would you want your parents to give you? Do you want to study alone? With someone? Tell me as much as you can.

AN INTERVIEW WITH SUSAN
(38 years old, California)

Susan has a B.A. in Occupational Therapy and an M.A. in Rehabilitation. She is a rehab counselor in California who was identified as an adult as having learning disabilities and ADD.

What is your advice to teachers?

"Help students be aware of their strengths. If we just go after the 'sore teeth,' people give up and leave school. If they work through their strengths, interests, and learning styles, students will be motivated to learn the skills they need and will forget about their 'sore teeth.' Set up an environment that will make them reach out and interact with other people."

What has helped you get through school successfully?

"I've learned to identify my learning style and to compensate for my weaknesses. I am a weak auditory processor. [*Note:* Susan requested a face-to-face interview rather than one conducted over the phone.] I am a strong kinesthetic learner. I take walks a lot. That is how I get my best ideas. When I get bogged down on a project I go walking and am able to get the whole concept. Then I can move forward. I allow my kinesthetic abilities to help me. For example, my statistics class was extremely difficult for me. I tape recorded lectures and would listen to them a few times at home, but it didn't help much. Then I started walking around the lake while I listened to the lectures. This helped me considerably. I now take frequent breaks, move around a lot, and balance my activities. I don't make myself sit at a desk."

Relaxation, Guided Imagery, and Visualization Techniques

*S*tudents with ADD/ADHD are often in a state of stress in school. It is therapeutic to teach children strategies to help them calm down and relax. Hyperactive/impulsive students, in particular, gain the most from learning techniques that relax their minds and bodies, recognize their internal feelings, and release inner tension. These strategies empower children with a feeling of peace and self-control.

There are a variety of techniques that have proven effective in helping us to slow down, and to improve focus and awareness. One book, in particular, is a gold mine of wonderful ideas, step-by-step exercises, and activities for teachers and parents to help children achieve this sense of relaxation and well-being. This wonderful book, *Centerplay: Focusing Your Child's Energy* (Fireside, 1984), was written by Holly Young Huth, a relaxation consultant and teacher specializing in early childhood education.

Fun and Laughter

Laughter is one of the best ways to release stress and feel good. The chemicals released in the body through laughter reduce pain and tension. So, there is probably no substitute for finding ways to have fun and to laugh with our children.

Breathing Techniques

Many of us know the positive effects of controlled breathing through our training in Lamaze or other natural childbirth classes. Controlled, conscious breathing has the benefit of relaxing muscles and reducing stress. Many believe it is useful in the management, perhaps cure, of some physical ailments and disease.

✱ Help students learn to take conscious, deep breaths to relax.

✱ Show students how to inhale deeply (preferably through the nose, but through the mouth is fine) and *slowly* exhale through the mouth.

✱ Students can do relaxation breathing in their chairs, seated on the floor cross-legged with eyes closed, lying down, or even standing.

✱ Teach students to isolate different body parts and relax them with each slow breath they exhale. For example, have students lie on the floor. Instruct them to tighten or squeeze their toes on the left foot, then relax with a deep breath. Now tighten their left knee and upper leg . . . then relax and breathe. Proceed in this fashion to the right side of the lower body, to the abdomen and upper body, each arm, hand/fingers, chest, neck, jaws, and face.

✱ It is particularly helpful for children to recognize that when they are nervous, stressed, and angry, they should feel the tightening of certain body parts. If they can recognize when fists clench, jaws tighten, stomachs harden, they have the power over their bodies to relax and gain control. They can begin to breathe deeply and "send" their breaths consciously to their hand (silently prompting themselves to relax—until the fist is released and fingers are loose). Teach children that when their bodies are relaxed, they are better able to think and plan.

✱ Help guide students to visualize that with each breath they take in, their body becomes filled slowly with a soothing color, aroma, sound, light, warmth, or other pleasant, comfortable feeling.

Ask students to think of a color that makes them feel very comfortable, peaceful, and relaxed. Then have them practice with closed eyes breathing in that color and "sending" it (blowing it) throughout the body. If a child, for example, chooses "turquoise," guide him/her to visualize the turquoise going down his/her throat, into the neck and chest, down to the stomach, and so on until the child is filled with the beautiful, peaceful, wonderful turquoise . . . and is relaxed and in control.

Yoga and Slow Movement Exercises

Centerplay teaches a number of yoga postures and slow movement games and exercises that are fun and appropriate for children. Prior to performing these movements, Holly Huth recommends dimming the lights and keeping a quiet environment. She teaches back, stomach, and sitting postures through pretending to be a ragdoll, scarecrow, popped balloon, candle, plow, bike, fish, bridge, snake, bow, boat, flower, crocodile, and others.

During these "postures" the children are told that quiet time is beginning and that if they need to talk, it must be very softly. Children spread out (if they want, with their blankets, carpet squares, mats) and are guided by the teacher. "It's time for us to become . . . "

Through the game of pretending, the teacher guides students to make slow movements that help calm them and engage their creativity. Some of the movements that are shared in *Centerplay* include:

— carrying a very fragile gift to someone

— pretending to be a peacock

— swimming through air

— scaling through space

— climbing a pyramid

— being a wave or the wind

Walking Meditations

Walking meditations can be done in a line or circle such as the following, from *Centerplay*:

Porcupine Walk

"We are going to pretend that we are following a porcupine that walks very slowly along the ground. We want to be the porcupine's friend, so we don't want to scare it. Very slowly, each one of you pretend that you're walking behind your porcupine. I will be leading the circle, so you can see how slow we have to go. Look down at the porcupine and be careful not to walk too fast or else you might step on the porcupine and get its sharp quills in your feet. Think about where your porcupine might be going . . . and be silent."

Visualization and Guided Imagery

The ability to visualize with colorful, vivid images, rich imagination, and detailed action are natural skills of childhood. These same skills have been found to be useful in empowering people to overcome obstacles in their lives. Many adults take classes and are being trained to develop these skills. For example, Kevin Trudeau's *Mega Memory* teaches how to dramatically improve memory skills through visualization techniques. Many cancer patients are being taught how to use their power of visualization to help stop the spread of cancer cells in their bodies.

One cancer patient who leads a support group in her community explained how she mentally prepares herself for treatments and has found success in battling her cancer through visualization. Through music (which she selects for different stages) and relaxation techniques, she brings herself to a state where she is prepared for "battle." She then clearly, vividly imagines her "good cells" attacking her "bad cells." The cells come in living colors, equipped with uniforms and battle gear. She plans different strategies for various battles. She begins at the top of her head and slowly has her "good cells" outnumber, overpower and destroy all of the "bad cells" as they march from one organ and body part to the next.

Huth shares a number of wonderful guided imagery activities in *Centerplay*. This one is in the form of a riddle:

Preparation: "Lie down on your blanket (pillow, mat, etc.) in your most comfortable position . . . just the way you do when you go to bed at night. Move around a little until you find the place that is familiar and cozy. Feel your whole body sinking down into the floor. Take in a deep breath through your nose—or, if you like, through your mouth—and let it out. Take another deep breath and just begin to notice your breath swaying you softly, helping you rest. Close your eyes. Try to close your eyes, because that way you can imagine better what I'm going to tell you. You can forget everything else and really be here. Now we are ready to go on a fantasy together. If you want to come with me, to imagine with me, that's up to you. If you don't want to, just rest quietly."

(Sailboat) "You are floating in the water, rocking back and forth, back and forth. Feel your whole body relax in the warm water. The gentle waves come and go against you. You are sturdy and strong. The sun shines and warms the wood that you are made of. The wind comes and blows you softly in the sea. Your big cloth billows and moves you slowly in the breeze. What are you?" (Teacher goes around to individual children and they whisper what they think is the answer to the riddle.)

In *Centerplay* the author shares many other long and short guided fantasies where the children pretend to take a journey (as a feather, leaf, cloud floating through the air, and so on).

Additional Visualization and Relaxation Techniques:

* **Use music for relaxation**. Music can be very helpful for relaxation, as a previsualization activity, to soothe away worries and distractions, and bring a sense of inner peace.

* **Use water.** We all know the relaxing, soothing, stress-reducing benefits of taking a hot bath. Water can also be used in the classroom (or outside the room) to evoke this sensation. Teachers may want to experiment with activities using plastic tubs or water tables.

* **Teach students to visualize themselves in situations where they are achieving and being successful.** Once students have had practice with guided visualization, encourage them to use the techniques of deep breathing and visualizing themselves doing what they want to do. For example, prior to taking a test, they can visualize themselves in detail working diligently taking the test. Encourage them to see themselves being persistent and reading each item carefully, relaxed and not getting nervous or excited, and being confident with their answers. Have students picture themselves finishing the test, going back and checking for careless errors. In addition, playing the theme song from the movie *Rocky* or another motivational song can help build confidence.

AN INTERVIEW WITH BRUCE
(37 years old)

Bruce is a very successful entrepreneur living in Manhattan. He was identified with learning disabilities and ADHD early in elementary school.

Memories of his childhood: Bruce basically blocked out his memories of childhood and cannot recall specifics. He does remember the feelings of anger and rage. "I tried so hard and everyone kept putting me down." Bruce describes himself as a survivor and recalls feeling that he was always hiding. "Secrecy was my safety. It protected me."

Bruce got through college by "studying morning, noon, and night." Mathematics and anything mechanical always came easily for him. Reading and writing are still very difficult and tedious tasks.

What have you learned that helps you now as an adult?

"I've learned that I have to exercise every day or I don't feel good. I also learned how to meditate. Learning to relax, calm myself, and control my mind and thoughts were some of the best things that ever happened to me."

Music for Transitions, Calming, and Visualization

Music can be effective and helpful for creating a mood, motivating, signaling, and using during transitional times in the classroom, home, and other settings (e.g., hospitals and surgical rooms, therapists' offices). Through music, children can greatly improve their abilities in critical and analytical listening skills, focus/concentration, and responding to specific directions and prompts. Some examples of using music during transitional times may include:

* "When you hear the drum for the first time, Table 3 may get up and return their books to the bookshelf"

* "When you hear the birds in this song start chirping, come quietly up to the rug."

Students can be trained in critical listening through activities such as:
"Count the number of times you heard the theme repeat itself in this selection" (e.g., "Bolero" by Ravel).

Visualization activities in response to listening to musical selections can be integrated with writing, drawing, and oral activities. Many of the recordings in this section are useful for visualization activities (e.g., "Bydllo"—visualizing an ox pulling a cart far off in the distance, moving closer and closer as the music gradually becomes louder). Teachers can play any of the recordings and allow for creative student interpretation. For example, ask students: "What does this music make you think of?" "Can you see pictures in your mind when you hear this music? Tell us what you see." A creative teacher will find countless ways to use music in the curriculum, to establish an environment that promotes individual learning styles, as well as to introduce and enhance music education and appreciation.

Music that gets you from one place to another (e.g., marches) is excellent for teaching children the discipline of moving their bodies appropriately. It requires focusing and counting.

Bertha Young, music specialist in the San Diego City Schools, has recommended musical selections to use for calming, visualization, transitions, and movement. Mrs. Young has 23 years of classroom experience in teaching grades K through 8, as well as in curriculum development and music writing. The following lists contain selections carefully compiled and used with permission by Mrs. Young. The selected choices of music include different instruments (e.g., trumpet, tuba, bells, guitar, piano, flute, as well as the human voice), and different musical periods (e.g., baroque, classical, romantic, modern, and contemporary). A variety of composers from several ethnic and cultural backgrounds are represented from these periods, and the examples of contemporary performers of differing ethnic backgrounds may serve as role models for students.

Music for a Calming Effect

These selctions are especially useful after recess, P.E., and other more active times of the day.

1. Barber, Samuel. "Adagio for Strings" from String Quartet no. 1, op. 11.

2. Beethoven, Ludwig. "Für Elise"
   (piano, approximately 3 minutes)

3. Bizet, Georges. "Berceuse" from *Children's Games (Jeux d'Enfants)*

4. Copland, Aaron. "Appalachian Spring Suite," Sections 1, 6, 7, 8 only. (Note: Section 7 is "Variations on 'Simple Gifts' "), Time-Life Record, Division of Time-Life Books, Time-Life, Inc., New York, New York. Record #TL 415, © 1967, Robert Irving, conductor. (Available in other recordings, cassettes and CDs with other conductors.)

5. Debussy, Claude. "Clair de Lune"
   (stringed instruments, approximately 3 minutes)

6. Delibes, Leo. "Waltz" from *Coppelia*
   (stringed instruments, approximately 2 minutes)

7. Halpern, Steve. *Spectrum Suite*
   (fourteen different color-themed songs each approximately 3 to 5 minutes long)

8. Holst, Gustav. "Jupiter" from *The Planets*
   (stringed section, approximately 1 minute)

9. Mendelssohn, Felix. "Nocturne" from *Midsummer Night's Dream*

10. Mozart, Wolfgang Amadeus. "Adagio for Glass Harmonica" from *Music and You, Grade 5*, 1988 edition, page 215, Record 8, Macmillan Publishing Co., 866 Third Avenue, New York, New York, 10022 (performed by Jamey Turner, Summer Chamber Festival Concert, June 24, 1986. Courtesy of

the Library of Congress, Washington D.C.), (4:24). May be available on other recordings.

11. Mussorgsky, Modest. "Bydllo" ("The Oxcart" excerpt from *Pictures at an Exhibition* (tuba section only) from *Music and You, Grade Two,* pages 34-35, Record 2, 1988 edition. Macmillan Publishing Co., 866 Third Avenue, New York, New York 10022 (performed by New York Philharmonic with Zubin Mehta, conductor. P 1980 CBS, Inc.) (2:54)

12. Offenbach, Jacques. "Barcarolle" from *Tales of Hoffman* (approximately 3½ minutes)

13. Puccini, Giacomo. "The Humming Chorus" from *Madama Butterfly*

14. Ravel, Maurice. "Bolero" (first half only)

15. Rimsky-Korsakov, Nikolai. "The Sea and Sindbad's Ship" from *Scheherazade*, Op. 35 Movement 1 (theme only)

16. Saint-Saëns, Camille. "The Aquarium" from *Carnival of the Animals* (approximately 2 minutes)

17. Saint-Saëns, Camille. "The Swan" from *Carnival of the Animals* (approximately 3 minutes)

18. "Sakura," a traditional Japanese folk song (performed on koto, approximately 1 minute)

19. Smetana, Bedrich. "The Moldau" (approximately 11½ minutes)

20. Tarrega, Francisco Eixea. "Recuerdos de la Alahambre" on album *Royal Family of Spanish Guitar,* imported from Europe (Netherlands) SR 9095. Previously released by Mercury Records.

21. Wagner, Richard. "The Pilgrim's Chorus" from *Tannhäuser* (trombone section)

Nontraditional Music for Calming

*1. *Environments:* Disc 1
Side 1—The Psychologically Ultimate Seashore
Side 2—Optimum Aviary

*2. *Environments:* Disc 3
Side 1—Be-in (voices in a park)
Side 2—Dusk at New Hope, Pennsylvania (drone of countless insects)

*3. *Environments:* Disc 4
Side 1—Ultimate Thunderstorm
Side 2—Gentle Rain in a Pine Forest

✱4. Environments: Disc 7
Side 1—Intonation (Om chant, good for meditation)
Side 2—Summer Cornfield (sounds of crickets and other insects)

✱5. Environments: Disc 8
Side 1—Wood-Masted Sailboat
Side 2—A Country Stream

✱6. Environments: Disc 9
Side 1—Pacific Ocean
Side 2—Caribbean Lagoon

7. *Steam: Past and Present.* stereophonic recordings on British Rail and England's Preserved Railways; thirteen separate steam trains. Recorded and compiled by Kenneth Granville Attwood.

8. *Tibetan Bells* by Henry Wolff and Nancy Hennings, Antilles Records. Manufactured and distributed by Island Records, Inc., 7720 Sunset Boulevard, Los Angeles, California 90046

Music for Moving from Here to There

A. Moving from out of classroom, back to classroom
(e.g., returning from assembly in auditorium to the classroom)

1. Berlin, Irving. "Alexander's Ragtime Band"

2. Chopin, Frederick. "Polonaise in A-flat major"

3. Elgar, Sir Edward. "Pomp and Circumstance March no. 1 in D major"

4. Gould, Morton. "American Salute"

5. Herbert, Victor. "March of the Toys" from *Babes in Toyland*

6. Rodgers, Richard and Hammerstein, Oscar. "Oklahoma—Finale" from *Oklahoma*

7. Sousa, John Phillip. any of his marches

8. Verdi, Giuseppe. "Grand March" from *Aida*

B. Moving from "here to there" within the classroom
(as from a reading circle to seat work)

1. Bolling, Claude. *Bolling Suite for Cello*, "Galop" only, performed by Yo Yo Ma, 1984, CBS Inc., 51 West 52nd Street, New York, New York.

2. Saint-Saëns, Camille. "The Elephant" from *Carnival of the Animals*

_____

✱ By Syntonic Research Inc., 175 Fifth Avenue, New York, New York 10010, or Atlantic Records, 1841 Broadway, New York, New York 10023.

3. Satie, Erik. "The Hunt" from *Sports et Divertissements* (fast, short piano music)

4. Tchaikovsky, Peter Ilich. "Dance of the Reed Flutes" from *The Nutcracker Suite*

5. Thomson, Virgil. "The Walking Song" (Acadian Songs and Dances) from *Louisiana Story Orchestral Suite* (approximately 2 minutes)

Music for Transitional Times

Use these selections to signal change from one activity to another, such as math to reading or from science to recess preparation.

1. Copland, Aaron. "Fanfare for the Common Man" (approximately 3 minutes)

2. Strauss, Richard. *Also Sprach Zarathustra* album by the same name. © 1968 Decca Record Co. Ltd., London. Exclusive U.S. Agents, London Records Inc., 539 W. 25th Street, New York, New York 10001. #CS6609. Also, second opening and ending of the album and movie *2001: A Space Odyssey*. Album #SIE-13 ST, MGM Records Division, 1350 Avenue of the Americas, New York, New York 10019, conducted by Karl Bohm (1:37 minutes)

3. Williams, John. "Star Wars Suite" (theme from the movie *Star Wars*, 1978)

4. Any concerto (baroque, or classical) music for trumpet(s) performed by Wynton Marsalis. Note—largo, adagio, or andante movements only, such as the following:

   Pachelbel, Johann (1653-1706). "Canon for Three Trumpets and strings in B-flat Major," Largo Movement only.
   Haydn, Michael (1737-1806). "Concerto for Trumpet and Orchestra in D Major," Adagio Movement only.
   von Biber, Heinrich (1644-1704). "Sonata for Eight Trumpets and Orchestra in A Major."

   All of the above performed by Wynton Marsalis on Album *Baroque Music for Trumpets* with the English Chamber Orchestra, manufactured by CBS Records, Inc., 51 West 52nd Street, New York. Digital Record #0-7464-42478-1.

5. Telemann, Georg Philipp (1681-1767). "Overture in D Major for Oboe and Trumpet" from Fifth Movement, "Adagio" only. Maurice Andre, trumpet player with Frans Bruggen, director. Produced by Teldec Records GmbH, © 1976, 1986, 1988. Musical Heritage Society (MHS) #912163K, a digital recording. Also on chrome cassette MHS 313163F and Compact Disc MHS 512634, 1710 Highway 35, Ocean, New Jersey 07712.

6. Torelli, Giuseppe (1658-1709). "Concerto in D Major for Trumpet, Strings, and Basso Continuo" from Movements 1, 2, and 3, only the "Adagio" sections. (Same source as above.)

7. Classical, baroque or contemporary flute music, such as:
   — Denver, John. "Annie's Song" from the album *Annie's Song and Other Galway Favorites*, RCA Records #ARL-1-3061 Stereo, 1980, New York, New York. Also available on stereo 8-ARS-1-3061 and cassette ARK1-3061, performed by Jean-Pierre Rampal, flautist.
   — Vivaldi, Antonio (1678-1741). *Works for Flute and Orchestra, Vol. III* "Largo" Movements only of:
      "Concerto in C Major for 2 Flutes" p. 76.
      "Flute Concerto in A Minor" p. 77
      "Piccolo Concerto in C Major" p. 79
      "Piccolo Concerto in C Major" p. 78
   with Jean-Pierre Rampal and Joseph Rampal (flautists), as recorded by Musical Heritage Society, Inc., 1980, MHS Stereo 4190, 14 Park Road, Tinton Falls, New Jersey 07724.

The following selections (8-11) on the CD *Hush* performed by Bobby McFerrin and Yo Yo Ma, (Sony Music Entertainment Inc. (1992) 666 Fifth Avenue, P.O. Box 4452, New York, New York 10101-4452) SK48177, DDD. Note: The following baroque compositions are performed by McFerrin, using his mouth in an unusual way, while accompanied by Yo Yo Ma.

8. Bach, J.S. "Air"

9. Bach, J.S., arranged by Charles Gounod. "Ave Maria"

10. Bach, J.S. "Musette" from *The Notebook for Anna Magdalena Bach*

11. Vivaldi, Antonio. "Andante" from *Concerto in D Minor for Two Mandolins*

A teacher may wish to dismiss students for recess, lunch, or other transitional times with music that has a repetitive theme. For example, Duke Ellington / B. Strayhorn's recording (or other recording artists') for "Take the A Train" has a main theme that repeats at least six different times. Students can be taught to listen to the music, identifying each time the theme repeats itself. The teacher may assign as follows:

"Group 1 may line up the third time you hear the theme. Group 2 may line up the fifth time you hear the theme," and so on.

RCA Records provided a recording of "Take the A Train" to *Music Alive, December, 1990, Vol. 10, No. 3,* a publication of Cherry Lane Music, Box 904, Rochester, Vermont 05767, ISSN 1051-8975 with cassette recording, P, © 1990, Guitar Recordings, Inc. #MA10390A.

Rock Music

Studies have also shown that the use of rock music may be therapeutic for some ADD/ADHD children. A study conducted at the Oregon Health Sciences University* tested the effects of rock music on eight ADHD young boys. The framework for this exploratory study was based on three concepts: "(1) The rhythmicity and intense repetitive beat of rock music stimulates an increased arousal of the cerebrum. (2) Prominent beat rhythm of rock music overrides environmental distractions and produces orienting responses in children with ADD. (3) Rock music with its repetitive beat tends to produce a reduction in skeletal muscle tension, resulting in reduced motor activity." The results revealed that for these eight subjects, the rock music did have a significant effect on activity level.

Over the past few years I have questioned many of my students about how they like to study at home and what helps them. I have had a few of my ADHD students tell me in their Learning Styles Interviews that they need to work while listening to rock music. As one student described to me, "I need the BOOM!"

In addition to the above recommended selections provided by Mrs. Young in this section, parents/teachers may wish to experiment with a variety of music, including rock (preferably instrumental selections without the distraction of words). Students may be given the opportunity to use headphones and a tape recorder during seat work and homework. If the child's productivity level increases (particularly for written output), it may be an option that is permitted in the classroom and during homework time. The key is to examine the student's focus and make sure it is the work at hand—not the music. As Mrs. Young points out, some students will respond well to the stimulation of music while studying. However, with some auditorally distracted students, the music (particularly a rhythmic beat) can be an interference, not a help. Therefore, parents and teachers need to be aware and evaluate the effectiveness for individual students.

*Cripe, Frances F. "Rock Music as Therapy for Children with Attention Deficit Disorder: An Exploratory Study." *Journal of Music Therapy*, XXIII (1), 1986, 30-37 © 1986 by the National Association for Music Therapy, Inc.

Communication with Parents and Mutual Support

We all know how important it is to elicit support from parents if we expect any success from their children, especially those with special needs. Children with learning or attentional problems don't outgrow their "disorders." They will generally need assistance, monitoring, structuring, and support for a number of years. Parents who are trying to help their children at home and wish to be supportive to the teacher's efforts, need the following:

* clear communication of the teacher's expectations;

* assignments recorded daily;

* accessibility of teachers; and

* teacher responsiveness and sensitivity.

When the parent is able to open a notebook, see a consistent format of recording homework assignments and receive feedback on a regular basis on how their child is doing, it is very helpful. Some teachers have weekly newsletters informing parents about what is being studied in class that week and when long-range projects are due. Some teachers send home notices to parents whenever a homework assignment has not been turned in, requiring the parent's signature. The form at the end of this section on page 142 is one that teachers and parents find helpful.

A child with ADD/ADHD or learning disabilities often experiences behavioral, emotional, and social problems that are evident in a number of situations, not only in the classroom. Many of these children have problems on the ball field, in church, and in social situations of all kinds.

Families often need help learning how to cope and deal with a "difficult" or "challenging" child. Parents need to hear that they are not alone and that many others are struggling with the same worries, fears, and frustrations that they are. Parent support groups are extremely helpful for this purpose. Networking with other people who share similar experiences and bringing in speakers and resources is very effective. Parents need to learn about their child's problems and how to help at home, as well as how to be their child's advocate and communicate their child's needs to family members, friends, teachers, and coaches.

Many parents benefit from parenting classes that teach specific strategies and techniques for effectively managing their child's behaviors. A "challenging" child in the home causes numerous stresses that could and does cause marital strife, tearing apart many families. Often families would benefit from family counseling or other therapy from specialists familiar with ADD/ADHD issues.

National Organizations and Resources for Parents

The following organizations are highly recommended to parents of children with ADD/ADHD:

Children with Attention Deficit Disorders (CHADD) is a national parent support and educational group designed to assist parents of children who perform poorly at school, display impulsive behaviors, are distractible, have short attention span, and respond negatively to discipline at school and home. CHADD has local chapters around the country.

Learning Disabilities Association (LDA) also addresses the needs of ADHD children and has many local and state chapters.

(See Bibliography and Recommended Resources for addresses and phone numbers of the national offices for CHADD and LDA.)

How a Site Team Can Help Parents

In some of our students' families, the parents are so bogged down in their own personal problems that they have little time or ability to concentrate on their children's needs. Nevertheless, most parents love their children dearly and want the best for them. They would like to get them whatever help they need, even though transportation, finances, childcare, and work schedules may prevent them from following through.

It has proven helpful to communicate to parents about services and classes available to them. Our support staff believes strongly in informing and educating parents. We try to find and provide support for families in many different ways:

1. Our team freely gives pertinent articles and literature to parents. We are happy to share our own personal copies of books, cassettes, and other resources that may be educational and helpful to parents.

2. We received a generous donation from our local Rotary Club to establish a lending library of materials and resources for parents and staff, includ-

ing books and videotapes on topics related to ADD/ADHD, learning disabilities, and behavioral management.

3. Our school nurse established an ADD/ADHD support group for parents in the community.

4. Our team communicates to parents about upcoming workshops and parenting classes that may be of interest to them. We do this through personal contact by members of our team to parents and through our school newsletter. Our consultation team has an article in each issue of the school newsletter about such topics.

Coping with a hard-to-manage child both at home and school is stressful, draining, and frustrating for both parents and teachers alike. It is helpful for parents to spend time in the classroom to acquire an appreciation of how difficult a teacher's job is—teaching, managing, and caring for thirty or more children and their many special needs. By attending a parent support group meeting, listening carefully to parents, and becoming well informed on ADHD issues that influence the home and social arena, teachers will also gain awareness and greater respect for parents. Once again, it is through the coordination of efforts and mutual support between home and school that we enhance the chances for our children's success.

WEEKLY PROGRESS REPORT

CHILD'S NAME _____ ROOM NUMBER _____ WEEK STARTING _____

WORK HABITS

_____ HAS BEEN WORKING HARD ALL WEEK

_____ HAS BEEN WORKING ONLY SOME OR PART OF THE TIME

_____ HAS DONE VERY LITTLE WORK THIS WEEK

_____ HAS FAILED TO COMPLETE HOMEWORK ASSIGNED

_____ PARENT/TEACHER CONFERENCE NEEDED

CITIZENSHIP

_____ WELL BEHAVED ALL WEEK

_____ HAS BEEN WORKING HARD MOST OF THE TIME

_____ GOOD BEHAVIOR MOST OF THE TIME

_____ DISRUPTIVE/UNCOOPERATIVE BEHAVIOR

_____ PARENT/TEACHER CONFERENCE NEEDED

ATTENDANCE: GOOD FREQUENT ABSENCES FREQUENT TARDIES

TEACHER COMMENTS

PARENT COMMENTS

TEACHER'S SIGNATURE _____ DATE _____

PARENT'S SIGNATURE _____ DATE _____

19

A Parent's Story: What Every Teacher Needs to Hear

A very special parent, Mrs. Linda Haughey, has shared her feelings and message to teachers. Two of her wonderful sons had been my students for a number of years, and I have the greatest respect for this very loving, caring family. I have learned much from Mrs. Haughey and greatly value her insight, wisdom, and support. I thank the Haughey family for sharing their story with us.

A Parent's Story[*] by Linda Haughey

I imagine that we all have childhood dreams. One of my many dreams was to grow up and marry a handsome prince, who like me, wanted a dozen little boys. Part of that dream came true. The handsome prince came along (without the official title), and instead of twelve little boys, we have been blessed with five wonderful sons whose ages are now 18, 17, twins 13, and 11 years old. Our bonus package came tied in pink ribbons! Our precious little girl is now five years old.

I can honestly say that we happily and busily balance these many ages and needs in our family today. But, of course, it hasn't always been that way. Like most families who have one or more children with ADD, each day can be a joyful surprise or a painful disappointment—sometimes both on the same day! One thing is certain, though: each day is not predictable, and we have learned to "go with the flow." We have had no choice! Our 17-year-old and our 13-year-old twins have all been diagnosed with ADD. It has been the painful part of our journey that has brought hope and confidence to our family.

Many special people have given of themselves to help change the directions of our children's lives, and, yes, the lives of each member of our family. When one

---

[*]Used with permission of Linda Haughey, © 1992.

person struggles in a family, all members are affected. Likewise, when there is self-esteem and success for one, the others reflect that also.

I can remember the exact moment in which a key unlocked the first of many doors. Each door represented a range of emotions and experiences, beginning with exhaustion, confusion, and plenty of questions. This is where I will begin our story.

We have, as a family, decided to share our story with the hope of helping other families like our own. We know how very difficult life can be on a daily basis. Most of all, we simply want to bring hope and encouragement to those families and the special people involved in their lives. Teachers *can* and *do* set the tone and make a difference in a child's life.

The phone rang as I walked through the front door of our home. Frazzled and frustrated from an attempt to make a brief stop at a local department store with my young children, the last thing I wanted to do was talk on the phone. That phone call, however, was the beginning of a new chapter of our family's life. It was the neuropsychologist who had been reviewing the developmental and psychological evaluations for our 5-year-old son, Christopher.

I explained to him that while shopping my son threw himself to the ground and began to sob. He cried, "Mommy, Mommy, get me out of here. I have to go home, Mommy." I felt his pain. He was actually in pain! Not the pain of touching a hot stove, but internal, unexplained torment. This kind of situation was all too familiar to me. It could happen anywhere, depending upon the circumstances. While I didn't fully understand why, his little body seemed to be over-responding to the stimuli in the store. I knew that discipline was not the solution.

The memory of that morning eight years ago is etched firmly in my mind. That phone call was the very first time that someone understood what I had just experienced with Chris. He not only understood, but also validated what I had known in my heart for years: Discipline is not the issue here. What was happening to Chris was beyond his control and very much a part of his delicate neurological makeup.

Relieved to know that it wasn't a total lack of parental skills causing these outbursts, I gladly set up an appointment to discuss the evaluation further. "At last," I thought, "there's light at the end of the tunnel." Little did I know how many dark tunnels our family would enter before the bright light!

The follow-up visit became the first of many future evaluations and consultations. Out of a constant need for new coping skills and a better understanding of the challenges we faced, we sought the help of those specialists who we hoped could fill in the blanks.

Our own pediatrician at that time would tell me there was nothing wrong with Chris that some good spankings wouldn't fix. Many of our friends and family members concurred. More often than not, I felt as if I were being judged as an inadequate mother, lacking skill and control over my son.

We had to work exceptionally hard with Chris to help him manage his anger and frustrations. His memory seemed to play tricks on him, and there were times that his interpretations of something we would say seemed to get jumbled when he tried to follow directions or repeat our words. I soon realized that those people who were offering their advice and criticisms had absolutely no idea how hard our job was. Nor did they understand that we were raising a child who required far more insight and coping skills than Dr. Spock offered in his helpful book!

Examinations and observations revealed that Chris was a bright child who had Attention Deficit Disorder with hyperactivity. This was accompanied by a history of learning disabilities, auditory and visual processing difficulties, and significant expressive language problems.

All of this meant, of course, that Chris would require much intervention throughout his young life: pediatricians, psychologists, a neurologist, speech therapy, occupational therapists, tutoring, special education, and extra help in the mainstream classroom. The doors of communication had to remain open between home and all of these special people associated with our precious son.

Our highly energetic and demanding child was much more prone to greater mood swings, distractibility, and angry outbursts than our other children. On the other hand, he was filled with a great sense of humor, consideration, thoughtfulness, and endless curiosity for the world around him.

I'm in awe of this child who was born fighting mad and ready to take on the world around him. It was obvious from the day he was born that his temperament would require a lot of patience and love. If his socks didn't fit perfectly across the tops of his toes, he would take them off and start all over. There were particular textures of clothing he refused to wear because he couldn't stand the feel of them next to his body. I later found out this had to do with sensory integration and the affect on his immature nervous system. It was literally painful to him!

Many of his developmental milestones, such as sitting and walking, were within normal range. Speech was significantly delayed, having developed a "twin language" with his brother Phillip. As a toddler, Chris experienced "night terrors": extreme, terrorizing nightmares that were almost impossible to wake him from. This, too, had to do with his immature nervous system. During the same period of his life, we discovered that Chris and Phillip both had obstructive sleep apnea.

When surgery was performed to remove the tonsils and adenoids to help correct the sleep apnea, Chris also had tubes placed in his ears to help drain fluid and to help him hear better. Within a month after the surgeries, Chris was talking in full sentences and sleeping through the night for the first time since his birth 2½ years earlier. We were also dealing with other health problems, such as chronic asthma, croup, allergies, and digestive problems. This is important to mention because many families with ADD children must frequently deal not only with the classic symptoms of ADD and the behavior problems often associated with it, but also with other chronic health issues.

All of these problems can create a tremendous pressure and burden for the child, the parents' marriage, and the entire family. It can be extremely expensive. Most insurance companies will not cover the cost of evaluations and treatment specifically designed to help the ADD child. The irony of this is that early detection and intervention are critical.

The reality is that most families cannot afford this out-of-pocket expense. They can be faced with the decision to enter into further debt and create new problems, or suffer the guilt and pain they feel because they are unable to obtain the necessary help.

We gave Chris and his brother Phillip an extra year of growth before placing them in kindergarten. It turned out to be the best decision possible. When the time came, they were eager to begin. The transition seemed to be going very well. Unexpectedly, within a month after kindergarten started, Chris began to have horrendous tantrums in the mornings before school. I'd exhausted every reason I could come up with to explain this behavior. All he could do was cry and say he couldn't go to school.

One morning I called ahead to the school counselor. When we arrived, she and Chris' teacher met us at the car and gently persuaded my angry, crying son to come up to the counseling office. We finally detected the problem. Chris was required to sit on a rug in the classroom, surrounded by other children. His personal space was being invaded! We've since discovered this is a very common problem for ADD children. Even something as simple as standing in a line to wait can require more endurance than the child may possess. Again, this is because their central nervous system is so fragile.

What may seem natural and ordinary to most of us may cause great distress and even pain for children like Chris. As curious as that may seem, many children like Chris have an opposite response to similar circumstances. They may be oblivious to what's going on around them. They may also have an unusually high pain threshold.

Considering all he has had to deal with, Chris has done remarkably well in school. We have learned to expect that every new school year there will be difficulty in the adjustment of getting back into school and meeting new changes and classroom expectations. Most years have not been easy. The most difficult year he has had was with a teacher who adamantly demanded that he would learn her way. Her rigid ways became a nightmare for him . . . and for us.

We have found that some flexibility is critical. Predictability and clarity are important in any classroom, and they're a must for ADD/ADHD children. Making changes and "shifting gears" for new projects is very difficult for them under the best of circumstances. Our most trying times in school often come from a lack of these necessary elements. A substitute teacher often represents chaos and behavior problems for a child with ADD. Expecting a math test and suddenly switching at the last minute to a surprise spelling test can create high anxiety and undue stress for the child.

Consistency in rules and schedules for the classroom invite predictability and more inner calm for the child. They know what to expect and what is expected of them. Flexibility in homework assignments and demanding projects can also make a tremendous difference. It can lighten an already heavy load.

Overall, we have had the privilege of watching Chris become a happy, confident, and responsible child. He is learning to cope and to compensate for the challenges in his life. He loves science, history, cooking, and gardening. Now 13, he has a zest for life that's infectious. He does homework and chores without being asked. He is sensitive to the needs of others. Chris seldom has a day go by that he doesn't do something extra nice for someone. The loving words we have spoken to him, he now speaks to us. "Great job, Mom." "Dad, you're the best!"

Miracle child? No. Loved child? Yes. Cared for by some exemplary and very special people who have given of themselves to make life better for Chris. A change of pediatricians many years ago helped to pave a path of greater discovery to meet our challenges. While he hasn't always understood all that we were dealing with, he keeps an open mind, trusts our judgments and intuition, and shows respect for our opinions. He draws Chris into the conversations and shows respect for him as well. He's had the wisdom to be able to help us when we needed it and refer us to other resources when necessary. His pride has never interfered with the health and welfare of our children. He continues to encourage our family and be there for us.

The speech therapists, occupational therapists, and developmental pediatrician, whose hearts were clearly in their work with Chris also made a significant difference in his life. They've helped him to become more aware of his body and his needs by identifying weaknesses and building on his strengths.

His grandparents, all of whom were mystified by much of what happened in the early years, have always loved and accepted Chris for his differences and qualities. Along with Chris' siblings, they have created a safe haven of acceptance and support.

All of this has been absolutely invaluable. There is, however, one other facet of this multi-modality treatment that has been the core of Chris' success: a school staff dedicated to their work and to helping children. As a parent, I've always acknowledged that much of the responsibility for my child's education falls on me. I have to coordinate and monitor the many elements that have to work in conjunction with one another to get the services he needs.

I'm not always sure how to evaluate programs or even know what's best. I have to remind myself I'm not the only one involved in this effort. It requires teamwork. If I've done my job and found trusted specialists, we can work together to determine what is best for my child. They know the programs, I know my child.

By a very fortunate set of circumstances, that's exactly what we got—an exceptional team consisting of resource specialist, teachers, nurse, and principal. The staff at our elementary school has worked together to create an atmosphere of cooperation designed with the best interests of the children in mind. Emphasis is placed on self-esteem, learning styles, and respecting individual differences. They have an excellent program to teach study skills and organizational techniques that has been extremely helpful.

I cannot stress enough the vital importance of all these factors in working with ADD children. In order to bring it all together, teachers and other staff must be knowledgeable of Attention Deficit Disorder and interested in applying different techniques to help these children. Recognizing the challenge of ADD and employing tactics to help the child will very likely mean the difference between success and failure. This is a lot of responsibility, and, yes, it's one more problem to contend with in the classroom. However, when you weigh the benefits of a whole child versus the tragedy of a broken one, how can we ignore the blatant reality of this problem?

Dealing with the ADD child is time-consuming and exhausting. Just when you think you've got things under control, you're met with new surprises and challenges. For example, this child who has been turning in his homework on a daily basis for the last week and a half suddenly shuts down and has difficulty turning in anything at all, including communication from home or a signed permission slip. That brings up another interesting point. Much of what is sent home frequently does not *reach* home. I can't begin to estimate the number of important materials I have not received due to our sons' forgetfulness or lack of organization. Please believe me when I tell you we have tried everything we can think of to help get those papers to and from school.

The problem is getting better as the children get older, but I have to remember it is not intentional. It is a part of the challenge they face. That is why I work extra hard at home in teaching organizational skills and talking with the children about all of life's topics as much as possible. Most important, I have to listen. In fact, that's usually more important than my talking!

It is important to note, too, that depression and isolation are common for the child and the child's primary care-giver. Because an ADD child can be demanding and in need of constant attention and direction, he can be unpleasant to be around. I have found that many people who do not have a child like mine don't have the understanding or tolerance to be with them for any length of time. Making new friends may be very easy. Keeping the friendships harmonious is another story! Once a child visits the home of a friend, it may encourage a fast ending to an otherwise promising friendship.

This can be a major factor in the depression and isolation. Since spending time with other families can create further problems for the child and parent, it may limit support and socializing for them. Some of my very closest friends are parents who, like myself, have children with ADD. I know I can pick up that phone and call on an understanding friend during a time of crisis or happiness! It makes a difference to share with someone who has been where I am. I didn't have that support when my sons were younger. Not much information was available concerning ADD. The fact that I also had two hyperactive little guys to guide was an additional drain on what energy was left. Today I make it a point to get more rest, exercise and time out, so that I can be a better mom. In dealing with the constant demands of these children, I believe it is very important that we have to care for ourselves in a healthy way in order to have a healthy attitude!

After all, just dealing with everyday stresses of living, and the added demands of the ADD child and other family members, can truly become a test of survival. What goes on at home can sometimes be more stressful to deal with than the appearances a child projects at school. This is because a child can "let it all hang out" at home. Usually it's the mom who becomes the target for those pent-up emotions and frustrations.

I have known families who, because of problems in school or maladjustments in the child, have been referred to a school counselor or psychologist. The problems the child is experiencing may be a direct result of ADD in the child or they may worsen ADD in the child. Once referred, it is then noticed that the child's parents have marital problems, and someone then assumes that the child's problems are the direct result of family problems. The parents then receive treatment.

Meanwhile, the child may be misdiagnosed and has still not received the help he or she needs because someone cannot see the real picture of what is going on with the child and his family. The traditional view in child psychiatry has been that most children's problems are the result of the problems of parents or families. If we live with a child whose needs drain our energies, resources, time, and budget, of course we're going to have marital problems. Any good marriage has some problems. Again, getting the right kind of help from the professional field, especially understanding, flexibility, and determination from the child's teachers, is invaluable.

We know first hand the distinct difference in the life of a child identified and helped in the early years as opposed to a child identified much later. The symptoms of the disorder are usually present at birth—for example, an infant who cries all the time and becomes overstimulated very quickly. As they grow older, they anger quickly and become more aggressive. Some children, like Chris, are walking advertisements for ADD. Other children, like Chris' twin brother, Phillip, and older brother, Scott, are seen as anything but your typical ADD child. That is, until the problem begins to unmask itself.

Experts say that only about half of those afflicted with the disorder have been properly diagnosed, and even fewer receive the comprehensive therapy the condition requires. Many of these youngsters in whom the condition goes unacknowledged are seen as slow, lazy, and undisciplined. Others like our son, Scott, are labeled as "bad kids" or the product of uninvolved, careless parents. Unsuspecting parents blame themselves or other circumstances such as health problems, a death or divorce in the family, or what they may perceive as their lack of parental skill for their child's poor behavior and performance.

When Phillip was eight months old he became very ill and his little body slowed way down in growth. Today he is a year and a half behind in bone growth development, and we suspected that the reason for his slowness in school was due to the habits he established during that period of time. One teacher remarked that she wanted to "put a stick of dynamite under him." That observation became a clear message that something else was probably going on and needed to be addressed.

This happened during the winter when Phillip was quite ill once again. He'd missed a lot of school and was having a difficult time catching up and staying caught up. With some reservations we requested testing toward the end of the school year. Dissatisfied with the results of the tests, we requested reassessment to be done in the fall when he was feeling better and starting fresh. The second IQ test resulted in a greater than 30 point difference and clearly identified Phillip as gifted.

Some learning disabilities were discovered, as well as a distinct possibility that Phillip also had ADD. This puzzled us. So much material had been written on ADD with hyperactivity. What about the child who appears bright, cooperative, and quiet . . . just maybe a little "spacey" or "slow"? Further outside evaluations confirmed our suspicions. Phillip had ADD without hyperactivity. Had he not been given the benefit of the doubt and received further assessment and cooperation from our school team, he would have been mislabeled, misunderstood, and underestimated.

We realize that he clearly has a pace quite different from Chris. He may need extra time to finish projects or even get started. He's very bright and intense. I believe it's quite common to think that because a person is slow, they're not bright. Wrong! It simply means they're slow! Many believe that because a person is diagnosed with learning disabilities that he or she is not bright. Wrong again! Chances are more likely than not that the child is extremely bright. They just need to learn in their own ways! I have to work very hard just to keep up with our sons. It seems as though they're usually far ahead of me.

It wouldn't be fair to discuss the success we've had without mentioning the rest of the story! It's necessary to know of all the caring people who were there for us—and those who could have made a positive difference and chose not to.

We were very fortunate to obtain an accurate diagnosis and appropriate intervention for Chris and Phillip. Although it has been a lot of work and a struggle finding the right combination of help, it's been more than worth the effort. Their self-esteem is intact. They both greet each new day with optimism and confidence. They've experienced varying degrees of success and can willingly move on to new challenges.

Our 17-year-old son, Scott, was not so fortunate. In retrospect I can see that as an infant many of the signs were there, for example, extreme fussiness and overstimulation. But because he was my first child, I had no way of knowing that all new babies weren't like that! He was an extremely bright child. He reached and passed developmental milestones quite early. He was confident and handled himself in an unusually mature manner. He was one of those children we all know: three years old, going on thirty!

Because of that, we put him into kindergarten at the age of five, never questioning his abilities and maturity. One more year of growth for Scott could have made a lot of difference then, but we had no way of knowing that. It wasn't a popular practice at the time to "hold children back a year." Kindergarten seemed to progress smoothly. It was in first grade that something began to happen. The "phone calls" (as I refer to the communication between school and home) began at that time. They were always the same: "Your child is so bright, but I just can't get him to turn in his homework." "He can pass a test and get an *A*, but he just won't finish his work in class."

It wasn't until fourth grade that he had a teacher who took a special interest in him and helped change his attitude about school and homework. She encouraged Scott, took time for him, and challenged him. While this made a tremendous difference in the way Scott was viewing things, he still lacked the ability to get work finished on time and stay on-task. At that time Scott was in a private school. We knew he needed more individual attention. Whatever it was that Scott needed (and we didn't know exactly what that was), he wasn't receiving it there. We decided to try public school.

It was in fifth grade that the behavior problems began to manifest themselves. There were more of "the calls." There was more of the inappropriate behavior. Where at least the test scores had been superbly high, they were now becoming lower and lower. Counseling didn't seem to help much. We were still at a loss for Scott's lack of motivation and low self-esteem. We had reasoned that it was caused by a traumatic event in his early years of life. When we ruled that out, we blamed home life and lack of skill. I was doing everything I felt I could do. It never occurred to me that ADD was the root of our problems. The high test scores threw us off course. The maturity that we saw in Scott as a very young child was deceiving. As we realized much later, he was mature, but not ready for school at age five.

By seventh grade Scott had been in three different schools (including kindergarten). He moved on to seventh grade at our local junior high. That year, without a doubt, was one of the most painful and saddest years in Scott's life. It was there that Scott's self-esteem plunged to the depths of despair. He encountered many new situations he had never experienced before, including racism, personal threats of harm and violence, fights, and displays of weapons at school. The classrooms were overloaded. Conversations with teachers revealed they were over-stressed. While in the G.A.T.E. (gifted and talented) program, Scott had a teacher who called me often to let me know how "lazy" and "disruptive" my son was in her class. She made it clear that she did not have the time or tolerance to deal with him. When was I going to do something about this? This same woman, I found out later, wrote in his school records: "This kid is a big fat zero."

Meanwhile, I had received a multitude of phone calls and met with Scott's teachers. One day his vice-principal told me she knew what Scott's problem was. First of all, we weren't disciplining him enough. Second of all, he was obviously (in her opinion) "a classic case of a child with learning disabilities" that had gone undetected. I requested and pursued testing through the school. We were repeatedly denied testing on the basis that Scott was "too bright." In other words, he hadn't met the criteria of falling two full years behind his grade level. He certainly wasn't performing to the fullest of his ability either. I can't help but ask myself over and over how many of our kids are falling between the cracks because our priorities are such that a child must fully fail before he can be given the tools he needs to fully succeed.

I set up an appointment with yet another outside source to have Scott thoroughly evaluated. Our young son was found to be in a full-blown state of depression. On top of that, he was diagnosed with Attention Deficit Disorder. Scott was placed on medication. Within a short period of time his attitude began to change and he was better able to focus. The suicidal thoughts he once had began to dissipate. The low self-esteem remained.

Self-esteem is the backbone of our children's ability to succeed or fail. When this is gone, all they have left is humiliation, anger, and deep-seated frustration that results in despair. That is when I see kids like Scott giving up. I am convinced that young people like Scott account for the majority of kids who make up the high dropout rate in this country.

In trying to "fit in" and find some place they belong, they pick unsuitable friends and act out destructive behavior patterns. When you combine that with a school setting of administrators and teachers who lack the knowledge and skill to deal with these children, it becomes a devastating, overwhelming problem.

That is exactly what happened to us in eighth and ninth grades as well. We moved Scott into a private school for eighth grade and on to a four-year high school for ninth grade. In matters of discipline at both schools, administrators chose to humiliate and insult Scott rather than address the issues that created the problems in the first place. We even brought in the psychologist who had been working with us to help mediate between school and home. These children become caught up in a vicious cycle: "I'm no good. I'll fail anyway. Therefore, I won't try. Then I'll have an excuse for failing."

In tenth grade I began to hear the words "I want to quit school." My heart sank even deeper. I couldn't blame him for feeling that way. All along I'd been searching for answers. For years I read books, attended conferences and meetings, and shared stories with my good buddy who had a son experiencing the same sort of trauma in another school district. We both knew our greatest obstacle was not our children. It was finding competent schools geared to the challenge and dedication of working with children like ours.

During the first semester of tenth grade, Scott brought home five *F*s and one *B*. The *B* came from an English teacher who respected Scott's abilities and eccentricities. He lit a fire under Scott. He took the time for him. He challenged him. Scott still talks about him with the utmost regard. Phone calls, conferences, pleas for help, and even punishing Scott didn't make much difference.

Just prior to the second semester I'd heard about a magnet school that was designed to meet the needs of children especially interested in theater and other arts. I visited the school and signed Scott up. It seemed too good to be true. Scott loves music and art, and his greatest strengths have always been in these areas. We had nothing to lose and everything to gain if this worked out.

I will never forget that first semester at our new school. The first phone call home was from Scott's art teacher. She said, "I want to thank you for sending Scott to our school. He brings a ray of sunshine into my classes." Not meaning to be sarcastic, I thought she had the wrong number. *I* knew that he was a ray of sunshine. He was a joy in my life. But his *teacher* saw him as a "ray of sunshine"! How I longed to hear those words. I thanked her with all my heart—and then I cried. At age 15 and so many teachers later, I knew we'd found a special place for Scott. I shared this with my closest friends and they cried, too. They know as I did that in those simple words came acceptance and hope.

Within a week I met our school principal for the first time. I briefly described our school history. She reached out to me and held my hands. She said, "Let me help you. I can make a difference." By 9:00 A.M. the following day she had Scott's records on her desk and me on the phone. In conversation with Scott, she told him she knew what it was like to have ADD because some people very close to her also have it. She said the hardest thing for him to do at this point in his life was to find his own niche—and that's exactly what they were going to help him do. By 4:00 P.M. that same day, Scott's teachers had individual consultations with him to make plans for his success. By the end of the semester he was bringing home a *B* average!

In discussions of discipline, Scott is treated with the utmost respect. If there is a problem, I receive a concerned phone call and suggestions for dealing with the problem. Our remarkable principal reviews his progress and report cards, always taking time to jot down a positive note to Scott. His schedule has been changed as needed to work in the classes he needs and to obtain tutoring. His wonderful resource teacher and her staff have become a "home base" where Scott can get a break away from the school pressures and put some of his ability and talent to work helping others.

In conjunction with the phenomenal intervention at the school, we found someone very special to help Scott with medication and a new approach to life. Since the assistance for ADHD children comes in many forms, we sought the most essential help in putting all of this together. Deciding to use medication was truly an agonizing dilemma. After trying three different psychiatrists over a period of a few years, the fourth turned out to be exactly the person to work with Scott. He helped to create an atmosphere of trust and acceptance that has allowed our son to be himself and begin to like it.

Today, Scott is no longer on medication. He has opted for healthy lifestyle changes. He is learning to direct his incredible energy toward positive thoughts and behavior. In a few minutes he can design an art format that looks professional, though he can hardly pay attention in the classroom. In the same way, he can rattle off meaningful lyrics to a song or the emotional words of a poem. Yet he still has trouble finishing his homework.

I remain eternally grateful to his first art teacher who has also become a friend and mentor. Although he no longer has a class with her, she still stays in touch with him. They both love animals and art. Her genuine interest and love for her students has become an inspiration. For us, she represents a beacon of hope in a dark sea of near hopelessness.

I love watching the changes take place in this wonderful young man. It's beginning to fall together because of people like the ones I've mentioned who helped make it happen.

It is not my intention to give the impression that once a child gets the appropriate diagnosis and intervention that everything is wonderful. There is some comfort in knowing what the problem is and that we are getting help for it. But this is an ongoing, tedious process that requires constant attention. These children don't outgrow ADD. The hope is that the older they get, and with each school level they reach, they will be learning new coping skills to allow them to compensate and reach their full potential as capable and competent adults. They will then be ready to share their unique gifts with the world.

It is not just a matter of getting the help, it is the way in which it is given. It is also in the way we speak to our children. This was so beautifully illustrated for us recently when our son brought home a paper that was clearly illegible. His devoted and knowledgeable teacher wrote a note at the top of the page: "Phillip, please write this more neatly so my poor ol' eyes can read it."

There is absolutely no substitute for a teacher who loves his or her job and wants to make a difference in the lives of our children. Trust and believe in your ability to change the future of a child. Dare to make a difference. Celebrate the magnificent gift of uniqueness in every child. A plaque I once saw summed it up this way:

"Teachers affect eternity.

One can never tell where their influence ends."

Medication and School Management

As discussed in previous sections, medication is only one of the interventions for improving a child's ability to function and succeed in school. However, medication can make a significant difference in the lives of individuals with ADD/ADHD. Over years of working with children with ADHD, I have witnessed many children improve dramatically once their physician prescribed and regulated the proper medication and dosage.

Parents do not easily make the decision to try their child on medication. Typically, parents agonize over the decision and frequently avoid the medical route for years. No parent wants to have their child take a "drug." They often are fearful and feel guilty. Avoid being judgmental and sharing your personal philosophy about the rights and/or wrongs of medication with parents.

It is between the parents and the physician to decide whether the child receives medical treatment. You would not try to dissuade someone from taking insulin for diabetes; therefore, you shouldn't make parents feel guilty by suggesting that medication for treating ADD/ADHD is improper. The school's role is to support any child taking medication. School personnel need to be aware of and sensitive to the issues involved with medicating children and fully cooperate as appropriate. Teachers in particular need to be involved with: close observation of the child, communication (with parents and doctor), and making sure the child is receiving the medication as prescribed and on time.

The author has no medical background. Parents need to discuss medications in depth with their child's physician. For more information, the Bibliography and Recommended Resources lists a variety of excellent books written by qualified medical professionals which address medical intervention for ADD/ADHD.

My school does an excellent job of facilitating referrals to outside agencies/physicians and working closely with parents and physicians to ensure that the child receiving medication is being carefully managed and monitored through our "team approach." Our school has acquired this excellence through the training and direction of an outstanding school nurse, Sandra Wright, MSN. Sandra has a strong background in education and actively participates in community advocacy organizations for the ADD/ADHD (including the establishment of an ADD support group in the community)—giving her intimate knowledge of the issues parents must deal with at home as well as in school.

Our nurse acts as liaison between parent and teacher in helping to manage the medication at school. Coordination and communication between all parties involved is essential for optimal results. Through frequent classroom observation and discussions with teachers, the nurse can keep the physician and parents informed of progress or lack thereof.

The questions and answers on pages 156-158 were written by Sandra Wright, MSN, to explore the school's role and management strategies for children who receive medication for ADD.

What Are the Most Common Medications for Treating ADD/ADHD?

There are two main categories of medications which are typically used in the treatment of ADD/ADHD:

Stimulant medications. These are the most commonly prescribed medications for ADD/ADHD and have been used and studied for many years. It is suspected that these drugs have an effect on the body's neurotransmitters and can enable the child to better focus attention, regulate his/her activity level and impulsive behaviors. These medications include methylphenidate (Ritalin®), dextroamphetamine (Dexedrine®), and pemoline (Cylert®).

When a child takes Ritalin or Dexedrine, they often require an additional dosage to be administered at school, since the drug wears off after a few hours. However, a long-acting, sustained-release form of the medication is sometimes prescribed.

Tricyclic antidepressants. These are also believed to work by acting on neurotransmitters in the brain. These drugs are often prescribed for a child who cannot take a stimulant drug, or are given to children who are showing signs of clinical depression as well as ADD. This category of drugs includes: imipramine (Tofranil®), desiprimine (Norpramine®), and amytriptyline (Elavil®). This group of medications may take two to three weeks to reach a therapeutic level.

There are other less commonly used medications for treating ADD/ADHD. Catapres (Clonidine®) is one such drug which acts in a completely different way from the stimulants or the tricyclic antidepressants. It is often prescribed in adults to lower blood pressure. However, its action to modify ADHD behavior is really unknown. Catapres comes in a transdermal patch as well as in tablet form, and can be helpful for the child who is hyperactive and aggressive or who has Tourette's Syndrome. (Tourette's Syndrome is a neurological disorder characterized by involuntary muscle movements or tics.) Some researchers describe Tourette's as having the same neurochemical imbalance as ADHD. Catapres may cause the child to be sleepy in class, but often the drowsiness decreases after the child has been on the drug two to four weeks. Again, it is important for the teacher to monitor the child's behavior and activity level.

When a child is started on medication therapy, there is always a trial period when the physician is trying to determine the appropriate medication and dosage for the child. Some children are fortunate to find immediate improvement with their medication. Others will take longer until an effective medication and dosage is determined. Some children will not benefit at all, and some cannot tolerate any medication. Twenty to thirty percent will be "nonresponders" to medication therapy.

What Are the Most Important Issues Teachers Should Be Aware of Regarding Management of Medication for ADD/ADHD?

The teacher is an integral part of the therapeutic team because of his/her unique ability to observe the child's behavior and ability to attend while on (or off) medication. These observations (by behavior scales, collection of work samples, responses to behavior management) help the physician to regulate the dosage and/or determine if the medication is effective. Teachers should feel free to contact the parent, physician, and school nurse with input, observations, and any concerns they might have. In fact, most physicians provide behavioral observation scales for teachers to fill out at various intervals.

It is also important for teachers to understand that medication, dosages, and times are often changed or adjusted until the right "recipe" or combination is found for the child. Because children metabolize medication at different rates, many experience side effects, or become tolerant to medication. It is common for these adjustments to become necessary.

What Are Some of the Side Effects of These Medications?

There are some possible side effects which may occur with medications for ADD/ADHD. For example, stomachaches, headaches, irritability, and sensitivity to criticism are common when beginning treatment with Ritalin. Loss of appetite and insomnia are side effects which are upsetting to the parents. Sometimes the medication is changed if these symptoms continue, but often the symptoms diminish with time. Mood swings or irritability as the medication wears off (commonly called "the rebound") can usually be altered by the physician adjusting the dosage or the times the drug is given. A very small number of children develop tics (involuntary muscle movements) in the form of facial grimaces, sniffing, coughing, snorting, or other vocal sounds on stimulant medication. In most cases these tics do not continue if the medication is stopped. Teachers can be very helpful when they observe these symptoms or changes in behavior by communicating these observations to the parent, school nurse, or physician.

Some children taking tricyclic antidepressants may become drowsy or sleepy in class, have a dry mouth, or become constipated. It is important to report these observations to the parent and physician. The dose may then be decreased or given primarily at bedtime.

Who Is Responsible for Medicating Students at School? How Is It Monitored? What Happens if We Forget?

Children receiving medication for ADD/ADHD often are prescribed a dosage to be taken during school hours. It is important that medication for ADD/ADHD be given on time. Generally, that means it is administered during the lunch period or right after lunch. With Ritalin, for example, the peak action is approximately two hours after the child has received it; the effects of the drug dissipate in about four hours. Many children experience aggressive, emotional, or impulsive behavior (commonly called the "trough") when the medication's effects wear off.

When the next prescribed dose is not given on time or is given late, these children are found crying, fighting, or otherwise "in trouble" on the playground or cafeteria. When the child returns to the classroom, he/she is not ready or able to focus on the lesson and is often disruptive. When it is obvious to the teacher that the child has not taken medication and is sent to the office, it takes another thirty minutes for the drug to begin working, wasting at least an hour of productive time.

Most elementary school children cannot remember without reminders to go to the office at the designated time for medication because of the very nature of ADHD. It becomes the responsibility of the teacher, school nurse, counselor, and/or office staff to help with the administration of medication.

A beeper watch for the older child or "coded" verbal reminders from the teacher or over the intercom may be necessary. A sticker chart kept where the medication is dispensed rewards the child for remembering. Color-coded cards given to the child by the teacher are all workable and helpful to the child. It is also very important to provide these reminders to students without breaking confidentiality or discussing medication in front of other students. Pairing the medication time with a daily activity is also a good technique because it helps establish a consistent schedule. In the nurse's absence, the office staff should be provided with a list of children who take daily medication (of any kind), sending for the child if he/she does not come in to receive it.

Does the Child Lose His/Her Free Will and Sense of Control With Medication for ADD/ADHD?

It is important for teachers to know that medication does not control the child. The medication helps to filter out distractions, allowing the child to focus on the task at hand. It diminishes impulsivity, letting the child make better choices. Medication therapy is most effective when combined with educational strategies specific to the child with ADD/ADHD, behavioral modification techniques, parental awareness and training, counseling, and management of the child's environment.

AN INTERVIEW WITH MIKE
(32 years old, graduate student in Colorado)

Mike was diagnosed in his twenties and treated for ADD.

What are your memories of school?

"Grade school through high school, I rarely did my homework. I got through on my test scores. On all of my scholastic aptitude tests I scored above the ninetieth percentile. I was lucky to be an avid reader. I could get the course syllabus and do the reading without even attending class. But I had a very hard time coping in school. I was highly frustrated, and considered by most of my teachers as a 'problem child.' I wasn't shy about challenging teachers."

Which teachers did you do best with?

"Those who had interesting things to say, lectured well, would go with the flow, and had a sense of humor. I did well with teachers who appreciated an original or challenging thought, who gave latitude for originality, and who weren't rigid."

What is your advice to teachers?

"Kids with ADD are going to need structure. When you find a kid not making it, start lending a little structure and see if it will help. I still need a little more structure from my bosses than my co-workers do."

What was it like for you, beginning Ritalin at 27 years of age?

"My chronic depression went away. I was in a hole and had a lot of problems. Economic: I couldn't hold a job. Relationship problems: My engagement was cut off, and it was devastating to me. Medication helped me organize my perspective and make long-term plans. It was a revelation to me that I can start something and be able to accomplish it within a reasonable amount of time—even something like cleaning my apartment. If only I'd been caught at eighteen or even eight."

What About Kindergarten?

*T*his section is devoted to how best to reach and teach the immature, impulsive, disruptive child at the kindergarten level. In schools everywhere teachers seem to be encountering an increase in the number of children who are more difficult to manage and have a host of special needs.

Many children are simply immature, needing a little extra time to develop the prerequisite social and emotional skills to handle the structure of kindergarten. In classes everywhere we are encountering an influx of "drug-exposed babies" and other youngsters who were medically fragile infants. These children are entering school with immature neuro-sensory systems and coping mechanisms. How many other young children—products of "dysfunctional families" and societal ills—must enter school tragically lacking the physical and emotional security and structure in their home lives? Kindergarten teachers are on the front line to meet the challenge—to find ways to provide for each child the necessary structure, nurturing, and education (academic, social, and behavioral) that will build their foundation for a lifetime of learning.

The information presented in this section comes from the "experts": sixteen kindergarten teachers from a variety of schools and backgrounds in San Diego County. These wonderful teachers willingly shared their teaching styles, specific strategies for cueing, transitions, and behavior management techniques as well as their philosophy and opinion of what makes a difference . . . what works for these children! The teachers I interviewed teach kindergarten in the following assignments: nine regular kindergarten classes, five special education/early childhood classes, two bilingual kindergarten classes. A number of these teachers are also mentor teachers in the San Diego Unified School District.

My thanks and appreciation to the following contributors: Betsy Arnold, Noreen Bruno, Allison Carpenter, Cindy Cook, Julia Croom, Levana Estline,

Christina Evans, Ellen Fabrikant, Brenda Ferich, Nancy Fetzer, Cathy O'Leary, Nancy Paznokas, Jill Prier, Adrienne Tedrow, Leilani Vigil, Peggy Walsh.

There are a number of similarities in all of the teachers I interviewed and in their classes:

* teacher provides classroom environment that is loving and nurturing—teacher is generous with hugs, smiles, praise, and affection

* close contact and involvement with parents

* specific, firm, and clear expectations

* lots of music, movement, and hands-on activities

* structure, consistency, follow-through

* children offered many choices

* individualized discipline and behavior management

* fun, exciting curriculum and activities

* room environment that takes into account different learning styles

* being well planned and prepared

* awareness that children's self-esteem and feeling good about themselves is most important

* respect for each child's individuality

In kindergarten, everything—every behavioral expectation and social skill—has to be taught. You need to explain and model each desired behavior and practice until all students know precisely what is expected of them.

Beginning of the School Year

From the minute the children walk through the door on the first day of school, they are taught the specifics of how you want them to behave throughout the day. Rules are established by the teacher alone or with children's input. Examples from two classrooms:

Classroom 1:

* Follow directions.

* Keep hands and feet to yourself.

* Use quiet voices.

Classroom 2:

* Keep hands and feet to ourselves.

* Raise hand for turn to talk.

* Toys, candy, gum are left at home.

One teacher does everything as a whole group for the first two weeks or so of the school year while she sets her standards and teaches all expectations and rules. This teacher models and teaches over and over every behavior:

* ✱ How and where to line up

* ✱ How to stand in line

* ✱ How to walk in line

* ✱ How to move to groups

* ✱ How and where to move to any station or learning center

* ✱ How to get the teacher's attention

* ✱ How loud to talk

* ✱ How to sit on the rug

* ✱ How to sit at the table

* ✱ How and when to raise hand

* ✱ What to do in new situations

Practice until students understand your expectations. It is important to be specific and consistent in those expectations. For example:

"Show me what to do when you have something you want to say."

"Show me how we get our lunch boxes and line up."

One teacher uses the story *The Day the Monster Came to School* [*] and a monster puppet to teach about rules. The class discusses the monster's inappropriate behaviors and the problems those behaviors cause in the classroom. After a lot of discussion and feedback from the children, the teacher prompts: "Tell what Mr. Monster *is* supposed to do." The kids make up three or four class rules. These are posted pictorially and a big book of rules is also made.

One of the teachers teaches her students this expectation:

"When I talk, you listen." After stating this over and over, she prompts students, "When I talk, . . ." Then students respond in unison, "We listen!" She does this every time someone interrupts. This technique is helpful because typically the same children repeatedly talk out and interrupt. She doesn't believe in singling out those children by saying their names, calling attention to their negative behavior. This avoids identifying the children as "troublemakers," and it helps them learn by hearing and saying the rule verbally.

Noise Level

Some teachers tolerate more noise than others. Teachers mentioned that many children are extremely reactive towards noise and hubbub. Classroom activities

---

[*] From *Back to School*, Macmillan Seasonal Activity Pack, pp. 8, 9.; © 1985 Macmillan Education Co., a division of Macmillan Inc.

are fun and exciting. However, the climate in the classroom needs to be calm, with a moderate noise level, not excessive noise . . . and not chaotic!

One teacher's expectation is that during free choice time, students use "indoor voices" with much practice of what that means. For work time, her students are taught that they may whisper to a neighbor. She spends time making a game out of teaching and practicing whispering. "Children enjoy it because they love secrets and it's like a game to them." For example, you can do the following:

"What do you think whispering is? When you put your hand on your throat (over voice box) and talk, you feel it vibrate." (Practice with students.) "When you whisper, it doesn't vibrate." (Practice with students.)

Structuring the School Day

Children need the predictability of knowing what group they are in, where it works, what it does, and so on. They need the consistency of routine and schedule.

One of the special education mentor teachers shared her structure. She stressed the importance of establishing a predictable sequence of activities from the first day of school. Everything in her class is in 15-minute increments, alternating between sitting and moving. Her sequence is as follows: Beginning at "rug time," they go over the rules and she explains the activities at the stations. She has a consistent routine of language arts activities with four activity stations related to literature and theme of lesson being taught. Students rotate to four tables of activities:

* **Table 1**—Art activity (e.g., painting)

* **Table 2**—Journal. Teacher writes a sentence or prompt for children to copy (e.g., We are thankful for . . .). At this table the children find their journal, copy prompt, and have available a variety of items they can use, such as stencils, crayons, magazines, and other pictures to complete the prompt.

* **Table 3**—Writing activity (e.g., tracing in different colors a letter being practiced that day/week).

* **Table 4**—Cutting activity related to the theme of the day/week.

After free choice, the children again come to the rug for an explanation of the day's math activities. These activities follow a consistent pattern—

Mondays—Sorting activities

Tuesdays—Patterns

Wednesdays—Measurement/graphs

Thursdays—Shapes

Fridays—Numbers

The same four tables operate for math activities related to the day's concept being taught. For example, on Fridays:

* **Table 1**—manipulatives and puzzles

✳ **Table 2**—journals and number books

✳ **Table 3**—writing/tracing numerals

✳ **Table 4**—cutting and pasting number activities

Many teachers (regular and special education) have a routine of centers, stations, and rotations.

Schedules and Consistency

Children want to know exactly what comes next. They need the security of knowing their schedule. One teacher shared how she uses two self-made charts—one for regular days and the other for shortened/minimum days. On the charts she drew clock faces and pictures of activities for their daily schedule.

Example:

9:00 — Picture of children coming through a door marked K3 followed by a picture of journals and books (the first activity of the morning)

10:00 — P.E. (picture of swings and monkeybars)

10:30 — Reading and math (picture of books and numbers)

12:00 — Lunch (picture of milk, banana, hot dog)

12:30 — Science and social studies (picture of plant, animals, and people)

1:30 — Dismissal (picture of children leaving door marked K3)

Kindergarten children generally aren't kept in a big group for long periods of time. There are a lot of activities occurring in small groups and short time periods to keep student interest and attention.

Behavior Management Techniques in Kindergarten

Time-Outs

Many teachers use some system of removing disruptive students briefly from the group's activity. A number of teachers reported that they don't have a designated spot for time-out in the room—they just send the child over to any table, chair, or area away from the group. Teachers emphasized the power of the group and children's desire to be a participant.

The important element of time-out that almost all the teachers agreed upon is that any time-out or time-away is brief and that the child is welcomed back to the group when he/she is ready.

✳ One teacher has a system where she gives three warnings and then sends the student to the "Think-About-It Chair." This chair is for "Oops . . . I have to think about what I am supposed to do."

✻ One teacher said she tries never to interrupt instruction when sending a child to time-out. She either points, or walks over to the child, taps his/her shoulder, and walks the child to a time-out area without discussion.

✻ The teacher needs to clearly communicate her expectations and consequences: "I'd like you to sit here. But if you do, you've got to keep your hands and feet to yourself. If you can't handle it, you'll have to go back there (away from the group)."

Giving the Child Space

Children who are losing control or who can't focus or stay with the group need space. A few teachers expressed that they use "time-in" rather than "time-out." Children with problems need time and space to get themselves back in control. One teacher said she uses the library corner as one designated spot and the playhouse area as another. She refers to this as a "cool down" area. She said that even though these are desirable areas of the classroom to be in during free choice, it is not reinforcing when they are by themselves there.

A few teachers mentioned that we have a tendency to hem children in—not giving them "outs." It is better for the child if we provide choices and allow them some space.

"Do you need some time? Do you need to move to a different area? Do you need time to get yourself together?" Whisper to the child, "Go to the pillow area; read a book." Give the child the chance to move away from the group and come back in when ready. Children with special needs react adversely when they feel people "closing in on them." Ask them, "Is there a better place for you to do your work?" Try letting the child determine where that space would be. When they are ready to come back, respond positively, "We are glad you are ready to join us again. Welcome back."

Set Consequences and Follow Through

"You have had a hard time keeping your hands to yourself and not pushing. You're going to spend the next recess with me today. You can go out to play tomorrow if you can keep your hands to yourself and not bother other kids." Talk to the child, looking directly into his/her eyes and touching him/her gently. Build on trust and expectations.

Heading Off Trouble With Diversionary Tactics

All teachers agreed that a key management technique is redirecting a child and heading him/her off at the path before the need for correction. This takes a perceptive, aware teacher who is watching his/her students for signs of "losing it" and is then effectively redirecting.

✻ Give the child a task that he/she likes to do. Most kindergarten children love to be the teacher's helper. Teacher's helpers are in charge of passing out papers/supplies, wiping down tables, and putting up chairs.

✻ During reading, the child may be asked to use the pointer or turn the pages of the Big Book. It is important to find what the child likes to do, identifying what is meaningful and motivating.

✱ When a child is starting to get disruptive, the teacher goes over to the child, looks directly into his/her eyes, and says, "You know, Mike, in about two minutes we're going to the snack table." This technique gives the child something to look forward to in little blocks of time.

✱ When a child is beginning to get restless and behave inappropriately, the teacher goes over to the child, makes eye contact, and says, "We don't do this in the classroom . . . In a few minutes you will be going outside and there you can do it."

Signals and Cues

Teachers use different signals and cues to get their students' attention and to focus them.

✱ One teacher rings a bell. Students are taught to quickly hug themselves and look up at her. She prompts, "I'm going to ring the bell. Who is going to be ready?" (She gently assists children who have difficulty.) She will not begin instruction until they all stop and look up at her.

✱ Another teacher uses, "Stop, look, and listen." At this cue, the children stop, put their hands behind their backs, and look at the teacher.

✱ There are many non-verbal signals teachers use:

— Stop sign: hand up

— Pointing to ear (listen).

— Pointing to and tapping chin ("look at me").

Teachers signal by playing a chord on the piano, ringing a bell, or flashing the lights. Some follow this signal with the word "freeze." Teachers physically cue their students by touching a hand, shoulder, or arm.

Teachers also use private cues, signals, and reinforcers worked out between an individual child and the teacher. Example: One teacher had a system with a girl who was having great difficulty staying with the group. "I'm going to put three checkmarks on the corner of the chalkboard. Each time you get up and move away from the table, I erase a checkmark. At the end of the period (about 10 to 15 minutes) I will give you a sticker for every checkmark still on the board." The behavior improved considerably and the teacher no longer needed to reinforce with anything tangible (just praise).

One teacher has a cue with a student who has great difficulty sitting. She explains that when her student feels he can't sit any longer, he gives her the two-thumbs-up sign. She then signals her aide to take the child outside for a few minutes of physical activity and then come back in quietly. She says that a brief period of swinging or running works to calm him, and he comes back in ready to work. The technique is also effective in heading off trouble—sending the child outside for two or three minutes of swinging (while the aide stands at the door) before the disruptive behaviors begin. Of course, this assumes the luxury of a classroom aide.

The Best Way to Manage: Positive Attention

All teachers mentioned that they always watch for positive behaviors and then name and recognize what children are doing right. They find the best, most meaningful, and reinforcing way to teach students appropriate behavior is through lots of specific praise, smiles, and hugs.

Many teachers have students applaud each other for individual accomplishments:

* ∗ "Let's give a big round of applause to . . . " (Children clap finger-to-finger in a large circular movement.)

* ∗ "Let's give ourselves a pat on the back." (Children reach over and pat themselves on back.)

* ∗ "Let's give the silent cheer for . . . " (making a "rah rah" hand motion in the air without using voice)

Checking for Specific Behaviors

"Are you using your inside voice?"

"Are your ears listening?"

"Are your eyes watching?"

"Are your legs folded?"

"Are your hands in your laps?"

"Where are you supposed to be sitting?"

"What do you do when you want to talk?"

"Where is your carpet square?"

Recognizing Positive Behavior

One teacher is careful to never say "good job." She instead describes the specific behavior she likes in a matter-of-fact voice—not effusively. For example, "I like the way you came over here and sat down next to Marcus even though someone else took your chair," or "I like the way Julie is working with her partner."

Other examples include—

"I like the way you are sitting on the rug, Mandy."

"I like the way Johnny has his eyes right up here. I can tell he is really paying attention."

"I like the way Tanneesha is sitting up."

"I noticed that Raul is walking nice and quietly. Thank you, Raul."

"I noticed the way you are sitting with your hands on your lap and your legs crossed."

"I noticed the way Cathy is remembering to raise her hand. That helps me teach so everyone can learn. Thank you, Cathy. Let's give her a round of applause."

"I really appreciate how Coby has been trying to wait his turn. Thank you, Coby."

One teacher uses praising words that correspond by letter-sound association with the letter being learned in class at the time.

i—incredible

w—wonderful

f—fabulous, fantastic

Catch the disruptive child doing something right, and compliment!

Resolving Conflicts Among Children

One teacher explained that many children have never been taught or shown how to handle problems in a positive way. They need to be taught and rewarded for this skill. She shared her technique:

Example: A child collides into another one, or someone hits somebody else or gets elbowed (either deliberately or accidentally). They consequently get mad at each other and run to the teacher for a resolution.

Teacher: "Can you tell Jason how you feel? I'll help you. I'll say it, then you can say it after me. 'I don't like it when you hit me like that. It hurt.' "

Student repeats.

Teacher (prompt to Jason): "I'm sorry, Bobby."

Student repeats.

Teacher (prompt to Bobby): "That's okay."

Student repeats.

This is followed by students shaking hands and the entire class clapping loudly and enthusiastically, with the teacher starting the applause.

The Impulsive Child Talking Out Disruptively in Class

Teachers generally seat this child right near them—within arm's reach for cueing. They explain that everyone has to wait their turn and why we have that rule. For example:

"Sally, I know you're really excited. The rule in my class is that we raise our hands so that I can hear what you say. Wouldn't it be sad if I didn't hear what you said because it was too noisy in the room? If you can work quietly for five minutes, you can help me with passing out the papers." (Redirect behavior.)

* Acknowledge child, but say, "Right now it's time for you to listen. It's my turn to talk. Raise your hand." If he/she does, call on him/her right away.

* Use a signal with that child. For example, the aide sits near that student and whispers, "Hold that question. Keep that one."

* "That's not appropriate. Not acceptable. James is speaking now."

* Call on the child as frequently as possible when he/she does remember to raise hand/wait for turn. Praise the child for being patient.

✳ When behavior persists, one teacher says, "Mark, that's yelling out. You need to go to the think-about-it chair." State it matter-of-factly.

✳ It's important to catch the student showing improvement: "Mark, I noticed that you are really catching yourself from yelling out in class. I am very proud of you."

✳ Give children chances to talk and share at pre-reading time or when introducing anything new (to reduce the need to blurt out at inappropriate times). Prior to reading a new book, show the pictures. Ask: "Does anyone want to share with us? Raise your hand." Then state, "It's my turn now." Whole language literature programs are conducive to this interchange.

Out of Control

One teacher said she will sit and wrap herself around an out-of-control child. She rocks him/her and says over and over calmly to the child what will occur. "When you are ready to calm down, you will go to lunch. If not, you will stay with me. You let me know when you're ready."

Teachers trying to calm an out-of-control child find rocking and a matter-of-fact, calm voice helpful. If the child feels "safe" it helps to control him/her. "I will not allow you to do that. Yes, I do love you, but I will not allow you to . . . "

Generally the child will be removed from the classroom with an adult, or the teacher summons assistance and she removes her class while the counselor or administrator deals with this child in the classroom.

What About Crying in the Classroom?

A certain amount of crying is to be expected in kindergarten classes, especially during the first few weeks of school. In most classrooms, if the crying persists beyond what is "reasonable," the crying child is removed from the classroom. One teacher said that it is all right to cry in her room. She tells children, "You can cry, but you can't scream and you can't jump up and down. It would sound like an earthquake in here." (She has very little crying in her room.)

Voice Control

Many teachers mentioned voice control as an effective management technique. One to one, look at the child in the eye, **lower** your voice and drop the pitch to get a child's attention, rather than raising your voice.

Studying the Child

With many ADD/ADHD children, the way they are able to cope and behave depends on the day, situation, and even time. It is important to try fitting the strategy to that individual child. Teachers need to ask themselves, "What can I do to prevent this behavior from happening?"

One teacher gave an example of a student who has extreme mood swings. She noticed over a period of time that the little girl cried around 11:00 every day. After she noticed the pattern, the teacher gave the child something she liked to do during this time (lead Number Rock music). If you start to see a pattern with a certain behavior, look at what time it occurs and any possible cause. Ask yourself: "Is there some positive behavior that the child could be doing at that time to head off trouble?"

Behavior Modification, Monitoring and Reward Systems

✳ Many teachers do not use a whole-class behavioral management system (such as red, yellow, and green cards) because they don't need it. As one teacher said, "You do the absolute minimum you need to do to maintain behavior."

✳ One teacher uses the colored cards for everyone. Every twenty green cards (good behavior) will earn a certificate and a prize. All of her students get a stamp on the hand and pat on the back at the end of the day if they had a "pretty good" day.

✳ Another teacher sends the colored card home with each child daily. She requests that parents reward with something small for every five green cards that come home.

✳ Most teachers use behavioral management charts or tickets home for a few children as needed.

✳ One teacher uses a chart broken into 15-minute periods. The child can earn a stamp for each section.

✳ Another teacher has a behavioral chart she uses with a child in which he/she earns stickers while being quiet (stickers count towards free time).

✳ One teacher has a weekly chart on which she draws faces: happy face = 3 points, straight face = 2 points, sad face = 0 points. Parents initial the chart and return it. Parents are asked to reinforce for every 10 points earned (some very small reward).

✳ One teacher has a contract with a child, whereby he earns a stamp for every 10 minutes of not shouting out in class.

✳ One teacher stressed how important it is to find what privileges will excite the child to work hard. Some children couldn't care less about stickers, but would love to work for the chance to play with bubbles, ride a trike, or care for the class rabbit.

✳ One teacher has a "Good Kid Club." All children have their names on a chart. If they behave (no more than two warnings), their card (with a picture of a panda on it) is still showing. If not, it is turned backwards. The child's card can be turned back again when behavior improves during the day. Each child gets a positive ticket to take home any day the card is still showing. Every ten tickets earns the child a grab-bag toy or book. Parents are encouraged to keep the tickets in a special place and may also choose to reward.

Almost all schools have other effective school-wide positive reinforcers for students who are behaving appropriately.

Involving Parents

All teachers stressed the importance of close communication with and involvement of the parents, particularly for children who are experiencing difficulty.

* Teachers invite parents to come in and see their child in action. They have the parent work with their child in a small group.

* Teachers confer with parents and send specific things home for the parent to do with their child.

Many teachers see parents almost daily, dropping off or picking up their children. Other teachers call parents regularly. Parental input is crucial. It is also useful to make home visits—particularly to homes of children experiencing difficulty in school. It is helpful to have some idea what the home situation is.

Children Who Want Your Attention and Need to Wait

One teacher uses a cue with children who come up to her when she is busy with another group or individual child. She covers his/her hand gently with her hand and rubs as she continues with the student(s) she is engaged with. This acknowledges that she is aware that the child is there waiting to speak to her and eliminates the calling out and pulling on her. Then she gets back to those children in order.

Handling Disappointments

Kindergarten children can become very upset if they aren't chosen for certain privileges or responsibilities. They don't deal well with not getting selected or having to wait their turn. One teacher uses an "oh well" signal. With a snap of the fingers in a big, sweeping motion she leads her children in saying, "Oh well . . . maybe next time." The teacher rewards and praises students who can do and say this when disappointed for not getting a turn. "I am so proud of you. You are so grown up." The teacher smiles at the child and gives a special signal to children who can use the "oh well" technique. This helps with "no fair" complaints.

When the Other Children Perceive a Certain Student as "Bad"

One teacher shared that children have a real sense of understanding and compassion. They always take the teacher's lead. Sometimes there is one child who is so disruptive that children think of him/her as "bad." The teacher always corrects and softens. For example: "There are no bad children. Sometimes Michael has trouble remembering the rules. It doesn't mean he is bad. Sometimes he can't help it. It is not always his fault. We need to help him. How do you think we can help him remember the rules?"

Learning Styles Environment in Kindergarten

Classrooms designed to meet students' different learning styles are colorful and warm, and offer many attractive activities. Rooms may have carpet areas, beanbag chairs or other big, soft chairs, sand tables, rice tables, water tables, computers, stuffed animals, playhouses, library areas, instruments, easels, listening centers, and so on.

These classrooms are inviting and child-centered, with children's work displayed freely. There are many puzzles, blocks of different kinds, and many different textures and things to feel and manipulate. It is an environment filled with love and respect. Teachers walk around and give personal attention to children and a great deal of affection (hugs, positive attention, and recognition).

Music and movement are embedded in all aspects of the curriculum and throughout the day. One teacher plays "new age" tapes, finding them very calming for children. A number of teachers like to play classical or baroque music during periods of concentration, such as writing, counting, or doing math activities with manipulatives. All teachers play songs and sing throughout the day. Teachers who use *The Animated Alphabet* program, by Jim Stone, for teaching letter/sound association find his songs and verses wonderful to play during activities that don't require as much focus concentration (coloring, pasting).

Teachers use music during transition times (e.g., clean-up). They combine music with movement for exercise, body awareness and coordination, following directions, and relaxation. Fingerplays, poetry, rhymes, and marches are used by all teachers. Again, students need to be taught how to move, how to march, and all prerequisite skills.

Special Early Childhood Programs for Children With Attentional Problems

The Animated Alphabet, by Jim Stone, is a wonderful multisensory phonics program. Letter-sound association is taught through all modalities: a clever verse sung to familiar melodies (auditory input), a picture card with corresponding mnemonic (visual input), and children making letter shapes with their bodies (kinesthetic). Through song, pictures, body movements, and toys, children are experiencing great excitement and success. For more information write to:

> J. Stone Creations, P.O. Box 2336, Grossmont Station, La Mesa, California 92044-0604

Mathematics Their Way is an exciting hands-on program for teaching mathematical concepts to children. It teaches free exploration, patterns, sorting, classifying, sequence, number, measurement, comparison, graphing, and much more through activities involving discovery, manipulatives, and group problem-solving.

Fun, Special, Thematic Activities

All teachers stressed how they do everything possible to make learning fun for their students—most use themes to build their activities around. Many children love to perform! In our school, kindergarten teachers create a number of programs that students perform for their parents and invited classes (e.g., Native American, teddy bear, spring, luau). These programs involve different languages, musical instruments, singing, movements and dance, costumes, and special foods.

Exercise

Children need the opportunity to move and exercise. Teachers build movement into the day at frequent intervals. Kindergarten children should have the opportunity to do a lot of climbing, running, and jumping. Some teachers have a regular routine of stretching, warm-up, jogging, and cool-down every morning—as well as physical education and motor skills training. In the classroom there are songs and rhymes with motions (hand and whole body) that are integrated throughout the day.

The Tactile-Defensive Child

There are some children, particularly those with ADD/ADHD, who have poor tolerance for being touched (the feel of anything rubbing or touching the body, such as certain textures, clothes, or being crowded in line). Teachers need to understand and respect a child's intolerance and accommodate. For some children this means that sitting on the carpet may be almost intolerable. One of the adults I interviewed for this book shared that he still prefers to wear silks and he cannot wear many other fabrics. As a child he refused to wear anything but flannel shirts.

In one special education class the teacher does a lot to build tolerance and acceptance for some degree of touching through numerous sensory activities. For example, she has a box of items for children to play and experiment with—feather dusters, rolling pins, fabrics of different textures, sandpaper, lotions, gloves of different textures.

A massage to the arm or back is also helpful to many children, particularly for calming and relaxing them. Read Section 19, What Every Teacher Needs to Hear.

The Child Who Has Trouble Sitting

I asked teachers specifically what they do for children with this difficulty. One special education teacher found that having children sit with legs crossed on the carpet is the best place and position for paying attention because hands are down, they have a base of support, and bodies are centered. Children sometimes need help sitting in this position. She has an adult sit right behind the child, also with legs crossed. This teacher also cues students with difficulty by singing:

"Everyone cross your legs.

Everyone cross your legs.

Everyone cross your legs.

And put your hands up on your lap."

Sometimes a child's inability to sit is blamed on behavior when in reality a child doesn't have the physical tone or ability to sit on the carpet and listen.

Additional Techniques to Help Children Who Can't Sit

✳ One teacher said that she tries to have an adult sit down with the child, touching him/her and rubbing his/her back or arm to help keep him/her seated and focused.

✳ Allow leeway. Some children cannot sit for more than a few moments. Teachers allow the child to get up and then try to redirect by assigning another task.

✳ Sometimes it is necessary to allow the child to sit in the back of the room and flail his/her arms and legs away from everyone else.

✳ Some teachers have signals with children that allow them to go outside with an aide for two or three minutes of physical release (running/swinging) and then return to class.

✳ Give the child space! ADHD children, with their neurosensory immaturities, need to know what is their "space." This includes the child's acceptable "space" on the rug, at tables, in line, and so on.

Transitions

Teachers use a variety of techniques, cues, and signals for transitions. In addition to those previously mentioned, the following techniques have proven helpful:

✳ One teacher sets a timer when her class breaks into language arts and math activities. A few minutes before the activity ends she warns, "We have about three minutes left before the timer rings." When it rings, she says, "FREEZE." Then she gives directions to the class, usually to clean up.

✳ Other teachers reward tables for good transitions. Table numbers are listed on the board. Every time a table does something well, the teacher praises specifically and puts a star by the table number. Clean-up time: "Table two cleaned up first. They get a star. Table three has the most stars—let's give them a round of applause. They will get to line up first."

Response Opportunities—Keeping Them Engaged and Focused

Teachers try to keep children actively responding and participating. Examples:

"Raise your hand if you think this is right."

"Put your thumb on your nose if you think . . . "

"Put your finger on the _____ as I walk around and check."

"Listen carefully because I'm going to ask questions of all of you."

"Show me with your fingers how many bears there were in the story."

"I'm going to ask Table 1 to give me a word that starts with a *b*, but they all have to agree." (If they give the wrong answer, the teacher says, "Oh. This table didn't agree. Talk about it some more until you agree.")

✶ Give instructions and ask if there are any questions. Then ask one or two children to repeat the instructions, targeting one of the children who has difficulty.

✶ "Every time you hear me say (magic word) clap your hands/wiggle your fingers." This technique helps focusing and listening skills.

Trust Building and Connecting With the Child

Teachers need to give the child the most they can at the emotional level. One of the hardest things for a teacher to gain is a child's confidence. Children need to trust you and know that you are going to follow through. As one teacher put it, "You have to mean what you say. Never make a promise that you may not be able to keep. And never break a promise!" Building on trust is a process that takes place over time and is different for each child.

It is important to try to find at least one other child for a student to attach to (someone accepting). For all children, especially those with special needs, having a friend makes all the difference in the world and can "save the day." Children with ADD/ADHD often have significant difficulty making and keeping friends. Teachers will find themselves in the role of facilitator, trying to find a friend for this child.

Team Teaching

In many schools teachers do a lot of team teaching. For example, two kindergarten teachers split students from two classes into six groups. One of the teachers has groups 1, 2, and 3 for one hour three times a week for art, contracts, math manipulatives, and free choice. The other teacher has groups 4, 5, and 6 for centers (easel, dramatic play, home center, Legos®, puzzles, computer). One kindergarten teacher teams with the first grade teacher next door. For an hour a day four times a week the students have their choice of centers that they may work at in either classroom, which are based on a thematic unit.

One of the advantages of team teaching is that disruptive children are all intermingled. Each teacher is getting a break from draining students, and all children get to experience different teaching styles and personalities.

Other Special Tricks

✶ One teacher uses a little "magic wand."

✶ Another teacher uses "special binoculars" to see children doing the right thing (appropriate behaviors).

✱ Many teachers use puppets or stuffed animals for special cues and communication with children.

✱ Many teachers bring in extra help for children. They use and welcome parent volunteers. They also find cross-age tutors very helpful, particularly during centers, rotations, and small group activities.

One teacher summarized her philosophy, which is consistent with all of the teachers I interviewed: "If my kids are happy and feel good about themselves, they will learn!"

The Challenge of Middle School and Junior High

*M*any of us recall with a shudder our junior high school experiences and are relieved that those difficult years are far behind us. Children have a great deal to contend with during this time of their lives:

* the changes and transitions to a new school;

* so many new students, many with different ethnic and cultural backgrounds together for the first time;

* several teachers, each with unique teaching styles, expectations, and requirements;

* fear of getting lost on campus and not finding their classes;

* often the feeling of anonymity and being alone;

* enormous social and peer pressures; and

* physical changes and anxieties of adolescence.

Children with any learning or attentional problems have all of the "normal stresses" to deal with that their peers have. In addition, they must cope with their specific difficulties, which generally intensify at this time.

Critical Factors for Our Students

Those same critical factors identified in Section 2 are the keys to what make a difference with middle and junior high school students as well. This is a period in

all children's lives when they need structure and the feeling of "connection," and being noticed and valued. This is a critical time for students to learn their strengths and how to study and access information. At this turning point in their lives they need to learn how to relate to others and get along with people from diverse backgrounds and cultures.

These years are important for keeping students motivated. It is essential that the curriculum be rich, relevant, exciting, and challenging to all students. Teachers of middle school and junior high should be masters of innovative teaching strategies to help students interact with each other and produce meaningful projects that tap their interests.

All of the strategies included throughout this book—especially in the academic and learning styles chapters—should be employed at this level.

The interviews throughout this book with ADD/ADHD adults and teenagers who share their personal stories and accounts of what happened to them during these years are very revealing. Of special interest is Dan's story in Section 29 (Exemplary Model Programs), which describes his personal success through the opportunity to have a "mentoring experience" when he was 13 and 14 years old.

Topics and Plans to Improve Junior High School

The following is a list of topics and plans to improve an ethnically diverse junior high school in a large metropolitan area. These factors were identified as areas of need and priorities by the community (including the staff and parents). Other junior high schools may find relevance and wish to explore some of these interventions, as well.

Campus Safety

* Increase instructional aide/secondary supervision to monitor campus
* Parent/student patrol
* Peer counseling program
* Monitor bathrooms
* Additional teacher supervision and stations
* Review locations of telephones and walkie-talkies to determine additional needs
* Use staff supervision time to include dialogue with students
* Have continuous classroom discussions of school rules, school safety, mutual respect, sexual harassment
* Post school rules in classrooms and hallways
* Survey staff regarding school safety

Addressing Student Behavior Issues

* Review staff responsibilities for addressing student behavior problems
* Peer student involvement in defining behavior issues and consequences
* Team (teachers, staff, parents, students) approach to behavior issues should be demonstrated to students
* Firm, sensitive, and immediate response to disruptive behavior
* Administration to continue to work with staff on discipline techniques for the classroom
* Expand site consultation team process to provide proactive interventions
* Establish a process to identify problems in their embryonic stage
* Review and revise disciplinary policy as necessary with staff, throughout the school year
* Peer teacher training to help others with discipline techniques
* Increase supervision of students during passing periods
* Minimize student passes during instruction periods

* Assist identified students with social skills needs

* Revise in-school suspension plan

* Regular meetings with targeted groups of students for proactive counseling

* Staff survey to determine effectiveness of implementation of the school discipline plan

* Administrative team to review the discipline plan for consistency, equity, and fairness of implementation

Getting Students to Know One Another

* Utilization of homeroom

  — Advisory period to replace homeroom

  — Advisory classes to be as small as possible

  — Structure advisory with lessons concerning specific issues (e.g., race relations, self-esteem)

* Planned lessons for first weeks of school to make all students feel they belong at the school

* Establish student committees (e.g., cafeteria, bus, hallways)

* Continue lunchtime activities (e.g., sports, computer lab, student council functions)

* Continue peer tutoring

* Explore with cafeteria staff alternative procedures

* Continue exploration of all possible means to foster mutual respect (students, staff, parents)

Staff Development Plans

Staff will receive inservice training on various strategies—

* Race/human relations

  — Fair and equitable treatment of all students as individuals

  — Skills for parent/teacher communication

  — Sensitivity to student and parent needs and perceptions

  — Additional programs that address tolerance, understanding, and getting along with others

* Instructional innovations:

  — Training in technology in the classroom

  — Socratic method

  — Cooperative learning

- — Learning styles
- — Multisensory instruction
✱ Enhance learning environment
✱ Teachers expand and share effective classroom strategies
✱ Teachers mentor each other via buddy system
✱ Develop a list of resources for teachers dealing with racism, ethnocentrism, classism, and cross-cultural curricula
✱ Increase knowledge and teacher responsiveness to cultural, ethnic, and gender diversity

Counselor Time

✱ Prioritize counselor responsibilities:
- — Evening student/parent counseling
- — Less time spent on data entry
- — Developing problem-solving skills among students
✱ Review and revise counseling responsibilities regarding discipline
✱ Increase interfacing with and utilization of social agencies and community organizations

Parent Involvement

✱ Seek parent involvement; acknowledge its many forms (e.g., helping with homework, positive role modeling, school committees, visiting classrooms)
✱ Explore a variety of communications methods
✱ Positive-parenting seminars
✱ Parent exchange/team building
- — Neighborhood coffee/tea
- — Provide space for a parent room/office on campus (with coffee, phone, resources)
✱ Explore ways to make parents feel comfortable on campus
✱ Explore contractual agreement for parent involvement

Special Concerns

✱ Encouragement and opportunities for students who are failing at the end of the year—teacher responsibility
✱ Budgetary considerations and impact on programs:
- — Reduction of district counselors and support staff
- — Increased class size at secondary level

Middle school, or junior high, is a transitional time when children are typically vulnerable and insecure. Students of this age may appear mature enough to need less adult guidance than in elementary school. However, it often seems that this is the stage when they need the greatest amount of interaction with adults and positive role models. Parental involvement, generally weak during junior high school years, should be encouraged. In order to effectively carry out a plan such as the one outlined in this section, parents must be a strong presence on campus, assisting staff and volunteering in a spirit of teamwork, collaboration, and support.

AN INTERVIEW WITH AMY
(17 years old, California)

Amy was diagnosed at a young age with learning disabilities and ADD.

Tell me about your favorite teachers in school.

"My best teacher was in second grade. She expected so much of you and she made learning fun. She wasn't mean, but she was firm. She gave me individual time, had me come up to the board, and really talked to me. When I had trouble concentrating, she had me sit at a table with walls around it, but it wasn't a punishment. It was just so I could work without distractions. It was a very supportive classroom.

"My history teacher last year was very understanding. You were supposed to read a whole chapter at a time, and at the end of each section, answer the questions. I worked really hard but couldn't get it done in time. Then I told my teacher that I have a learning disability. I am dyslexic. He gave me all the time I needed. I was never frustrated or nervous in his class."

How about your worst classes?

"In tenth grade my math class was so difficult for me. I would raise my hand for ten minutes and the teacher always ignored me. He would walk right by me and never listen to me or help."

What is your advice to teachers?

"Teachers should be understanding of the child's needs. If the kid says, 'I just need a little more time on this,' the teacher should say, 'O.K. Would you like more time tomorrow? Do you want to take it home or do it in the Learning Center?' Sometimes teachers are so difficult, you just want to cry. You get so frustrated!"

Actual Case Studies
With Intervention Plans

*T*he following examples are case studies of two students who have required a great deal of intervention and team planning. These two students illustrate the challenge of reaching and teaching children with ADD, with or without hyperactivity.

Case Study A: Steven
An ADD Student With Extreme Hyperactivity

Steven came to our school this year as a third grader after experiencing much frustration and failure in his previous two schools. He had most recently been attending a parochial school; his school records and teacher reports indicated that he was capable of doing the work, but "chose" not to. They viewed him as a major discipline problem. He had significant behavioral and emotional problems and was underachieving.

When his mother came to register Steven, she met with the school nurse and me, asking that he please be evaluated to see if he qualified for special education. She was very distressed as she recounted his history, describing his previous school not recognizing Steven's special problems and needs and being very punitive in their approach to him. Steven was also having significant problems at home. His mother described him as sweet and loving, but often difficult to manage. He was frequently explosive and angry, could not maintain friendships, and had low self-esteem. She felt he was bright, but had great difficulty doing the work in school. Steven's mother was very anxious and concerned about her son, and hoped he would do well in our school.

His mother also brought a letter from the family physician requesting that the school assess Steven, indicating that Steven very likely had attention deficit disorder with hyperactivity. However, he had not prescribed any medication. Both parents, particularly his father, were uncomfortable with the idea of medication. In addition, Steven had seen a therapist for about a year, but therapy was discontinued. Steven also received private tutoring in reading and math.

School Action

First, we assured the mother that Steven would be welcome at our school and that we wanted to work closely together to ensure Steven's success. We requested a four-week intervention period during which we could observe Steven, his teacher would have time to get to know him, extra assistance could be provided by regular educators, and we would informally assess his needs. Since his classroom had other students who were in my resource specialist (learning handicapped) program, I would work immediately with Steven along with my other students when I served his classroom. This would also be part of the informal diagnostic process. Steven received a full assessment a few weeks later (which included academic, psychological, health, perceptual-motor, and memory tests). He did meet the eligibility criteria for special education services. A significant discrepancy existed between his ability (measured IQ) and his achievement in reading, math, and written language. This discrepancy was determined to be caused by a learning disability in visual-motor integration and visual sequential memory. It was also obvious to all that Steven displayed certain behavioral characteristics (e.g., high activity level, inability to sit or control impulsive acts, talking out) to a severe degree.

We had an Individualized Educational Plan (IEP) meeting during which time we all met (both parents, teacher, principal, nurse, psychologist, and resource specialist). We discussed test results and observations. We identified learning strengths and areas of weaknesses and determined that Steven qualified for special education. We planned and wrote goals and objectives and identified a few behaviors to work on to help Steven improve.

After about five weeks of regular communications with the classroom teacher and trying some additional interventions, it was clear that Steven required much more assistance in addition to the special education services he was now receiving. We asked his parents to come in for another meeting and shared all of our observations, what we were currently working on, and that additional intervention would be required.

It is critical that such meetings be conducted in a spirit of cooperation, sensitivity, caring, and respect for the parents' feelings and comments. It is counterproductive to bombard parents with large group meetings where they feel intimidated and defensive. Fortunately, his parents knew we were all on the same side. The school nurse and I discussed current recommendations of a comprehensive treatment plan for ADHD.

Steven had a strong need for physical outlets. Prior to this meeting, his parents were considering the possibility of enrolling him in martial arts classes. His classroom teacher told how impressed she was with his agility and felt he had a talent and strength for gymnastics and acrobatics. She recommended he pursue more training in this area or in dance, which Steven demonstrated he likes and for which he has a natural ability. Unfortunately, some of the flips and cartwheels he was doing were in the classroom!

The issue of medication came up. Steven's parents were given literature and resources to read and were provided with classes by specialists in the community that addressed medical treatment for ADD/ADHD. We asked if we could share our concerns and observations with their physician. Both parents agreed and at this point were willing to pursue medical intervention, including outside evaluation with physicians who specialize in this field if needed.

The following is my summary and input at this meeting. This letter, along with test results and teacher input, was forwarded with written parental consent to the family physician:

Regarding Steven X:

Date:

Dear Dr. _____ ,

I am very concerned about Steven's ability to function at school, both in the large classroom and in the small group settings. It has been my observation over the past month that Steven is unable to maintain attention or remain seated for more than a few minutes. His excessive movement and impulsivity (e.g., talking out inappropriately in class, frequently falling from his chair, doing flips in the class when the teacher turns her back) are extremely disruptive and have a strong negative impact on his ability to achieve. Steven is missing much of the teacher instruction because he is unable to settle down, listen, follow directions, and follow through on assignments.

I believe Steven wants to comply with rules and behavioral expectations to please his teacher. However, a great many of his behaviors seem to be beyond his control and awareness. His classroom teacher has already moved Steven several times because he is unable to sit near the other children without bothering them constantly. He is unable to complete any assignments without someone sitting directly with him and keeping him on task and focused. We are going to try having Steven use a study carrel (partitioned office area) to help block out distractions for him and give him more "space." We are also going to begin a behavioral contract to use in the classroom for monitoring behaviors and communicating with parents on a daily basis. Our school counselor will be assisting the teacher with this.

In the small group setting, I have been using behavior modification with positive reinforcement and a great deal of structuring and cueing. Even with these interventions, and only five other students in the group, Steven is having significant difficulty attending to task and controlling disruptive behavior.

Steven is a very likable and affectionate boy. We are all willing and eager to do whatever is necessary and possible to help him succeed at our school. However, he is in need of far more assistance than we are able to provide for him.

We have a number of students at this school with medically diagnosed ADD/ADHD. Our team believes in working closely with parents and physicians to help coordinate efforts on behalf of the child. Please feel free to contact me at any time.

Sincerely,

Name, title
School name
School phone

Follow-Up

Steven was placed on medication in November. Throughout the following weeks up until Christmas vacation, we were monitoring use of the medication and communicating with parents and physician as to its effect.

There were definite improvements in Steven's behavior. He was better able to remain in his seat without excessive motion and the need to get up and roam. He was better focused on instruction. However, Steven was having difficulty with all the activity and change in routine around the holiday time. Steven's class and the other third grade classes were doing a lot of special activities, frequently working together. We recognized the need to come together again as a team and form a consistent plan that all the teachers and aides who worked with Steven throughout the day would adhere to, and that his parents were aware of.

The following intervention plan was written, distributed, and explained carefully to all parties.

Intervention Plan

Student: Steven X

Date plan is written:

Members of team present:

School and Grade:

Behavior Modification

Steven will be monitored for behavior and work completion by all school personnel (teachers, aides, tutors) throughout the day. A weekly behavior modification chart is used, broken up into segments of the school day (approximately 1 hour each). Steven is to carry the chart with him from class to class (except lunch).

Note: Steven's third grade teacher did a lot of team teaching with the other two third grade teachers. The three classes rotated for various subjects and activities during the week.

During each time segment, the teacher (or aide) will signal Steven when he begins to act inappropriately (talking out, excessive movement, noises, etc.). The signal will be to quietly and privately get Steven's attention and to cue him by holding up one finger (as first warning), two fingers (second warning), or three fingers (last warning). If Steven gets four fingers up during that monitoring session, he loses the opportunity to get a star on his chart for that period of time.

If he does not need more than three fingers up, he will receive the positive reinforcement on his chart.

Work completion will be monitored and reinforced on the chart during those same time frames. Steven's work receives a separate star or teacher's initials if he has been putting forth good effort and has accomplished a reasonable amount of work during that time.

Rewards / Reinforcement

It was decided that if Steven receives ten stars for work completion on his weekly chart by Thursday afternoon, he will earn the privilege of playing computer games with a friend of his choice in the classroom (or resource room) on Friday. Any stars earned Fridays for work completion will count towards the following week's reward. The classroom teacher was given a variety of software programs (math games that Steven enjoys) by the resource specialist to use for this purpose.

Note: Once Steven meets with success at the ten-star level for work completion, the criteria will be gradually raised.

It is recommended that parents provide a lot of praise and positive reinforcement when Steven demonstrates good effort in work completion and behavior throughout the week. They may also wish to reinforce his efforts with a special privilege at home.

Organization, Structuring, and Study Skills

1. Steven receives a weekly packet of homework from his teacher every Monday that includes assignments due on Friday. The resource specialist or classroom aide will see Steven individually on Mondays to go over the homework packet and clarify as needed. Parents need to make sure this packet is removed from his backpack, helping him organize and structure his time at home to complete and return homework by Friday.

2. Steven uses the *Skills for School Success* program in his classroom. On the assignment calendar in his binder any additional assignments (projects, tests, book reports, field trips, etc.) should be recorded on the "due date." Teacher, classroom aide, or student buddy will monitor and make sure that his assignment calendar is kept up-to-date and accurate. Parents need to check the calendar and know that regular homework (in packet) is due on Friday.

Additional Assistance

1. As Steven needs additional practice with basic skills building, a packet of additional activities will be prepared for him and sent home as parents requested. The resource specialist will gather and prepare extra math drills, games, and practice activities that he can keep at home and work on as needed. The classroom teacher will let parents know which stories/units Steven is reading in class and suggest activities to work on at home. However, this additional work is not required.

Note: Realistically, most parents find it almost impossible to keep their children caught up with regular homework, and additional academic practice, particularly worksheets and drill, is not to be expected or recommended. However, both parents requested the above and we complied.

2. District counselor will start seeing Steven in a group with some other students with similar needs to work on appropriate ways to deal with anger, impulse control, and other social skills, as her schedule permits.

3. Teacher will arrange to have sixth grade cross-age tutors come to class and assist Steven (keeping him on task) as needed during seat work time.

4. Steven will continue with his present schedule in the resource specialist program with a combination of in-class and pull-out services daily.

Environmental Modifications and Observations

1. Steven will be given a large working space—no one else sitting next to him sharing a table. He will continue to use privacy boards to block out distractions during seat work. He will be seated next to well-focused students. These environmental modifications will need to be monitored and changed if they don't work.

2. The school nurse, district counselor, and/or resource specialist will make classroom observations, if possible, when Steven is in rotation and with his own and other third grade teachers. The nurse will continue to monitor and communicate with the physician regarding Steven's adjustment/behavior as medication and schedule are regulated.

Communication With Parents and Assistance

1. Parent facilitator (a service we have through special education in our school district that consists of trained parents working for the district who have children in special education, and who are knowledgeable and familiar with the system) will contact parents for support and assistance if needed.

2. Parents will continue to receive information from the school team regarding appropriate parenting classes in the community, ADD support group information, literature, etc.

3. Resource specialist (RS) will share plan with parents and site staff. All teachers and aides will be trained by RS regarding the finger warning system and charting of behavior. Nurse will send copy of plan to physician. If Steven begins receiving private counseling again, therapist will also be given a copy of plan.

4. Team will meet with parents in five weeks for a progress review.

Evaluating Progress

As a result of the large amount of input, communication, and commitment from everyone working with Steven, he ended up having a successful third-grade experience. He made some friends and finally kept up with most of the classroom assignments. Most important, he started feeling good about himself. A child with such significant needs required much more intervention than most children with learning disabilities and/or ADD. It isn't possible to execute such an intensive intervention plan for a large number of students. However, every school could target a few (or even one or two) students to zero in on rigorously.

Steven's classroom placement and progress in the following grades need to be carefully monitored. We know that the challenge is far from over and that Steven is going to continue to need extra assistance, management, and structuring of his life. We are hopeful and optimistic that he is now on the road toward success and will continue to make great strides academically, socially, and emotionally.

Case Study B: Randy
An ADD Student Without Hyperactivity

Randy (fourth grade) had attended our school since kindergarten. In second grade he was referred by his teacher to our site consultation (student study) team. His teacher shared how intelligent he seemed to be. He had strong math skills, his comprehension was high, and he was a talented artist. However, he had a very difficult time getting any work done. Writing and reading were laboriously slow. He seemed to daydream a lot and had trouble listening and paying attention.

He was receiving a number of interventions within our regular education program, including basic skills tutoring and small group one-to-one assistance from the teacher, classroom aides, and cross-age tutors. His assignments were being modified so he had less to write and extra time to complete them.

We tested Randy and found him to qualify for special education. He, like Steven, had a very high ability level, but was significantly underachieving due to learning disabilities in visual-motor integration and visual-sequential memory skills. We had an IEP meeting, and Randy became one of my students. Throughout the rest of the school year he received a great deal of extra assistance in reading and writing skills. As I worked with Randy, it became clear that his greatest need was to be able to focus on instruction, get started, and complete tasks.

Team Collaboration

Randy's second-grade teacher and I met again with his parents a little later in the school year and devised additional interventions to work on, including rewards for work completion, shortened assignments, accepting oral rather than written reports which were so extremely frustrating for Randy to complete, and a home plan for monitoring his homework and getting his assignments back into his backpack for school. We expressed our concern about his inability to focus or pay attention in class, discussing the possibility of an attention deficit disorder. We would also pay close attention to his classroom placement next year.

The following year, in third grade, Randy had another wonderful teacher who spent a great deal of time and effort trying to meet Randy's needs. His teacher understood and accommodated Randy's difficulty with writing and speed of output. He did everything at an excessively slow rate—moving, organizing himself, and especially writing. Randy wasn't at all disruptive in class. He tended to be quiet and could easily go unnoticed.

We worked collaboratively to ensure that Randy was receiving assistance in both the classroom and a small group pull-out. Environmentally, he was provided with a study carrel, seating up close, teacher cueing, private signals, etc. We used Randy's talent and love for drawing as a reward, and he was usually the designated illustrator in cooperative learning groups and projects. In spite of all the assistance and teacher concern, Randy continued to do poorly in his day-to-day assignments. He was definitely gaining fluency in reading and writing skills. However, he was still very disorganized, did not turn in assignments (even ones that we worked together on and he completed) and did everything at a snail's pace.

Randy's teacher and I worked closely with him—talking to him and involving him in decisions and plans that we wanted to try. We provided assistance (from teacher, aides, or peers) in writing down assignments, helping to organize his materials at school, and making sure he got his things in the backpack to go home in the afternoon. We both kept in close communication with Randy's parents about long-term assignments, upcoming tests, and so on. Our frustration mounted through the year when very few assignments (shortened to be reasonable for Randy) were turned in, various behavior modification and incentives proved unsuccessful in motivating Randy to improve study skill behaviors, and Randy's self-esteem was, if anything, deteriorating.

Additional Interventions

We met again as a team with his parents and planned additional strategies. Once again we discussed the possibility of ADD being a part of the picture, in addition to Randy's learning disabilities. His parents decided to have Randy see a counselor (child psychologist) they had heard about. We also gave them more information and resources regarding ADD, parent support groups for LD and ADD, materials to read, and people in the community to contact. We were delighted that they were going to involve a private counselor, letting them know that we welcomed an outside person on the team who could assist and work with us to help Randy achieve.

It was interesting that the therapist, during his one-to-one sessions with Randy, decided that his problems were due to low self-esteem. He felt that the teacher wasn't trying to accommodate his needs. He didn't believe Randy had any difficulty with focus and attention unless he was bored. He told us that Randy was a very bright boy who needed time to do things his way, and that we needed to nurture his creativity.

We found this to be very frustrating and an unfair interpretation of what was going on in Randy's classroom. We invited him to observe Randy in the classroom. Once the therapist did finally come in to observe for about an hour, he was able to see some of the many adaptations, modifications, and interventions that the teacher did indeed employ for Randy. He also observed Randy's distractibility and his inability to get any independent work done that we were so frustrated about. I mention this to encourage teachers, parents, and site teams to invite, indeed urge, outside doctors, therapists, and others working with our students to see them in the setting of their daily lives—the classroom.

Medication

Randy was passed on to fourth grade the following year, although his achievement had not met the fourth grade level in most skills. We took great care in his classroom placement and teacher. His new teacher was chosen because we felt Randy would do well with her teaching style and personality. She is lively, has a wonderful sense of humor, and provides many hands-on projects and cooperative learning activities. She also is structured and organized, and has excellent home-school communication. She provides immediate feedback and a lot of encouragement to her students. She also does not let anything slip by and makes sure that her students keep up with requirements.

Unfortunately, Randy still displayed the same behaviors and difficulty with study skills. His teacher and I worked closely, and we shared the load of monitoring Randy, calling parents and communicating with them when assignments weren't being turned in, and so on. After the first few months of school, his parents finally decided to pursue a medical evaluation for Randy with one of our city's top specialists in attentional disorders. Randy was diagnosed as having ADD, and a trial of medication was initiated. Immediate improvement was found in his ability to stay on task and attend to instruction. He appeared more alert and increased his rate of output somewhat. However, organizational problems, completing and turning in homework, and other long-term problems did not improve.

Later in the school year, we met again as a team to formulate and write a comprehensive intervention plan for him. The following is a copy of this plan.

Intervention Plan

Student: Randy X

Date plan is written:

Members of team present:

School and Grade:

It was decided at the team meeting with parental agreement and cooperation that the following plan will go into effect for Randy:

1. Continue services in resource specialist program with RS and her aide going into classroom twice a week, and with Randy's group coming to resource room four times a week for half-hour sessions. On Wednesdays, Randy comes with unfinished classroom work/projects to RS and/or aide for assistance, if needed.

2. Resource specialist to begin training Randy on computer/keyboarding skills. This typing/keyboarding training will be increased next year, as

Randy will need to become more proficient in word processing/typing as he approaches secondary school.

3. Teacher will continue to monitor homework assignments and send home slips for parental awareness and signature for any assignments not turned in.

4. Teacher will collect Randy's homework directly from him every morning.

5. Teacher or study buddy will check before the end of the school day that assignments are recorded and books are taken home. It is Randy's responsibility to check with teacher or study buddy before leaving at the end of the day.

6. Parents are to check backpack, binder, and assignment sheet daily. It is recommended that Randy's parents structure an after-school routine with him to help him plan and follow through on homework assignments. School and home need to work together to help him learn to be organized and accountable. The possibility of an after-school tutor (perhaps a high school student) was discussed.

7. Parents to structure together with Randy's input:
    — a place in the house to do homework
    — a time he will do homework
    — where he will keep all supplies/materials
    — daily time and place for parents to check his backpack, binder, and assignment sheet
    — who to call if uncertain about any assignment
    — consequences if work is not completed
    — positive reinforcement (reasonable reward or privilege given when Randy meets expectations for the week)

8. Parents to try techniques such as:
    — Helping him write a *Things to Do* list daily. This list is an action plan that he can refer to and cross items off as he completes them.
    — Randy responds to a "beat the clock" incentive to keep him on-task. Parents may try setting a 10- or 15-minute timer while he works. Check for completion and accuracy in small time increments.

9. The school will continue to inform parents of classes or workshops in the community that address issues affecting students with ADD and Randy's needs.

10. Nurse, teacher, and resource specialist will observe Randy carefully and provide feedback to parents and physician as needed regarding any changes in behavior and output that may be resulting from the medication.

11. Teacher will continue to employ the numerous learning styles strategies and environmental modifications she is currently using in the classroom:

— Cueing Randy

— Using study carrels/privacy boards

— Teaching with multisensory, interactive techniques

— Cooperative learning (students working on activities with buddies and in small groups)

— Clear expectations, follow-through, and communication

— Modification of Randy's assignments as needed: More time for output and test-taking, shortened written assignments, and allowing Randy to dictate some work or share his knowledge orally, rather than writing it on his own.

12. We will continue to look for some positive motivator that Randy may be interested in working for. So far, we have not succeeded at home or school in finding an effective incentive.

13. As Randy responds to loss of privilege when he doesn't perform, he will continue to lose some recess time to complete assignments as needed. (This needs to be monitored carefully so that Randy isn't regularly missing recess since he also needs his recess time.)

14. Principal will speak to Randy to let him know that she is interested in how he is keeping up with his work. She will also be monitoring and positively reinforcing him.

Evaluating Progress

Since Randy is a special education student, his progress will be reviewed at annual IEP meetings with parents, teachers, and other team members. The challenge continues in finding ways to help Randy achieve to his potential, feel good about himself and school, and find the right mix of ingredients at school and home to help him succeed. Little by little, the pieces are coming together. Our goal for his last two years in elementary school is to wean him from all of the extra assistance he has required, and to help him become self-motivated, self-aware, and equipped with study skills so he can do well in junior high and high school.

Summary

Both of these case studies illustrate the reality of how difficult it is to find what works for any given child. Most critical in helping these children is the educator's commitment, caring, and effort. It takes a tremendous amount of extra work on the part of the adults involved to make a difference. What we plan doesn't always work. We need to keep on trying and revising our plan. We can't afford to give up.

How Administrators Can Help Teachers and Students Succeed

As mentioned briefly in Section 2, administrative support is important in providing an effective educational experience for ADD/ADHD students.

Administrators need to be trained, together with their teachers, in learning what ADD/ADHD is and is not. They need to increase their sensitivity and awareness of why these children behave the way they do and the appropriate interventions that should be implemented at school.

In order for teachers to employ effective academic and management strategies, they need to have opportunities to attend workshops, seminars, conferences, and other professional growth activities. Administrators who understand and respect this need will allow, encourage, and support all teachers in their quest to improve their skills.

Administrators should ensure that teachers have time within their working week to meet with other teachers (particularly at their grade levels), share ideas and strategies, and plan together. It is also helpful for teachers to observe and even coach each other. Teaming and collaboration require time. Administrators should support any collaborative effort and make this a priority.

Administrators need to be aware of what kind of instruction is taking place in all classes, as well as the emotional climate in the classroom. Innovative techniques, cooperative learning, and hands-on projects are not always the quietest of activities. Administrators should appreciate and encourage teachers to experiment with "new" approaches that actively involve students in the classroom.

There are teachers who are not effectively teaching their students. They may be "burned out," inflexible, or unwilling to change or grow. Consequently, they are shortchanging their students. These teachers should be strongly motivated and encouraged by administrators to improve their teaching skills through whatever means are available.

Any teacher who is harming children by humiliating, embarrassing, criticizing, and intimidating them must not go unchallenged. Administrators have the responsibility to place the children's needs first and must deal with such teachers firmly.

Administrators should make sure their staff is trained in ADD/ADHD and learning disabilities—and how to provide multisensory instruction and appropriate interventions. Every school site committed to reaching and teaching all students should include at a minimum training in the following:

* Cooperative learning

* Study/organizational skills

* Learning styles

* Multiple intelligences (Howard Gardner)

* Teacher expectations and student achievement

* Gender and ethnic equity and student achievement

* Tools of technology (computer literacy)

* Higher ordering questioning techniques (e.g., reciprocal teaching, Socratic seminar)

Administrators need to support teachers who have very disruptive students in their classes. Many students who are extremely difficult to manage in the classroom are ADHD children. If any teacher has a disproportionately high number of ADHD or other special needs students, administrators should look into the possibility of lowering the number of students in that class, furnishing more aide time, and providing other creative ways to assist teachers. Look carefully at the composition of each class. Many times the "dynamite" teacher, who is skilled in working with students with special needs, gets overloaded. Reward these excellent teachers, who care about their students and are willing to take on more than their share, by providing extra assistance and support.

A teacher cannot effectively teach a class when a student is out of control and very disruptive in the classroom. When such incidents occur, and regular behavior management techniques don't work (e.g., time-outs in classroom), it is important that the student be sent out of the classroom.

Administrators need to assist by providing for other out-of-classroom areas with supervision for time-outs and "cooling off." They should be responsive to teacher calls for help, and explore all means and options at the school site to find appropriate interventions. It may be necessary to arrange for a child to have a temporary period of being in school for only half days rather than full days. In-school and out-of-school suspensions are other possibilities.

In some cases, depending on whether the school has other support staff on site, the administrator may need to be the person (together with the teacher) who makes recommendations to parents regarding psychological, academic, and medical assessment, tutoring, counseling, parenting classes, and so on.

Other Positive Ways Administrators Can Help

1. Be available and willing to attend parent-teacher meetings/conferences when requested as a supportive third party and team member interested in helping the child.

2. Get involved individually and personally with the students—talking with them, welcoming them when they arrive at school, calling by first name, giving pats on the back, smiles, and hugs, applauding achievements, and doing anything else that elicits a positive response from students.

3. Promote a proactive team approach to working with students who are experiencing difficulty in school. If a school site does not have support personnel (nurse, counselor, psychologist, special education teacher, speech therapist), a team can be created that consists of a few knowledge-able, caring staff members who are willing to undertake this responsibility.

4. Encourage upper-grade classes to team up with lower-grade classes. Have these older students go into the lower grade classes to help students in need. A cross-age tutor can often effectively sit next to an ADHD child, calm him/her, and keep the child focused and on task.

5. Make positive phone calls to parents when targeted students are caught doing something good. Calling parents with positive news is very effective, and unfortunately, little used. One principal makes a major effort to track down a parent with "good news" (including at work or even shopping) and finds that parents are very surprised and appreciative. Parents seem to always expect negative phone calls and, therefore, many dread and avoid returning calls to the school.

6. Encourage and arrange for parents of "challenging" students to spend the day "shadowing" their child at school. This means being in the classroom and following the student throughout the day. This is a very effective method of curbing disruptive behavior in middle and junior high school students particularly. While the parent is on the campus for the day, it is helpful for that parent to meet with the team (teacher, principal, and other support staff members) to discuss and plan strategies beneficial to the child.

7. Sometimes it requires major involvement on the part of administrators to maintain a child at school, and to facilitate "speeding up" a necessary special education evaluation/placement for children unable to function in a regular classroom. There are ADHD children who even though they may be only six years old, can become so aggressive, violent, and out of control that they destroy an office, attack six-foot adults, and wreak havoc throughout the school!

We have had a few students over the years at my elementary school who have been "extremely challenging." I have a great deal of respect for how our administrators lend their direct support to teachers and become actively involved with the child, the family, and the pursuit of appropriate intervention. They demonstrate compassion, flexibility, and the ability to maintain their sense of humor and perspective.

An effective administrator truly cares about children, is visible and accessible, has an open-door policy with staff and parents, and creates a working climate where all parties feel appreciated, comfortable, and part of the team. The administrator is the key person who can set the emotional tone of the school and work to eliminate negative forces which create unnecessary stress. The administrator must communicate through example and expectations that the school's priority at the school site is the success and positive self-esteem of every student!

Team Teaching and Teacher Partnerships

*T*eam teaching is advantageous for a number of reasons—both to students and teachers. If teachers are able to find a partner in the school willing to team with them, one of the main benefits is being able to teach your area of strength and interest. Teachers can put greater planning, energy, and enthusiasm into teaching what they enjoy and feel more skilled at. No one teaches every subject well. This strategy allows teachers to plan only certain subject areas and to teach the same lesson to both classes.

The Advantages of Team Teaching

At my school, for example, two sixth grade teachers decided to team teach last year for math and social studies. One has a love of mathematics and is very skilled at teaching the subject with manipulatives and hands-on strategies. She is much less enthusiastic about teaching social studies. The other sixth grade teacher feels less comfortable about teaching math but is highly creative and truly enjoys teaching social studies and all of the related projects. Students in both classes reaped the benefits of enthusiastic teachers and a highly enriched curriculum.

Teachers who team teach report that another advantage is being able to share students for part of the school day. It is common for a student who is "acting up" in his/her classroom to be well-behaved that day in the other classroom. The opposite, however, can also occur. Students who are familiar with the structure and expectations in their own classroom may have difficulty in the other class with different teacher expectations and rules.

Nevertheless, team teaching allows teachers to "get a break" from certain students who may be irritating them that day.

Students benefit from team-teaching because of their exposure to different teaching styles and personalities. Again, students are being enriched and motivated by teachers who are enthusiastic about their subject matter.

Enrichment Wheels

Enrichment wheels are another way to rotate students and allow them to have the experience of interacting with a variety of teachers and students from different classes and grade levels. At my school, all third through sixth grade classes participated last year in the wheel for one hour per week on Friday afternoons. Students across the grade levels were mixed and rotated to each of the teachers during the course of the year. Teachers worked with each group of students for a period of a few consecutive weeks before the groups rotated. Teachers chose an area of interest that they were responsible for teaching throughout the year to all groups. Topics and activities included: music, folk dance, Spanish immersion, Japan, the rain forest, clay, jazzercise, travel, and cooking. Students gained from exposure to and involvement in the wide variety of enrichment activities and from the social interaction in their multi-age, heterogeneous group.

Teaming for Disciplinary Reasons

Teacher partnerships for disciplinary purposes are often helpful. As discussed in the Behavioral Management section, it is often effective to have students who need "time out" or "time away" to go to other classrooms (rather than to the counseling center or office). Some teachers find it helpful to arrange a quiet desk in their room for students to use for a time-out. Students are sent to the partner class (same grade or different grade) for a specified period of time without acknowledgment or attention by students in that room. Some teachers prefer to send the student with work that must be done. Others prefer to have the child do absolutely nothing. In either case, the receiving class is rewarded for not paying attention to the student during this time.

Network, meet, and plan together frequently. Teachers who are able to work together and share each other's ideas and strategies are usually the happiest and most successful. If your administration allows for coverage of your classroom, it is helpful to observe your peers during instruction. All sites have a wealth of ideas, skills, and expertise. This needs to be shared by teachers working together, communicating with and observing one another. A spirit of cooperation and collaborative effort is much more productive than one of competition and isolation. An observing teacher-buddy can also be very helpful in sharing strategies and interventions for the hard-to-manage/hard-to-teach student in your class.

Using Tutors and Volunteers to Help Students in the Classroom

When students are unable to maintain attention and are acting out with negative behavior in class, teachers are in great need of more assistance in the classroom. Unfortunately, with budget cuts in many districts, classroom aides have been reduced and teachers are struggling even more. Many of our students are unable to work or complete assignments independently without someone keeping them focused and on task.

Creative Ways to Bring More Assistance Into the Classroom

Peer tutors. Give students in your classroom opportunities to teach other students. Make use of all the students in your class to ease the teaching load by having them pair up and work with each other. This is too valuable a resource in every classroom to waste since students often learn best from their peers.

Cross-age tutors. In many schools, classes of different grade levels form partnerships. Upper-grade classes (e.g., fourth grade) go as a whole class once a week into the lower-grade class (e.g., first grade). Students are assigned buddies and given specific tasks to do. For example:

* Read books to younger students, ask the questions, and write down their answers.

* Assist students with art projects.

* Interview the younger children and record their responses.

* Older children take dictation from the younger children.

In addition, the upper-grade students gain an appreciative, captive audience for sharing some of their own creative work. They can read their own stories or books they have written and show off their special projects to the younger children. This system is very popular at my school and beneficial for all students involved. We notice a bonding between students that carries over onto the playground, on the bus, and in the cafeteria.

Cross-age tutors can also be used for specific students only. Lower-grade teachers need to find an upper-grade teacher willing to release a few students more frequently. Students who are very difficult to maintain in the classroom without one-to-one attention need a rotation of cross-age tutors who can come assist (and yet not miss much of their own instruction in class).

Additional Sources of Assistance

✳ **Parent volunteers** are another valuable resource that should be utilized in the classroom whenever possible.

✳ **Senior citizens**. It can be a wonderful partnership to access retired seniors to volunteer in classrooms. Churches, synagogues, retirement homes, and senior citizen groups can be contacted for this purpose.

✳ **Partnerships between elementary and junior/senior high schools** may be possible, with interested secondary students coming to the elementary schools to offer their time and assistance.

✳ **School/business partnerships** are forming across the country. My school is fortunate to have both a business partner of a major publishing company, as well as the partnership of a Navy unit. The students particularly love when the Navy people (from the TACRON division) come in uniform and volunteer in the classroom. They have been involved with some very special projects with the children, for example, helping the sixth grade students put together a video newscast.

✳ Many counseling centers train **student conflict managers** to help resolve problems that arise on the playground.

✳ **Use of peers** (same age or older) is very helpful with students who have ADD/ADHD. They often respond well to social skill intervention and modeling from peers better than from an adult.

✳ Allow **the student with special needs** to also be a peer or cross-age tutor. They gain in self-esteem and academic/social skills through the experience of helping others. Typically, children with special needs can work very effectively with a younger child.

School Documentation and Communication With Physicians and Agencies

When a child is being evaluated by a physician or agency for possible ADD/ADHD, the school will be asked to furnish information about the child. In all cases, be sure that the parents have signed a release-of-information form that grants the school permission to communicate and share information and records with the doctor or agency.

Questionnaires and Rating Forms

Frequently, there are questionnaires and rating forms that teachers (or school counselors, school nurses, and other support personnel) are asked to fill out. Typically, the teacher will be asked questions such as:

* Describe the child's strengths.

* Describe the concerns/child's difficulties.

* Describe the current educational functioning levels and performance.

* Has the child had any testing or school assessments?

* Does the child receive any special education services?

* How does the child get along with other children? adults?

* What services are available at the school?

* Has the child ever repeated a grade?

Many times there is a list of several behaviors, and the teacher needs to indicate by a check mark in the appropriate box whether the behavior is observed:

not at all, moderately, or very much. Sometimes the rating scale is by numbers (1–5).

In addition, teachers may be asked how the child is performing in a variety of academic skills: far below grade, somewhat below grade, at grade, somewhat above grade, far above grade.

Even though it is sometimes an inconvenience to complete these forms (especially when teachers are swamped with other paperwork and responsibilities), it is very important to do so. Teachers need to take the time to fill out the forms and write their observations/concerns in as detailed a manner as possible. This is a professional responsibility that needs to be taken seriously.

There is no specific test that determines if a child has ADD/ADHD. The diagnosis involves a number of factors, with behavioral assessment (e.g., through rating scales and observations) comprising a significant part of the evaluation and diagnostic process.

DECKER
FORREST

Teacher Documentation

Teacher documentation of specific behaviors exhibited by the child is very helpful to a diagnostician. Examples include: emotional/behavioral outbursts, frustration exhibited by tearing up papers, inability to stay on task/work independently as noted by completing only one or two math problems during a 20-minute independent seat work period, and so on.

Teachers use a number of systems for jotting down notes to themselves to save as "mind joggers" for documentation, reasons for referrals, parent/teacher conferences, and other purposes. Some teachers have a ring of index cards with each student's name on a different card. Whenever something occurs in class that the teacher wants to recall, she jots down the incident and the date on that student's card. Some teachers carry a pad of stick-em notes in their pocket. When they want to write themselves a note regarding a student, they use the stick-em and place it in their lesson plan book. Later, they transfer all of these notes into a folder that they keep on each student. These anecdotal records together with a collection of work samples are very useful sources of documentation.

When records are requested from the school, someone (generally a member of the student study team) needs to make copies of the previous report cards and any documentation in the child's records that may indicate that those behaviors which are of concern have existed for a while. When previous teacher comments and reports indicate that the child displayed difficulty with attention, listening, self-control, and distractibility for the past few years, it is very important clinically.

Besides report cards, it is worthwhile to include any documentation at the school site that indicates the need for disciplinary action, (for instance, copies of classroom, playground, lunch, and bus referrals to the office or counseling center). Copies of any consultation team/SST referrals and action plans and school assessments, reports, IEPs, etc., should be copied and sent.

Sample Cover Letters to Physicians/Agencies

The following letter is a sample of one sent to the doctor along with other appropriate documentation, records, and reports.

Date

Regarding: Lucas Z.

To whom it may concern (or Dear Dr. _____):

Lucas has been referred to our school site consultation team in first and second grades. He was also assessed for special education in first grade, with an IEP held on (date).

Enclosed are copies of his IEP, assessment reports, and referral forms. He was referred for testing in first grade due to academic difficulty in all areas—reading, math, and written language. He displayed poor self-control, having great difficulty settling down, staying on task, and controlling impulsive behaviors. Lucas's first-grade teacher described him as "cooperative, enthusiastic, seems to be bright."

My notes from the site consultation meeting on (date) include the following comments from Lucas's first-grade teacher: "Lucas is very inconsistent in his attention to task. He seems to have an auditory strength. He is lovable, with an outgoing personality. His behavior is erratic and impulsive. He can settle down, but flits from one idea to the next. He is always blurting out answers and directing everything, but he can't stay still." His kindergarten teacher also described Lucas as needing to "develop self-control."

As a result of this meeting, the team worked with Lucas and the teacher. Recommended strategies for students with possible attention deficit disorder were shared with his teacher. Lucas was to continue with basic skills tutoring, speech/language services for articulation needs, small group, peer/cross-age tutoring, and working with the counselor on specific behaviors (contracts, charts, positive reinforcement). Our district counselor was to recommend some free or affordable parenting classes to mother.

Later that year, the school tested Lucas. He did not qualify for special education because he did not meet the eligibility criteria. (See psycho-educational testing and reports.)

This year (second grade) Lucas was referred again on (date) to the site consultation team by his teacher, (name). She was and is still concerned about the same behaviors. He is noted as having a very high activity level, lack of self-control, and impulsive behavior. He is continuing to receive interventions of school counseling, small group assistance, basic skills tutoring, and many in-class interventions (change of seating, behavior modification, close communication with teacher and parent, someone working with him and assisting directly for much of the day). The team has met with Lucas's mother and discussed our recommendation that she pursue a medical evaluation for Lucas.

We are very concerned about Lucas. He is still trying hard to please and is very sweet and likable. He continues to receive maximum intervention within regular education. His behaviors are continuing to interfere with his success in the classroom. We appreciate your assistance in helping this child.

Sincerely,

Name, Title

Phone Number

The following letter is a communication between the elementary and receiving junior high school alerting the team of an incoming student with very significant needs. The letter is also a plea for the school to do whatever is possible to keep trying to obtain the needed help for this boy. It also illustrates the frustration and reality that, unfortunately, teachers and schools have to deal with—children with severe needs which we cannot meet because "our hands are tied." Frequently (due to lack of funds) programs don't exist, or the child doesn't qualify for them. In this case, the parent did not agree to school recommendations for program placement—without parental approval, the school cannot act.

Date:

Student: Damien N.
Birthdate:
Grade:

Dear _____,

Having worked intensively with Damien over the past few years, I would like to share my observations and recommendations at this time. My concern for

Damien is that he will very likely have a difficult time adjusting and coping next year in junior high school. My hope is that he will receive a great deal of assistance in his transition to the secondary setting, especially with his social and emotional needs.

Damien has been medically diagnosed as having attention deficit hyperactivity disorder (ADHD) as well as learning disabilities. He displays all of the classic behaviors associated with ADHD, including: high activity level/great need for mobility, extreme distractibility and impulsive behavior, difficulty staying seated, always touching and playing with objects around him and invading others' space, very sensitive to noises around him, and oblivious to social cues, resulting in difficulty functioning with adults and peers.

Damien has episodes of out-of-control behavior during which he is unable to remain in the classroom. On these days, he typically has not received his medication. Teachers need to be aware of and sensitive to his needs. Usually, when Damien receives his medication, he is capable of far more self-control and the above-mentioned behaviors are more manageable.

Damien is a bright, capable boy with a lot of potential. He has a strong interest and aptitude for math and science. I would like to see him have every opportunity to participate and advance in math and the sciences. Damien has always been weak in reading and language skills (writing and oral expression) due to a learning disability in auditory sequential memory skills. In spite of some difficulty, Damien still has the ability to do most of the work at his grade level (with some modification and assistance).

He underachieves in his classes every year. Due to his low tolerance for frustration, he often resists or refuses to do work that he perceives as too difficult. Often days that go by when he will not produce any work in class or only a minimal amount. Typically, Damien is not motivated by incentive programs (rewards, privileges). Great care has always gone into placing Damien in classes with teachers who are nurturing, sensitive, and skilled in working with children with special needs.

Damien is a loving, affectionate boy. He is very good with younger children and is sweet and warm-hearted. He is also quick to anger and is often upset and tearful. Adults who know him well can see beyond his behaviors which are often disruptive and inappropriate. He is very vulnerable and likely to be "led into trouble" if the opportunity arises.

My greatest concern for Damien is the strong social and emotional factors that impede his functioning at school. He is very easily frustrated and "shuts down" frequently in class and in the resource room. When he doesn't feel like working or participating (which occurs frequently and unpredictably), he will not open books, join the rest of the class, or answer teacher questions.

Damien is very moody, and it is impossible to predict how he will function on any particular day. His moods and behavior fluctuate drastically. He very rarely smiles or shows signs of being happy at school. He is quiet, soft-spoken, and rather shy. Often he appears sullen and possibly depressed.

Socially, he has a very difficult time and has never had any close friends at school. Other children basically tolerate him but don't seek him out as a friend.

Damien does not pick up on social cues (facial expressions, tone of voice, etc.) as most children do. This is one of the characteristics of ADHD, and one which causes him trouble and conflict with others. He is often in the middle of a conflict and frequently isn't aware of his part in it. Damien is in great need of training in social skills and appropriate responses, as well as control of impulsive behavior. He has received a great deal of counseling in school, including assistance/training in conflict resolution and dealing with anger and frustration appropriately However, his needs are such that in-school counseling is not sufficient.

We have spoken to Damien's mother on several occasions regarding the importance of having him see his physician for a medical examination and follow-up. His medication may need to be regulated or changed. He strongly needs outside counseling for the severity of his behavioral and emotional problems which need to be treated and carefully monitored. We are not equipped to deal with all of Damien's needs adequately at school. Further intervention and assistance is needed.

As you can see (attached assessments, IEPs, recommendations), our team has been very concerned about Damien for several years. Every school year we have had several team meetings regarding how to best meet his needs. Damien's mother is very difficult to get in touch with and often does not speak to us when we call. We have gone to the home, met his mother at her workplace, written letters, and involved a parent facilitator. Damien has had extensive assessment—in addition to annual review meetings, we have conducted a few "review of placement" IEP meetings as well. Damien has qualified and been eligible for more intensive special education services in a smaller class setting that may have better addressed his needs. However, the parent has never agreed to or permitted a change of placement or followed team recommendations for more intervention.

We hope you will be successful in helping Damien obtain the appropriate care and assistance he needs. Please let me know if I can be of any assistance to you.

Sincerely,

Name, Title

Phone Number

School Referrals, Assessment, and Special Education Placement

*T*eachers and parents who are concerned about a student's performance, behavior, or achievement in school should have an open avenue for requesting and obtaining assistance. The first step should always be a parent-teacher conference. Teachers must always communicate with the parents, sharing some positive observations about the child along with any concerns. When teachers discuss concerns during the conference, they should also share the strategies they plan to implement (for example, moving the child's seat up closer to the teacher, providing some small-group or one-to-one assistance for the child from the teacher and/or aide).

Parents should always take their concerns directly to the teacher as a first step as well. This is proper protocol in most schools and is often communicated to parents at the beginning of the school year by the administration.

Once parent-teacher contact has been made, an action plan and strategies are implemented by the teacher. If more intervention is needed, the student should be referred to the student study team (SST) or consultation team (CT), if one exists at the school.

Note: The terms student study team (SST) and consultation team (CT) are used interchangeably; terminology varies from school to school. There are probably other names for this team, as well.

Have You Tried These Interventions and Modifications?

Before the referral process, ask yourself if you've tried numerous interventions to help a particular child. The following list of interventions will help you answer this question.

Environmental

* Seating up front, close to teacher
* Giving student extra workspace away from distractions (e.g., the door, centers)
* Limiting visual distractions/clutter
* Designing room to accommodate different learning styles
* Seating among well-focused students
* Turning off the lights
* Using music during certain periods of the day to calm and relax students
* Use of study carrel or privacy board for seat work

Organizational

* Assignment calendar used daily
* Teacher, aide, or student buddy to assist with recording of assignments
* End-of-day check by teacher/aide for expected books/materials to take home
* End-of-day clarification of assignments/reminder to students by teacher
* Things-to-do list taped to desk
* Beat the clock for work completion

Increased Home/School Communication

* Daily or weekly home/school communication to be signed by parents (indicating behavior and work completion)
* Increased phone contact with parents, remembering to share positive observation as well as concerns
* More frequent conferences/planning meetings with parents

Teaching Techniques and Individualizing for Students

* Consistent expectations and consequences
* Allowing extra time for processing
* Allowing extra time for completing tests
* Increasing the amount of modeling, demonstration and guided practice
* Providing for frequent breaks and opportunities to move
* Providing significantly more positive reinforcement
* Regular feedback and progress check

✱ Private, personal cueing

✱ Modified, shortened assignments

✱ Contracts/positive reinforcement for on-task behavior, work completion, increased time in seat, and improvements in impulsive/disruptive behaviors

✱ Accommodating written output difficulties (e.g., allowing oral responses, dictation rather than writing, reducing written requirements)

✱ Extra one-to-one assistance (e.g., teacher, aide, parent volunteer, cross-age tutor, student/peer buddy)

✱ Teaching calming, think-before-you-respond strategies

✱ Providing frequent breaks and opportunities to move

✱ Many opportunities for hands-on activities and projects

✱ Multisensory instruction: using clear verbal presentation, many visuals, color, movement

✱ More modeling, demonstration, and guided practice

✱ Frequent opportunities to work cooperatively with a partner or small group

✱ Many opportunities to be able to verbalize in class and respond in a "safe" climate without fear of ridicule

✱ Encouraging and allowing use of computer

Teamwork

✱ Involving your Site Consultation/Student Study Team

✱ Meeting with the parents to build a partnership for helping the student

✱ Buddying up with another teacher/classroom for time-away/time-outs as needed

✱ Letting student know you are interested in helping him/her: dialogue with student, encourage open communication

Student Study Team/Consultation Team Process

The student study team or consultation team is a multidisciplinary team of professionals serving the school site who meet regularly, usually for an hour or two to:

✱ hear the concerns and discuss students who have been referred, and

✱ plan as a team some appropriate interventions to be implemented.

Members of the team (always including the classroom teacher and sometimes the parent) leave the meeting with an action plan and assigned tasks. Members of the SST may include:

* classroom teacher

* school counselor

* special education teacher/resource specialist

* school nurse

* principal

* school psychologist

* speech/language therapist

* adaptive p.e. teacher/motor skills teacher

* any appropriate person at site or as invited by the team when planning for a specific student

In my school district, the consultation team is a function of regular education, not special education. It is important to make that distinction clear. Not all students who are referred to the consultation team are referred for academic problems or are candidates for special education. The district counselor coordinates and facilitates the consultation team. It is the teacher's responsibility to sign up on the calendar and schedule time to attend a consultation team meeting. Teachers are asked to bring work samples to the meeting and to fill out a referral form which contains the following information (see pages 214-216).

Identifying Information

Student name, address, identification number, teacher, grade, room number, parents/guardian name, home phone, work phone, ethnicity, language of instruction, etc.

Checklist of Items That Appear to Describe the Student

Health/Physical Factors

_____ 1. Health problems _____ frequent complaints

_____ 2. Frequent absences/truancy

_____ 3. Appears pale, listless, apathetic

_____ 4. Extremely active and restless _____ fidgets

_____ 5. Possible deficit: vision/hearing

_____ 6. Poor motor coordination: _____ fine _____ gross

_____ 7. Growth or development lag

_____ 8. Physical injuries (not from physical abuse)

Speech/Language Factors

_____ 1. Limited speaking vocabulary

_____ 2. Difficulty relating own ideas

_____ 3. Incomplete sentences _____ poor grammar

_____ 4. Responses are inappropriate

_____ 5. Difficulty following directions

_____ 6. Articulation: mispronunciation of speech sounds

_____ 7. Stuttering: speech blocks, breaks, poor rhythm

_____ 8. Voice: quality is hoarse, harsh, too soft

Education Factors

_____ 1. Academic difficulties _____ Reading _____ Math _____ Written Lang

_____ 2. Poor retention of subject matter

_____ 3. Poor handwriting or reversals _____ messy work

_____ 4. Difficulty staying on task _____ inattentive

_____ 5. Difficulty comprehending directions _____ subject matter

_____ 6. Difficulty changing activities

_____ 7. Easily discouraged, often frustrated

_____ 8. Work completion: _____ rushed _____ slow _____ fails to finish

Personal/social Factors

_____ 1. Generally withdrawn, timid, fearful

_____ 2. Poor self-control _____ temper outbursts _____ inapprop. language

_____ 3. Poor peer relations _____ fights _____ disturbs others

_____ 4. Seems unhappy _____ moody _____ cries easily

_____ 5. Feelings of inadequacy, low self-concept

_____ 6. Fantasizes _____ exaggerates _____ lies

_____ 7. Challenges authority _____ defiant _____ impulsive

_____ 8. Shows little empathy/concern for others

Student Strengths

Teacher is asked to identify the child's strengths.

Parent Contacts
dates, purpose/outcome

Teachers must have already discussed their concerns with parents prior to referral to the student study team. We ask teachers to tell parents in advance that they have made the referral to the team for the purpose of brainstorming and planning some additional ways to help their child. Parents are also told that they will be contacted after the team meeting to share the intervention plan. Many schools invite the parent to the consultation team meeting. At our school we have found that for the initial meeting (due to time constraints), it is more productive not to invite parents. However, if parents ask to attend, they are certainly welcome, and in some cases we do request that parents attend.

We schedule three to four 15- to 20-minute slots for our weekly consultation team meetings. We are also fortunate to have coverage from a certificated staff member during this time to go to the teachers' classrooms while the teachers attend the CT meeting. When we schedule follow-up CT meetings, parents are frequently invited at that time.

A proactive consultation team (student study team) encourages this identification process at their school. They prioritize early identification of problems and want teachers to bring to their attention students who are displaying any number of difficulties—not just those who teachers think may need special education. Teachers are encouraged to refer students who are exhibiting health, behavior, attendance, academic, or social problems. Throughout my school district there is a staggering number of students who are referred because they are displaying the characteristics and behaviors associated with ADHD.

Special Education Referrals

Special education referrals may come directly from a teacher or parent requesting that a student be tested to determine if he/she qualifies for special education services. This referral process begins a legal timeline during which the designated case manager

* prepares paperwork;

* informs parents of legal rights;

* obtains parental permission in writing;

* contacts all parties involved to prepare their assessment plan for the parents to agree to (in writing); and

* has a multidisciplinary team assess the student, write their report, and meet with the parents in an IEP (Individualized Educational Plan) meeting.

We strongly encourage teachers and parents to refer their students through the consultation team/SST process first (although this is not a requirement). It is a requirement that a variety of interventions and modifications be implemented for a period of time and documented before a student is permitted to be assessed for special education. The SST/consultation team process is an ideal means of gathering resources and putting heads together in an effective, efficient manner to address the needs of students and make this intervention plan. Then, if more help seems warranted to meet the student's needs, it is appropriate to pursue assessment for special education. Any special education referral must include documentation of interventions that have been implemented. (See page 211 "Have You Tried These Interventions...?")

Student study teams may recommend and form an action plan that involves a number of possible interventions. Often particular team members will leave the meeting with the responsibility for:

* observing the student in various settings;

* helping the teacher create a behavior modification plan (contracts, charts, reinforcement systems);

* meeting with parents to further share and discuss concerns;

* making home visits if warranted;

* employing classroom strategies and modifications (including instructional, behavioral, and environmental); and

* providing small group, one-to-one assistance from available resources.

Obtaining a Comprehensive School Evaluation

Students who are referred for special education are required to receive a thorough, multidisciplinary assessment bound by legal procedures and timelines. Not all students who display the characteristics of ADD/ADHD will require special education assessment or services. If the student is achieving in the classroom and his/her behaviors are not significantly interfering with his/her ability to function successfully, there is no need to pursue the route of special education. Many students with ADD will be able to perform and achieve at a successful level when appropriate teaching strategies, environmental/organizational modifications, and other regular education interventions are employed. This is, indeed, our goal.

However, there are many students who will continue to have significant difficulty functioning and achieving, in spite of numerous interventions. These students should be assessed and any services they may qualify for should be provided. A psycho-educational evaluation includes:

* observations;

* examination of school records and history;

* health/developmental history from parents;

* vision and hearing screening;

* academic, cognitive, psychological, perceptual-motor testing; and

✱ depending on other indicators and needs displayed by student, an assessment of speech/language and motor skills by appropriate professionals.

Many students with ADD/ADHD also have specific learning disabilities. It has been my experience over the past several years that at least one-third to one-half of my LD (learning handicapped or learning disabled) students display the behaviors and characteristics associated with ADD/ADHD even if they do not have the medical diagnosis or receive medical intervention. "The incidence of identifiable learning disabilities among children with ADHD may be as high as 30 to 40 percent, according to some researchers." (Lisa J. Bain, *A Parent's Guide to Attention Deficit Disorders*, p. 26.)

Who Is a Learning Disabled Child?

To be classified as having a learning disability, it must be proven that the student (1) has *at least* average intelligence, and (2) has a significant discrepancy or gap between his/her intellectual ability (determined by the school psychologist) and his/her academic achievement. Reading, math, and written language levels and standard scores are determined on one-to-one achievement tests given by the educational specialist, special education teacher, or resource specialist. The student does not have to be performing far below grade level, at least in the state of California. He/she does have to be seriously underachieving relative to his/her measured ability or IQ. For example, if a student has an IQ of 100, standard scores on the achievement tests of around 78 and below would indicate a significant discrepancy. Scores above that would probably not. However, other factors could be taken into consideration.

A very bright student, for instance, with an IQ of 135 may be scoring at grade level with standard scores of around 100 in reading, math, or written language. This child would meet the first part of the criteria for being classified learning handicapped or learning disabled, since there is a significant gap between his/her ability and achievement.

Note: This criterion may vary from state to state.

Processing Deficits

The other part of the criteria for being classified as learning disabled and eligible for special education is that the significant discrepancy between ability and achievement must be due to a deficit in one or more areas of "processing information." The child is *not* having difficulty achieving academically because of social or cultural deprivation, physical or mental handicap, or emotional distress (such as problems occurring in the home). Children with learning disabilities have a significant weakness in either the *reception* (taking in), *integration* (processing, organizing, retrieving, and making sense of), and/or *expression* (output) of information and language. They have difficulty manipulating symbols (which affects reading, writing, and math). Each child is unique and presents a different profile of strengths and weaknesses.

Note: Even if a student is tested and meets the eligibility criteria, whether that child is placed in a special education program is always an IEP team decision, with parents an integral part of the team. Any special education services are always contingent upon parental approval.

What Are Auditory Processing Deficits?

Auditory processing deficits may include a deficiency in discriminating sounds, sequencing sounds, recalling what is heard, and comprehending or assigning appropriate meanings to the auditory input. When there is a deficit in auditory processing, the student typically has a hard time following teacher lecture, conversation, or learning that is delivered at a rapid or even normal rate. Generally, these students need more time to process, comprehend, and/or deliver information. Teachers should present the auditory information at a slower pace, repeat it, and give the student more think time. They must also provide a lot of visuals to help the student compensate for his/her auditory processing weakness.

If the student has difficulty with auditory discrimination, he/she usually has trouble recognizing and hearing the difference between similar sounding words (pin/pen, bad/bat, hut/hot). ***Note:*** Students with other primary languages often have difficulty hearing the fine difference between similar sounding vowel sounds, particularly the short *i* and short *e* sounds. These students, however, do not have a learning disability.

The majority of students I have taught in my years of teaching children with learning disabilities have significant weaknesses in auditory sequential memory. This is the ability to recall the correct order or sequence of the things they hear, particularly letter sounds and symbols. Students with this difficulty are inevitably poor spellers and usually have great trouble memorizing math facts, memorizing information for content area tests, and following directions. Children with auditory sequential memory deficits generally have significant problems learning to read, recalling letter/sound association (particularly vowel sounds and consonant blends), and decoding or sounding out words with many errors in sequencing of the sounds/syllables.

It is sometimes hard to sort out during the assessment process if students who perform poorly on tests of auditory sequential memory (measured by repeating verbally a series of words or numbers immediately after the examiner) had difficulty with the task because of a memory deficiency or due to inattention. Many ADD/ADHD students do poorly on this task but may not have a learning disability in auditory sequential memory. Conversely, many ADD students actually do have a learning disability in this area as well.

What Are Visual Processing Deficits?

Visual processing deficits may include significant weaknesses in *visual perception* (e.g., discriminating the difference in size, shape, or position of objects and symbols in space, causing numerous reversals, inversions, rotations), *visual-motor integration* (copying correctly from the book to paper, board to paper, writing within the lines, organizing written work adequately), and *visual-sequential memory* (recalling what they see, particularly letters, numbers, and other symbols, in proper sequence).

Students with visual sequential memory problems typically have serious difficulty remembering the "little words" when spelling or reading. They may have good sounding out skills and apply phonetic strategies effectively to decode and spell the longer words. It is the basic sight vocabulary (of, said, from, who, what, etc.) that they don't recall when they read and spell. They may also have great difficulty recalling math facts.

Students with perceptual problems make letter reversals and inversions past age seven, and generally have trouble reading clock faces, keeping their place when reading (skipping lines, rereading lines), and following directions and position in space. Many have weakness in fine or gross motor skills.

I don't recall ever having an ADD/ADHD student in all of my teaching experience who did not have some weakness with written output. My learning disabled students who also have ADD/ADHD typically test as having a deficit in visual-motor integration. They often have terrible spacing between letters and words, form letters in an awkward way, exhibit difficulty in cutting and coloring, produce illegible work, etc.

It is interesting to observe that many children who receive medication for treating ADD/ADHD show a significant improvement in penmanship, general neatness of product, and the ability to organize written work, stay within lines and write/copy at a more appropriate pace. However, this is certainly not always the case.

Some students who have ADHD are in serious need of a special education placement. Their needs are such that they are not able to be met in regular education, even with a tremendous amount of assistance. These children are usually referred immediately because of the seriousness of emotional, behavioral, and social problems they present. The school team should prioritize these referrals and expedite the process as needed for these children. If the student is known to an outside agency, permission should be obtained from parents to communicate and share information with the agency or physician. Parents must be included in information-sharing meetings and planning strategies. Shortened time periods between SST meetings and follow-ups will probably be necessary—during which time observations can be made by SST members and a variety of interventions can be put into place.

AN INTERVIEW WITH BRAD
(34 years old)

Brad, a chaplain in the Navy, was diagnosed at 28 years old as having ADD and dyslexia.

Who helped you and made a difference?

"My mother was very supportive. She played an important role in my decision-making process. My mother would let me run things by her—like an article or things I was planning to do. She helped by acting like a filter, so I wouldn't make a lot of the mistakes that would come back and bite me. She gave me a lot of psychological approval.

"When I was diagnosed, I worked with a specialist for three years. She was excellent. She helped me improve my socialization skills and communication. With dyslexia, it's all tied together. The inconsistency in how you process language filters down on many levels. My mind skips from A to B to G to D to F. It was clear to me what I meant to say, but not necessarily to the listener. She helped me with my writing. I would run past her some of the writing assignments I was working on, and she would help me see when it wasn't linked together . . . it didn't flow. Through her help I developed an 'internal clock.'"

Tell me how you improved socially.

"I had no problems meeting people and getting dates. But after two or three dates, that was it. I knew when the dates were successful and the girl was interested, and I would ask to get together again. But, I wanted to know then the date and time of the next date. It wasn't an issue of insecurity, but I was seeking clarification. Everything in my world was black and white. There was no gray area. One of the ways the specialist helped me was to deal with the gray area. I realized it was O.K. to ask a girl if I could give her a call later . . . no pressure."

How do you remember ADD affecting you when growing up?

"Teachers attributed my problems to laziness or inattention to detail, even though I spent hours doing my work. I spent so many more hours than anyone else did. I always wondered why I didn't get an *A*. I would fall asleep during class. At school I would sit ten minutes and be ready to get up and move somewhere else. I always blurted things out in class and couldn't wait to talk. All the kids did that to an extent, but I was 'big time.' I didn't interact well socially. I had friends . . . I did the things everyone else did, only at the wrong time. Others got away with it, but I didn't. They knew when and when not to do something. I didn't realize there was a time and place for everything. I was doing things that were appropriate for kids maybe a few years younger.

"When we would get together and visit family, there were only two things I would talk about—the Navy and rabbinic school. Anything else . . . I was a wallflower. Looking back I can see that there were thirty people there and several separate conversations going on at the same time. I couldn't focus or follow any of them. By the time I got involved in a conversation, I was behind everyone else."

How has your life changed since you were diagnosed?

"Once I found out, I set my own agenda. You can say, 'Look. I can do this work, but I'll have to have extra time. Maybe I need to have an extra semester or year.' I had no problem with spending an extra year in rabbinic school—my ego was not on the line. Once I knew, I was able to ask questions . . . I wanted to find out everything. I started Ritalin at twenty-eight. It improved my ability to concentrate tremendously. I was able to sit down in front of the computer and write a paper. I was able to take notes in class, and interact much more effectively. I didn't fall asleep in class. I only took (take) 25 mg a day, which isn't much, but it has really helped my ADD. Some of my grades went from *C*s to *A*s, which is very gratifying when you're in an academic environment."

section
29

Exemplary Model Programs

This section turns the spotlight on three outstanding programs in the nation that make a tremendous difference in the lives of students. Other school districts may wish to investigate further. They are:

* Project for Attention Related Disorders, San Diego

* Key School, Indianapolis

* Mentor Program, Minneapolis/St. Paul

In the San Diego Unified School District, the PARD Project (Project for Attention Related Disorders) is a systemwide, collaborative approach among school personnel, medical/psychological communities, and families to best support children who have ADHD. It was developed in part through a federal grant (Maternal and Child Health Program, Health and Human Resources, Healthy Tomorrows Program).

In Indianapolis, the Key School has achieved almost celebrity status for its teacher-initiated reforms and innovations. It is based upon Harvard psychologist Howard Gardner's theory of multiple intelligence (MI). The Key School is, to quote Gardner, "The most innovative education experiment in the country."

The Mentor Program in the Minneapolis/St. Paul area is an outstanding program designed to provide senior high school students the opportunity to explore and study their career interests in depth by working directly as a protégé with a professional in that field.

Project for Attention Related Disorder (PARD)

PARD was started in 1989, as a result of a three-day conference on ADHD held in San Diego. This conference brought to the surface the frustration and concern of school personnel, parents, and community professionals regarding children with attentional problems accessing appropriate care and intervention. At that time there was no systemwide approach to identification or intervention when a child displayed focusing or attention problems. Most school personnel did not have the awareness of or skill to help ADD students, and it was difficult to obtain a diagnosis of ADD since so much of the diagnosis depends on subjective observation. Often, little or no information from the school accompanied these children when they visited a physician in the community.

The San Diego schools were fortunate to have Jeff Black, M.D., F.A.A.P., as its consulting pediatrician and Dorothy Davies Johnson, M.D., F.A.A.P., specialist in neurobehavioral disorders and learning disabilities. Together, with an advisory community group from the school and community, they wrote a grant proposal outlining the following goals and objectives of the PARD project—To improve the physical and mental health and educational outcome of children identified with ADD/ADHD by:

* increasing the knowledge base of individuals working with children who present ADHD (school personnel, parents, physicians, and other community providers);

* improving the coordination of school/community services to ADHD children and their families; and

* establishing an ongoing school-based system for identifying, evaluating, and managing ADHD children.

The Health Services Department in the school district put together an itinerant team of school personnel to serve as consultants to schools. The team consists of a school nurse practitioner (one day/week), district counselor (one-half day/week), and psychologist (one-half day/week). All the people on the core team came with training and day-to-day experiences in dealing with the frustrations and joys of having a child with ADHD. Mentor teachers from the district also lent their ideas and expertise in giving direction to teachers.

Dorothy Davies Johnson, M.D., F.A.A.P., wrote a manual, *School-Physician Collaboration for the Student With Attention Difficulties: Handbook for Intervention,* which includes information, assessment, and follow-up tools, and strategies. In addition, the PARD project contracted two community resources with strong experience and existing programs for children and parents.

Education is a major goal and component of the PARD project. School nurses were trained to be the primary coordinators of the assessment-gathering component, responsible for referral to community physicians and ongoing communication regarding the child's progress. Counselors and psychologists in the schools were trained in social skills development and parent support. Teachers and administrators were offered several workshops and inservices throughout the district on ADD/ADHD.

Another valuable service was offered by PARD. Schools were able to request and schedule a day for Dr. Johnson to come to the school. During these scheduled visits, Dr. Johnson spent time observing a few targeted students that the school wanted assistance in helping, and then met with the consultation team and teachers of those students in a "debriefing session." Later in the day the full staff received an inservice on ADD/ADHD.

Pediatric consultants polled the medical community and enlisted the assistance of approximately seventeen physicians who agreed to see a couple of PARD project participants each month. Physicians were offered inservice opportunities by Dr. Johnson. **Note:** The PARD project was originally directed to low-income children with medical needs who had previously not had access to care. The process has ultimately been successful for the entire system in terms of diagnosis and treatment, since the forms for data gathering and referral can be used for any child, regardless of socio-economic status. Intervention strategies are also taught systemwide and are not limited to project participants.

The systemwide changes in San Diego that have occurred as a result of PARD are very positive and recognized by all parties. In the school system, there is generally a greater awareness and sensitivity to children with attentional issues, and the medical community is now more receptive to the school data that is sent to them.

It has been a wonderful opportunity and privilege to work with PARD as a mentor teacher in the San Diego schools. I have learned a great deal as a result of my involvement with PARD and its dedicated, knowledgeable leaders, especially Susie Horn and Dr. Dorothy Johnson. I have asked the coordinator of PARD, Susie Horn, R.N., to share the most recent assessment of PARD's effectiveness in San Diego:

"The PARD process of data gathering and referral has been extremely effective as evidenced by 1991–92 nursing statistics. Evaluation for ADD were done for 642 children, with 415 receiving diagnosis and treatment. We have addressed over forty school sites regarding ADHD and school strategies effective in working with ADHD students. Our district inservices for all employees have been well attended and well received. In the 1992–93 school year we will be working on new teacher training to provide the current techniques for teaching these most challenging students.

"Several difficult areas that PARD will be addressing in the next two years are meeting the needs of secondary students, parent support, and working with publishing companies to develop curricula for the unique needs of ADHD students. It has been extremely rewarding working with dedicated colleagues to support students, teachers, parents, and community providers who deal with attention deficit and hyperactivity disorder."

For more information about PARD, write to: San Diego Unified School District, Student Services—PARD Project, 2716 Marcy Avenue, San Diego, California 92113.

Key School

The Key School is a unique magnet school that was created through the efforts of eight elementary school teachers who taught together in Indianapolis. Through their belief, commitment, and hard work, they managed to obtain approval from their school district and additional funding from another source (the Lilly Endowment) to plan and establish the Key School in 1987.

The Key School is based on the latest research and philosophy of multiple intelligences, thematic teaching, and qualitative, meaningful assessment. The founding teachers (the "Key Crew") were successful in obtaining the input and assistance from a number of community resources. They also received direct involvement from Howard Gardner, author of *Frames of Mind*, and other scholars whose ideas they were implementing, such as Mihaly Csikszentmihalyi, Professor at the University of Chicago and author of *Flow: The Psychology of Optimal Experience.*

Teaching Staff and Students

The teaching staff at Key School includes eight classroom teachers and seven specialists. There are around 150 to 160 students attending the school who have been selected by a district lottery. African-Americans comprise 40 percent of the student body. About 40 percent of the children are from single-parent homes. One-third of the school's population is eligible for free lunches under federal guidelines. Students are grouped heterogeneously in mixed-age groups. Primary classes have a combination of students from grades 1 through 3. Intermediate classes have a mix of students from grades 4 through 6.

The curriculum at Key School is unique, emphasizing the seven intelligences identified by Gardner in *Frames of Mind*:

* Linguistic

* Logical-mathematical

* Musical

* Spatial

* Bodily-kinesthetic

* Interpersonal

* Intrapersonal

The curriculum includes almost daily instruction in music, physical education, art, computers, and Spanish. Traditional subjects are taught as well. Key School uses an interdisciplinary, schoolwide, thematic approach, with themes changing every nine weeks.

Other Special "Key" Features

1. **Project-oriented curriculum** with students required to produce a project that reflects the theme every nine weeks.

2. **Pods**. Students spend periods of forty minutes, four times per week, in multi-aged groups called "pods," where they are engaged in an activity of their choice over an extended period of time. Some of the specialized "pod" activities include architecture, choir, drama, physical sciences, mind, and movement.

3. **Flow center**. Students spend time in the flow center on three days of the week. This is a special room equipped with puzzles, games, and manipulatives. A teacher in the flow center spends time carefully observing and recording students' choices of activities, preferences, and level of involvement.

4. **Integrated arts program** taught by specialists. All Key students are exposed to and participate in a rich arts program. For example, all students learn to play a musical instrument.

5. **Weekly staff planning and evaluation sessions.**

6. **Extended day and after-school electives** which include activities such as photography, computers, and gymnastics.

7. **Advisory committee** from local businesses, universities, and cultural institutions.

8. **Extensive use of community resources** as part of the enrichment and after-school programs.

9. **Required parent commitment and involvement**. For example, parents must attend three of the four parent/teacher conferences if their child is to remain at the school.

A Pioneering Approach

Key School has taken a pioneering approach to assessment that is meaningful and reflects a child's true development. Some ways they assess and keep records on students' development and progress include:

1. **Videotaped portfolios**. The school tries to capture the child's interests and accomplishments. One way they do this is to videotape students' culminating thematic projects every nine weeks.

2. **Taped interviews** with the students.

3. **Student reflective logs** about the themes and their individual projects.

4. **Nontraditional report card**. It evaluates progress, participation, and motivation in numerous areas including:
    — Linguistics/language arts
    — Spanish
    — Musical instruments
    — Vocal music
    — Logic/mathematics

— Science

— Computer

— Research skills

— Spatial/visual arts

— Geography

— Bodily/kinesthetic skills—physical education

— Interpersonal skills/social studies

— Learning community/citizenship

— Leadership

— Flow activity

— Intrapersonal/Pod area

— Presentation of individual projects.

For more information about Key School, see sources:

Blythe, T. and Gardner, H., "A School for All Intelligences," *Educational Leadership* (April, 1990), 33–36.

Bolanos, P.J., "Restructuring the Curriculum," *Principal*, Volume 69, No. 3 (January, 1990), 13–14.

Cohen, D., "Flow Room, Testing Psychologist's Concept Introduces 'Learning in Disguise' at Key School," *Education Week* (June 5, 1991), 6–7.

Lytle, V., "The Best School in the Country?" *NEA Today* (September, 1991), 10–11.

Olson, L., "Children Flourish Here," *Education Week*, Volume 7, No. 18 (January 27, 1988), 16–19.

The Mentor Program

The Mentor Program provides capable and motivated high school students in the Dakota County, Minnesota area with an opportunity to learn at an advanced level. The students are able to experience career choices in a professional way as the protégé of an expert. By working with an expert in a field of their choice, students are able to learn skills that could not be taught at such a challenging level at their high schools. They also have a chance to get a realistic view of a career in which they have an interest. Students, often referred by teachers or counselors, apply for the program.

Mentor Seminar

Prior to connecting with a mentor, students must complete a 60-hour preparatory Mentor Seminar. In this integral phase of the program, students work with their

Mentor Program instructors to improve their self-awareness, communication, and independent learning skills. The seminar helps to insure that students understand and are comfortable with their personal goals for the mentorship, have a basic understanding of the field they want to further explore, and feel comfortable interacting with adults in the workplace. While the Mentor Seminar was developed for high school students, the skills taught can readily be modified for younger students. In addition, isolated segments of the course may be all a younger student needs to pursue an interest or feel more successful in his or her learning.

The following information about the Mentor Program was graciously provided by Dr. Jill Reilly, developer and current coordinator of the program. Dr. Reilly, author of *Mentorship: The Essential Guide for School and Business,* also shares her insight and recommendations on how younger students may access the benefits of mentoring, which could be a significant learning experience for the ADD/ADHD student in particular.

During the *Self-Awareness Unit* students' individual talents and interests are assessed along with their individual learning styles.

Students explore the educational requirements for entry into their chosen field and the basic duties and lifestyles which accompany that position. During this time students also consider additional personal circumstances—such as ADHD—which will affect their mentorships, and develop means to articulate their needs and cope in new circumstances. The Self-Awareness Unit assures the students and their instructors that the field in which they hope to be mentored is appropriate, that students have sound strategies for coping in their new environment, and the Field Experience will be a good use of both the mentors' and the students' time and energies.

In the *Research Unit* students find more recent, complete, and/or advanced resources in their individual fields of interest. They need to identify and locate libraries that hold professional periodicals in their fields and learn to use these resources. In this way students obtain the most current information in small portions. For ADHD students, databases and other technological advances in library sciences can alleviate frustration and ease students' searches for relevant materials. Learning to identify and locate community resources such as museums, theaters, businesses, clubs or organizations, wildlife centers, or specific individuals can offer alternatives to students who prefer not to read through telephone or face-to-face informational meetings. In the Research Unit students compile an annotated bibliography of their sources and may also complete a project that further expands their background and readiness for mentorship. Students have created everything from multi-media artwork to computer programs, and explored such diverse fields as neurosurgery and news reporting.

Finally, students polish their *Interpersonal Communications* skills. In this unit they consider the impact of their verbal and nonverbal expression on those with whom they come in contact. This unit stresses evaluation of individual skills and practice for improvement on students' abilities to handle introductions, telephone usage, appropriate dress, and personal presentation, etiquette, multi-cultural issues, conflict resolution, and personal assertiveness.

Reilly notes that if one skill must be taught to students, it is assertiveness. She observes that frequently young people are not taught to carefully consider and express their own needs in a learning situation. In order to assert those needs, students must first think about them. Consider the value of an ADHD student being able to state politely and respectfully, "Ms. Jones, I've discovered that I will learn much more quickly—and happily—if I can actually do something with my hands to help me/if I can get up and walk around the classroom for a few minutes every now and then/if I can see how this will be used in my daily life/if I can tape-record your lecture so that I can hear it over again a few times at home." This strategy may not always be effective, but, surely, the chances of having others recognize the students' needs increase measurably.

Mentor Program Field Experience

When students complete the Mentor Seminar and their individual needs are clear, program instructors approach professionals in the community about the possibility of becoming a mentor. If they wish to consider offering a student a Field Experience, the mentor, student, and Mentor Program instructor meet to further discuss and plan a mentorship. At this meeting any of the three people involved may decide that the Field Experience will not be viable. If each person agrees to the Field Experience, the mentor and student begin to develop a learning plan that outlines the knowledge, skills, and abilities that the student would gain. After a few meetings they decide on a learning project that will allow the student to demonstrate that he or she has indeed fulfilled the learning plan. The instructor monitors the Field Experience and offers assistance as needed, but is not involved in the day-to-day activities of mentor and protégé.

The Mentor Program Field Experience takes place in the last two periods of the school day. Students meet with their instructor once a week and leave school to work with their mentors the other days. Other, less time-intensive experiences can be developed for younger students. Mentors might be recruited to come to the school instead of having students meet at mentors' workplaces, and younger students will probably want to meet with their mentors less frequently. Once every two weeks, or even monthly can make a big difference to them. Also, younger students may not sustain their interest in an area beyond a few weeks or days. The school might also bring experts to work with an entire class, grade, or even the whole school, then allow the experts to work individually with a few truly committed students.

Benefits of the Mentor Program

The benefits of matching students with adults willing to share their skill, expertise, and enthusiasm are considerable (proven by the eight years of research compiled from the Mentor Program and other programs like it throughout the world). Many students find the experience and education they received through this type of relationship and on-the-job training to be the most exciting and valuable in their lifetimes. Students have gained diverse experiences such as learning about bird behavior and breeding, writing legal briefs in Federal District Court, creating a multi-media advertising campaign for a new community business, designing repairs for a 747 jet airplane with an aerospace engineer, and composing original music and producing it in a major recording studio.

Dr. Reilly has found that mentors also benefit from these experiences. Protégés expose mentors to their enthusiasm and fresh new ideas. Students are willing to work and eager to learn. Mentors have also found that they have been able to clarify their own goals by explaining them to a student and have gained skills in and insights into interacting with a young person.

For more information on the Mentor Program and establishing a similar program for any age group refer to: Reilly, J.M. *Mentorship: The Essential Guide for School and Business*, Dayton, Ohio: Ohio Psychology Press, 1992.

Or, write to: The Mentor Program, Dakota County Secondary Technical Center, 1300 East 145th Street, Rosemount, Minnesota 55068.

Children of all ages, abilities, and backgrounds can benefit from the opportunity to be mentored and guided in an area of interest. What a powerful learning experience it would be, particularly for our struggling students, to gain competence and self-esteem through a personal, one-to-one relationship with an expert. This kind of experience also brings additional resources to our schools on behalf of our children. What school can afford an electron microscope or a 747 jet? What school doesn't benefit from happy, healthy students learning about something that intrigues them?

The Role of Parents

Parents are in the position of being able to facilitate finding a role model or mentor to develop their child's interests and skills. Parents can connect their children with friends or relatives with a similar interest, take them to visit facilities that relate to the child's interests, or call professionals and ask if they would be willing to give 15 or 30 minutes to share their interest. These experiences can lead to ongoing mentoring if both parties are willing to sustain their interest. The following story illustrates how this was done successfully—

Dan's Story

Dan was a child with ADHD. He had a history of physical and emotional distress which centered around his experiences in school. By first grade, he had a lengthy medical history including chronic asthma, ear infections, and allergies. His behavior was impulsive and his teacher frequently telephoned home to tell his parents that Dan wouldn't stay in his seat and that they should try to better control his behavior at school. By fifth grade, Dan had been on Ritalin for several years. His health problems increased to include several surgeries. Although he achieved fairly well, but not "up to his potential," he had been held back a grade due to emotional immaturity. Dan now had much difficulty with peer relationships. His parents pursued every avenue they could find in their search to help him, but not enough changed.

During sixth grade Dan learned to cook, an activity that really held his interest. At the beginning of seventh grade he learned about a restaurant with a sports theme that interested him. He asked if he could see it. His mother, Marla, promised to take him when she could make time and afford the cost. One night Dan's mother and father unexpectedly ended up at the restaurant. Marla mentioned to the hostess that her 13-year-old son really wanted to visit the restaurant. The hostess said that if Dan wanted to visit about 1:00 P.M. on a weekday, she would take him on a tour of the kitchen and he could watch the chef at work. The hostess gave Marla her card.

On their next mutual weekday off, Marla and Dan had lunch at the restaurant. When Marla made reservations, she reminded the hostess of their conversation. Dan not only enjoyed the meal, but he met the chef, Peter, and watched him work. Peter told Marla and Dan that he was impressed with Dan's mature behavior and interest. He said that Dan could come back and observe sometime during the summer.

As soon as school ended for summer vacation, Dan called Peter and asked if he could come in to visit. It was a long ride from his home to the restaurant, 30 minutes, but his parents agreed to transport him. Once each month Peter allowed Dan to come in. First Dan observed, but gradually Peter allowed him to assume certain tasks. Dan loved it! Peter and the rest of the cooking staff began to include Dan in their exchanges of records and in their friendship.

One day after about four months, Peter asked Marla for a "parent-chef conference." Peter asked if Dan was really learning anything and if he liked it. Marla's first thought was that Dan was "messing up," but she told Peter that Dan was baking desserts and showing her "meal presentation" tips. Peter said he was concerned about whether Dan was truly interested. Marla thought he was.

Months went by and Dan continued to help out. He got As in cooking, and his organizational skills improved as did his relationship with others including his peers. Gradually as he began to perceive himself as competent in his work at the restaurant, Dan seemed to feel more competent in other areas.

Dan was really excited when Peter told him that he had graduated and could come in every other week. After over a year invested, Peter told Dan that he really needed him to help with preparation for Saturday nights. Dan was really "staff" now, and Peter gave him his own staff T-shirt. Soon after that, some of the young staff members asked Dan to go to a concert with them. Dan's confidence swelled.

Dan continues to work at the restaurant. Currently he's working on his driver's training anxiously awaiting the time he can transport himself to the restaurant more often. Dan plans to graduate from high school in three years instead of the usual four and is taking effective steps toward that goal. When he graduates, he knows he wants to enroll in a four-year college hotel and restaurant management program. He has even selected colleges to apply to. So far, Marla reports that Dan has maintained the academic credentials which will help to ensure his college admission.

No one can be sure what contributed to Dan's personal growth—age, the neurochemical changes of puberty, and the attention Dan received at school and at home probably all helped. What seems pivotal, however, is the attention and skill Dan has gained from Peter. Dan knows what he enjoys and that he can become a competent professional one day. He also knows that Peter cares about him and believes in him. In terms of his education, and how he feels about what Peter has taught him, Dan told me the following:

"Peter is such a good communicator. He takes his time and tells me how to do things. He taught me what it means to do 'teamwork.' Peter 'cultures me' and he has fun when he's mentoring me, too. Peter is my top learning experience!"

Child Advocacy:
Going the Extra Mile

When people make the personal commitment to do all they can for children, with open hearts and willingness to give beyond their job descriptions, there is no limit to what they can accomplish. I have been extremely fortunate to be part of such a caring, nurturing, and committed team of professionals for the past several years at Benchley-Weinberger Elementary School, one of the magnet schools of the San Diego Unified School District. Ours is a multi-ethnic school of approximately 500 students, with the majority of our population bussed in from various parts of the city. Our mission statement and program goals reflect the collaborative vision of our school community.

Mission Statement

It is our mission to provide a magnet program that promotes the development of talents and abilities that will lead to the academic and social literacy of our students while continuing to develop responsibility and respect for self, others, and the community. We seek to provide a program that no longer views teaching as instructing "to" the learner, but rather makes a dramatic paradigm shift to doing things "with" the learner at a conscious level. We, the staff at Benchley-Weinberger, are committed to enhancing and valuing the special contributions of each child, including their talents, diversity, and uniqueness.

Program Goals

The Benchley-Weinberger staff recognizes that our focus is promoting academic excellence and self-esteem utilizing a collaborative school/community approach to developing life-long learners through:

✳ attention to learning styles

✳ providing a variety of teaching strategies

✳ providing a nurturing environment for learning

✳ developing respect for cultural diversity

✳ recognizing individual talents and abilities of students and staff.

I strongly believe that what makes the difference for our children are the people we have at our school—

The Human Factor

1. **Teachers who:**

   — believe in and are committed to learning style differences;

   — make strong efforts to meet the needs of all learners;

   — accept each child and appreciate his/her uniqueness;

   — are creative, challenging, and maintain high expectations of all students;

   — have knowledge and training in effective, interactive, multisensory teaching strategies;

   — work collaboratively as a full team;

   — implement interventions and modifications, putting in extra time and effort for the success of each child; and

   — encourage and welcome parents and volunteers in the classroom.

2. **Administrators who:**

   — encourage and support personal growth opportunities for all teachers and staff;

   — make the effort to know the children, welcoming them personally with a smile and a hug;

   — encourage and support current teaching strategies in the classroom;

   — make personal, daily contact with students, and frequent contact with families;

   — involve themselves in student study/consultation team, supporting the collaborative effort;

   — respond sensitively to students' individual needs and placement; and

   — place child's needs as top priority.

3. Parents who:

— are interested and actively involved in the education of their children;

— support the school's efforts;

— communicate with teachers;

— take advantage of educational opportunities to increase their knowledge, awareness, and skills; and

— educate themselves regarding their children's needs, in order to support their children and be effective advocates.

4. A Support Team (nurse, resource specialist/special education teacher, counselor, psychologist, speech/language therapist, adapted P.E. specialist, etc.) that:

— is proactive, prioritizing early identification and interventions for children;

— works cooperatively with teachers and parents;

— is knowledgeable and well-versed in learning disabilities, ADD/ADHD, and appropriate interventions;

— gets involved with parent education;

— is highly involved with staff development/teacher education;

— is visible and accessible to children, parents, and staff;

— interfaces with social workers, professional counselors, and physicians who may be involved in child's care;

— makes referrals to appropriate social agencies or educational resources;

— makes observations in the classroom to facilitate assessment and educational interventions; and

— prepares substantial documentation for outside agencies involved in ADD/ADHD assessment or counseling.

5. School aides, office staff, and other school personnel who:

— are caring, nurturing, and supportive;

— are helpful, respectful, and welcoming to parents and families;

— give of themselves to the school, supporting teachers, and children; and

— uphold the school philosophy of respect for the individuality of each child.

Every child needs someone at his/her side—caring, encouraging, listening, protecting, guiding, and supporting. We all must make the personal commitment to be strong advocates for children, which means taking action and letting our voices be heard at the political level. Our schools are filled with fine, dedicated professionals who work exceptionally hard to educate our children and prepare them to effectively meet the challenges of the future. Every day we face the demoralizing impact of major cuts in funding, resources, personnel, and programs that are necessary for children. It is time that children become the top priority in our communities and in our nation.

Bibliography and Recommended Resources

Articles and Books

Academic Therapy. "Preventing Management Problems," Vol. 23, Jan., 1988.

Archer, Anita & Gleason, Mary. *Skills for School Success.* North Billerica, Massachusetts: Curriculum Associates, 1990.

Armstrong, Thomas. *Awakening Your Child's Natural Genius.* Los Angeles: Jeremy Tarcher, Inc., 1991.

Armstrong, Thomas. *In Their Own Way.* New York: St. Martin's Press, 1987.

Bain, Lisa J. *The Children's Hospital of Philadelphia: A Parent's Guide to Attention Deficit Disorders.* New York: Delta Books, 1991.

Bash, M.S. & Camp, B. *Think Aloud: Increasing Social and Cognitive Skills, A Problem-Solving Program for Children.* Champaign, Illinois: Research Press, 1985.

Bodenhamer, Gregory. *Back in Control.* New York: Prentice Hall Press, 1983.

Burns, Marilyn. *About Teaching Mathematics.* Sausalito, California: Math Solutions Publications, 1992. (Distributed by Cuisenaire Company of America.)

Cummins, Kathy K. *The Teacher's Guide to Behavioral Interventions*. Columbia, Missouri: Hawthorne Educational Services, 1988.

Dunn, Rita & Kenneth. *Teaching Students Through Their Individual Learning Styles: A Practical Approach*. Englewood Cliffs, New Jersey: Prentice Hall, 1978.

Fowler, Mary Cahil. *Maybe You Know My Kid: A Parents' Guide to Identifying, Understanding, and Helping Your Child with ADHD*. New York: Birchlane Press, 1990.

Frank, Marjorie. *If You're Trying to Teach Kids to Write, You've Gotta Have This Book*. Nashville: Incentive Publications, 1979.

Gardner, Howard. *Frames of Mind: The Theory of Multiple Intelligences*. New York: Basic Books, A Division of Harper Collins, 1983.

Gattozzi, Ruth. *What's Wrong with My Child?* New York: McGraw-Hill, 1986.

Goldberg, Ronald. *Sit Down and Pay Attention!: Coping With ADD Throughout the Life Cycle*. Washington, D.C.: The PIA Press, 1991.

Goldstein S. & Goldstein, M. *A Teacher's Guide: Attention Deficit Disorders in Children*. Salt Lake City: Neurology, Learning and Behavior Center, 1989.

Graves, Donald H. *Writing: Teacher and Children at Work*. Portsmouth, New Hampshire: Heinemann Educational Books, 1983.

Grayson, Dolores A. & Martin, Mary D. *Gender/Ethnic Expectations and Student Achievement: Teacher Handbook*. Earlham, Iowa: Gray Mill, 1988.

Heacox, Diane. *Up from Underachievement*. Minneapolis: Free Spirit Publishing, 1991.

Huth, Holly Young. *Centerplay: Focusing Your Child's Energy*. New York: Simon & Schuster, 1984.

Ingersoll, Barbara. *Your Hyperactive Child: A Parent's Guide to Coping With Attention Deficit Disorder*. New York: Doubleday, 1988.

Johnson, David, Johnson, Roger, & Holubec, Edythe J. *Cooperation in the Classroom* (Revised). Edina, Minnesota: Interaction Book Co., 1990.

Johnson, Dorothy Davies. *I Can't Sit Still: Educating and Affirming Inattentive and Hyperactive Children*. Santa Cruz, California: ETR Associates, 1992.

Kelley, Mary Lou. *School-Home Notes: Promoting Children's Classroom Success*. New York: The Guilford Press, 1990.

Levine, Mel. *Keeping a Head in School*. Cambridge: Educator's Publishing Service, 1990.

McCracken, Robert and Marlene. *Stories, Songs, and Poetry to Teach Reading and Writing*. Winnipeg: Peguis Publishers Limited, 1986.

Morrison, Marvin L. *Word Finder: The Phonic Key to the Dictionary*. Gulfport, Florida: Pilot Light, 1987.

Moss, Robert A. *Why Johnny Can't Concentrate: Coping With Attention Deficit Problems*. New York: Bantam Books, 1990.

Osman, Betty B. *No One to Play With: The Social Side of Learning Disabilities*. New York: Random House, 1982.

Parker, Harvey C. *The ADD Hyperactivity Workbook for Parents, Teachers and Kids*. Plantation, Florida: Impact Publications, 1988.

Rief, Sandra. *Systematic Phonics*, Birmingham, Alabama: EBSCO Curriculum Materials, 1993 revised edition available (1-800-633-8623).

Routman, Regie. *Transitions from Literature to Literacy*. Portsmouth, New Hamphshire: Heinemann Educational Books, 1988.

Silver, Larry B. *The Misunderstood Child: A Guide for Parents of Children With Learning Disabilities*. Blue Ridge Summit, Pennsylvania: TAB Books, 1992.

Sloane, Howard. *The Good Kid Book*. Champaign, Illinois: Research Press, 1979.

Turecki, Stanley. *The Difficult Child: A New Step-by-Step Approach by a Noted Child Psychiatrist for Understanding and Managing Hard-to-Raise Children*. New York: Bantam Books, 1985.

Vail, P.L. *Smart Kids With School Problems*. New York: E.P. Dutton, 1987.

Weisberg, Lynne and Greenberg, Rosalie. *When Acting Out Isn't Acting: Understanding Child and Adolescent Temper, Anger and Behavior Disorders*. Washington D.C.: The PIA Press, 1988.

Weiss, G., and Hechtman, L. *Hyperactive Children Grown Up*. New York: The Guilford Press, 1986.

Note: See Section 12 for a list of additional mathematics resources.

Recommended Videotapes

Why Won't My Child Pay Attention? (featuring Sam Goldstein, Ph.D.), 1989. Available from: Neurology, Learning and Behavior Center, 230 South 500 East, Suite 100, Salt Lake City, Utah 84102. (Runs approximately 76 minutes)

Phelan, T. *1-2-3 Magic: Training Your Preschoolers and Preteens to Do What You Want.* Glen Ellyn, Illinois: Child Management Press, 1990. (Runs 2 hours)

National Groups and Associations for Support

Children with Attention Deficit Disorders (CHADD)
1859 North Pine Island Road, Suite 185
Plantation, Florida 33322
(305) 587-3700

CHADD has chapters all around the country. CHADD publishes a semi-annual newsletter called *CHADDER*, and a monthly newsletter called *CHADDER BOX*.

CHADDER and *CHADDER BOX*
499 N.W. 70th Avenue, Room 308
Plantation, Florida 33317

Learning Disabilities Association (LDA)
4156 Library Road
Pittsburgh, Pennsylvania 15234
(412) 341-1515

LDA (formerly ACLD) also addresses the needs of ADHD children and has many local and state chapters.

In addition to CHADD and LDA, many communities have local ADD support groups, workshops, and resources for parents and professionals. Check with your school support staff, physicians/clinicians who specialize in the field, or local hospitals. They will very likely be able to direct parents to resources in the community.

ADD Warehouse
300 N.W. 70th Avenue, Suite 102
Plantation, Florida 33317
(800) 233-9273

This is an excellent catalog of books, videos, and other resources on the topic of ADD/ADHD.